D1582651

WALL STREET MONEY MACHINE

VOLUME 5

FREE STOCKS

"When it is too expensive to buy something, it is better to be selling."
—WADE B. COOK

WALL STREET MONEY MACHINE

VOLUME 5
FREE STOCKS

WADE B. COOK

Lighthouse Publishing Group, Inc.
Seattle, Washington

 Lighthouse Publishing Group, Inc.
Copyright © 2000 Wade B. Cook

Library of Congress Cataloging-in-Publication Data
Cook, Wade.
Wall street money machine, volume 5, free stocks: how to get the stock market to pay for your stocks - free! / Wade B. Cook
p. cm.
Includes bibliographical references and index.
ISBN 1-892008-67-X
1. Speculation. 2. Stocks. 3. Futures. I. Title.
HG6041.C64 1999
332.63'228–dc21 99-17010
CIP

Book Design by Judy Burkhalter
Edited by Leslie vanWinkle
Dust Jacket Design by Mark Engelbrecht
Dust Jacket and Inside Photographs by Zachary Cherry

Published by Lighthouse Publishing Group, Inc.
14675 Interurban Avenue South
Seattle, Washington 98168-4664
1-800-706-8657   206-901-3027 (fax)

Source Code: WSMMV5-01

Printed in United States of America
10 9 8 7 6 5 4 3 2 1

Laura Marie, you're wonderful.

BOOKS BY LIGHTHOUSE PUBLISHING GROUP, INC.

THE WALL STREET MONEY MACHINE SERIES, WADE B. COOK

Wall Street Money Machine, Volume 1
Wall Street Money Machine, Volume 2: Stock Market Miracles
Wall Street Money Machine, Volume 3: Bulls & Bears
Wall Street Money Machine, Volume 4: Safety 1st Investing

Stock Split Secrets: Profiting from a Powerful, Predictable,
Price-moving Event, DARLENE AND MILES NELSON

On Track Investing, DAVID R. HEBERT
Rolling Stocks, GREGORY WITT
Sleeping Like A Baby, JOHN C. HUDELSON
Making A Living In The Stock Market, BOB ELDRIDGE

Real Estate Money Machine, WADE COOK
101 Ways To Buy Real Estate Without Cash, WADE COOK
How To Pick Up Foreclosures, WADE COOK
Real Estate For Real People, WADE COOK

Blueprints For Success, WADE COOK AND VARIOUS OTHER AUTHORS
Brilliant Deductions, WADE B. COOK
Million Heirs, JOHN V. CHILDERS, JR.
The Secret Millionaire Guide To Nevada Corporations, JOHN V. CHILDERS, JR.
Wealth 101, WADE B. COOK

A+, WADE B. COOK
Business Buy The Bible, WADE B. COOK
Don't Set Goals (The Old Way), WADE B. COOK
Wade Cook's Power Quotes, Volume 1, WADE COOK

Living In Color, RENAE KNAPP

COMING SOON

Beginning Investors Bible, DOUG SUTTON

CONTENTS

PREFACE

FREE! The word and concept have been the advertising foundation for billion dollar corporations, the heartbeat of huge marketing campaigns and the nexus between companies and customers for eons.

Of course, people always think there has to be a catch. And you know, there usually is. The company giving a toothpick sampling of their new teriyaki chicken as we walk by their store in the mall is obviously hoping we'll come back and spend money there. The software company giving us a free software program is just as obviously hoping that we'll go on and indulge ourselves in their other products. The Stock Market Institute of Learning, Inc.™ sending out FREE informational CDs is hoping to get people excited by knowledge, so they will want more education. It makes so much sense, and that is the catch.

So you read the title to this book: *FREE STOCKS: How to Get the Stock Market to Pay for your Stocks*, and what do you think? Is there a catch? I'll be right up front and say there is, but it's not what you think. Oh, from time to time, throughout the book I'll mention other products and services which I believe will truly help you, but no, that's not the catch I'm talking about. There is a way to get FREE STOCKS, which, if you get to the bottom-line root meaning of FREE, is simply that you do not pay for your stocks yourself. I'm talking about quality stocks, and here's a wild shift from the normal use of the concept FREE– you get to choose your own batch of stocks! You can be as diversified as you want. And get this–you can pretty much start with any amount of money you have.

So what's the catch? It is simply that *you must give up an old concept that there is something outside of yourself*–some new business deal, some wild new stock, some multi-level plan that will "poof" make you rich and famous. *You must be prepared to study, practice and take on a certain element of risk.*

Okay. Here's the trade-off to this obligation of study, practice and accepting a certain element of risk. If you start with about $5,000, in two years or so, following my LOCC™ (Large Option Covered Calls™) plan, you will have around $50,000 in stocks that you did not pay for. You could sell them, keep them, or have them continue to produce $6,000 to $12,000 *per month* depending on how safe you want to be.

If you can start with $25,000, then in six months or so, you will have just a little under $25,000 in stocks, which you will own for FREE. You could reclaim your original $25,000 and spend it elsewhere, or continue to use it to generate more FREE stocks.

If you have more than $25,000 to work with, just take the previous numbers times how much you have. Some of you with more money should learn about the basic LOCC™ system in Chapter Three, and move on to some of the additional cash flow methods.

So, here's the catch: this is not a get rich quick plan. This is also not some ambiguous, nebulous method that only a few people can master and use. It is also not a theory, but an in-the-trenches, workable, cash flow stock market machine. This plan takes a simple, yet overlooked aspect of the stock and options markets, and puts it to full use. The results are dynamic and far-reaching.

LOCC has a beginning, middle and an end. It is based on four to six month stock option cycles and is an excellent strategy for the busy person. It puts the emphasis where it should be: on generating income so you can retire. That is what I do as an educator–I show people how to get retired. You may forget this as you race on to having millions, or building new businesses, but I won't forget it. I help people build monthly income, even if it's only $800, or $4,000, or $8,000 a month. Yes, huge assets are nice, but let's go for simple ways to build steady monthly income so we can do more of the simple, yet wonderful things that life has to offer.

These two testimonials sum up my desire for my students:

"When I started learning from Wade Cook, I was a millionaire, but I worked 65 to 85 hours a week and I saw my family very little and I had very little time to myself. I now have all the time I could ever imagine to spend with my family. I now have the most rewarding life I could have ever imagined. I now know my wife and kids. Thank you, and thank God."

–JACK R., TX

"I am assisting elderly parents and two neighbors that are in ill health...I have set up several scholarships, and today made a very nice contribution to an annual collection for the area soup kitchens. Thank you for making a change in my life and allowing me to take the fruits of this crop to those who can really appreciate it."

–CRAIG H., CT

In the last chapter of this book, after you've learned how to get your own FREE stocks, I'll explore several retirement scenarios. It's not about having more, but about doing more with what you have. Look at this quotation by Woodrow Wilson:

You are not here merely to make a living. You are here to enable the world to live more amply, with greater vision, with a finer spirit of hope and achievement. You are here to enrich the world, but will lessen yourself if you forget the errand.

–WOODROW W. WILSON

You must understand that everything you read here flies in the face of the "conventional stock market wisdom." Most brokers and other financial professionals, if they are willing to admit their naivete, will wonder where they have been. Simple things/methods/systems like LOCC have been all around them, but they have fallen prey to their company's desire to sell the next investment, and not look for ways to truly help their clients with that age-old quest for income.

Discovery consists of seeing what everybody has seen and thinking what nobody has thought.
—ALBERT SZENT-GYORGYI NAGTRAPOLT

This book gets to the "why" (and the "how") behind many things, not just with my LOCC plan, but with other aspects of the stock market.

The man who knows how will always have a job, the man who knows why will always be the boss.
—DIANE RAVITCH

Some of the so-called professionals will always criticize my efforts, but I want you to take time out and you be the judge. I'm offering a life of FREEdom, generated by income the market will give you, and having your favorite stocks literally purchased for you by the market. These FREE stocks will then produce yet more income in an ever-increasing stream of monthly income.

What stands between you and this new FREEdom is knowledge, and the wise use of it. Knowledge and information become power, but they are only potential at first.

As a general rule the most successful man in life is the man who has the best information.
—BENJAMIN DISRAELI

ACKNOWLEDGMENTS

It takes a team to write a book like this. I am also sincerely grateful for the help of my many Team Wallstreet™ instructors who have not only taught our students well, but have shared many of their innovative and up-to-date ideas. The members of our research and trading department David McKinlay, Barry Collette, George Park, Greg Harrop, Jay Harris, Paul Lund, Rich Simmons, and Richard Lowman have given me extremely valuable help on a timely basis. Thanks also goes to Lighthouse Publishing Group, Brent Magarrell, Gina Lynd, and Leslie vanWinkle who have been very helpful in typesetting and editing this book, and Mark Engelbrecht who designed the cover. There have also been many other contributors to this effort. Also thanks to the Executive Staff at Wade Cook Financial Corporation, Carl Sanders, who has since retired, Robert Hondel, Cindy Britten, and Robin Anderson. They run the show so I can write. Also, heartfelt appreciation to my assistants Patsy Sanders, Angela Johnson, and Cindy Little. And last, but not least, thanks goes to my wife, Laura, for her love and support.

1

HOW TO GET THE STOCK MARKET TO PAY FOR YOUR STOCKS

A few years ago, when I designed the LOCC™ (Large Option Covered Call™) system, I thought I had hit the mother lode. This system is a machine. A machine for generating cash to purchase stocks. A machine for generating consistent cash flow—and in sufficient quantities to better any lifestyle.

LOCC truly lets anyone live a more quality life, but after all, this formula is just an enhanced covered call. A covered call that buys and pays for itself! Let's review a few basics, then we'll get on to some really cool angles for making this system work even better.

Writing covered calls is a way to literally play the market from the opposite angle of most everyone else. Everyone else puts the emphasis on buying, we put it on selling. They buy risky options, we sell risky options.

Most people get fooled into old, lethargic ways of thinking and acting. They buy and hold their investments—even bad ones. The so-called professionals do stupid things like dollar cost averaging down (or up) without picking better price points (or any sell points). They ignore the ability to "rent" out stocks and generate income. This lack of knowledge negates their ability to use this income to buy more and better investments. Most people never learn how to work with low-cost, limited-risk options.

1

Writing covered calls has rules:

- Buy the stock on dips; sell the call on strength.
- Use volatility to your advantage.
- Use careful margin trading to double your rate of return.

Writing Large Option Covered Calls does what the name implies, captures premiums–large ones. LOCC has rules like:

- When in doubt, go for more cash flow.
- Aim for deals where you get called out for 100% of the maximum profit.
- Shoot for 80% to 100% five to six month returns.
- When in doubt, be a seller not a buyer.

We can also use a call option as a replacement for the stock. We're covered, but by an option to purchase the stock. This ties up less cash and can produce spectacular results. In short, we can do Bull Call Spreads and even wider Longhorn Spreads. But let me get back to the idea of "renting" out stocks.

One of the best selling features of real estate is the simple fact that real estate buys and pays for itself. Why? Because you have a second person (renter) bringing in cash every month. If the property goes up, great–in 30 years your $200,000 property is worth $400,000 and it's free and clear. If it goes down, then great–your $150,000 property is free and clear. Either way, someone else paid for it for you.

Now, with this little known and seldom used powerful cash flow formula I'm going to introduce to you now, this Large Option Covered Call, you can get the stock market to pay for your stocks.

> *Do you wish to become rich? You may become so if you desire it in no halfway, but thoroughly. Do you wish to master any science or accomplishment? Give yourself to it and it lies beneath your feet. This world is given as the prize for the men in earnest; and that which is true of this world, is truer still of the world to come.*
>
> –F.W. Robertson

Writing a LOCC is just what it says–selling big (expensive/fluffy) option premiums against a stock position you own. By writing (selling) a call in this way, you are agreeing to sell your stock at an agreed upon price on or before a certain date, called the expiration date. It is mandatory (if the position is still open) to sell your stock if your option is exercised, and you will have your stock bought from you. This will happen if the price of your stock is above this agreed upon price at expiration. In fact, it all happens electronically.

Often you won't know if your stock has been bought away from you until the Monday after the expiration date. If your position is still open (not exercised) before this date, you can reclaim control of your stock by buying back the option, hopefully for a much less expensive price than what you originally sold it for. (See Chapter Seven for buy back information.)

Writing a call generates income in one day. Option income hits your account the next day. These calls (and puts) are bought and sold in a regular brokerage account whether you work with a live broker or online. I much prefer a live broker who "gets it" and who is trained and experienced in these strategies. Most are not.

Generating income has been the theme, indeed the mission of all my financial education books and workshops. In this case we get paid this income to agree to sell our stock at this fixed price. If the stock rises substantially above this fixed price, or strike price, we do not participate in this extra increase. We have given up this upside by agreeing to sell it at a certain price. The upside is gone–it was sold for cash. You probably should not sell a covered call if you think you have a flyer–a stock you think will take off.

Extra Large Option Premiums

At any given time, the stock market usually has a group of stocks with extra large option premiums. In past time periods, this group has been varied. Today, at the beginning of the millennium, the power-packed group includes the high-tech stocks, and especially the Internet stocks.

Even just a few years ago "high-tech" meant computer software and applications. Today, having seen the industry grow so fast, the perimeter of the group has expanded. Now it includes the Internet with its wide array of products and service providers. It includes those who create and maintain the behind the scenes systems for using the Internet. Also within this group now are high-speed fiber-optic switching and transmission companies, broadband and wireless companies, and a host of other big and small companies that provide equipment and products for the use of various services that help business customers and consumers communicate.

The Internet is here to stay. The players will come and go—some fretting and strutting their fifteen minutes on the stage, others investing in season tickets and reaping their profits from the safety of the balcony. I, for one, want to personally thank Microsoft. They have done so much to create, expand, and make available so much good through their software, functionality and stable environment for computer users. Isn't it ironic that companies that did not exist, and would never have existed without Microsoft's pioneering innovations, now whine to the obtrusive Feds? The billions of dollars they've made as a result of Microsoft's existence is not enough—they want blood. *"America loves winning, but they hate winners."*

> *After having been in this country for only a few years, I wrote this, a generation ago:*
>
> *'In Britain, eminently successful business leaders are Knighted. In America they are indicted.'*
>
> *Today, this is still as conspicuously true. Never before has our astigmatic Department of Justice fought more frenziedly to indict highly successful American enterprises. Too often it is not recognized that our unparalleled prosperity has been brought about by the brainiest of our business leaders. Politically, pre-eminent business success has become suspect.*
>
> —B.C. FORBES (1950)

All of this high-tech activity, including a government agency run amok, plays into the market sentiment and creates volatility. This volatility (the large swings in stock prices) is simply what drives up the price of options. (See Chapter Five for more on volatility.)

It is these expensive call options that I like to sell. A simple example and then I'll conclude this section, so you can get on to making deals–ultimately having hundreds of thousands of dollars in stocks that the stock market has bought and paid for–just for you.

A stock is $200. It can make giant (even intra-day) moves of $20 to $50. We buy 100 shares of the stock. One hundred shares at $200 is $20,000. Don't stop reading if you don't have $20,000. Margin means a stock brokerage firm will loan us a percentage of the stock price–say 30%, or 50%, or even 70%. We'll use 50% for this example. They will loan us $10,000 to buy the stock. They will use the stock as collateral for the loan. We have, at this point, $10,000 of our own money tied up. (See more about the cautions of margin investing in *Wall Street Money Machine, Volumes 1* and *4.*)

We now sell a call option against our stock, agreeing to sell the stock at a fixed price. Option contracts are in one hundred share batches–we can sell one contract. If we had 800 shares of the stock, we could sell up to eight contracts. If the option strike price is $200, then we agree to sell the stock–actually, we agree to let someone buy our stock for $200. If the next month out $200 strike price is $7, our one contract would bring us $700 (100 x $7 = $700). This money gets into our account the next day. We can use it for whatever we want–even taking it out for a trip to Yosemite, after we go to the movies.

But look! The option out five months from now is going for $45. There is now more time–that's what we are selling–the time and the "implied volatility," or what I prefer to call the "speculative value," of the option.

This is a large premium. A different, more staid stock might see a five month premium at $13, but not $45. Selling one contract of this large premium option generates $4,500. Again, actual money in our account in one day. Because this money is ours, whether the stock goes up or down, whether we're called out or not, it can be used any way we like. Immediately, it lowers the cash we have tied up from $10,000 to $5,500. We have $4,500 of our original $10,000 back and ready to work elsewhere. The market gave us $4,500 of this $10,000; like a "renter," the market is paying for our security, in this case the underlying stock.

Our job here was to capture the large premium. To make it ours. We have done that. We had every hope that this stock would go up, or at least stay up above $200. We'll explore in Chapter 11 what happens if the stock you own goes down in value, but for this scenario we'll sell the stock. Our original money comes back in, the $5,500, and we get to keep $4,500. Using $5,500 to make $4,500 is a powerful formula. The market just gave you $4,500. What can you do with it? It's yours–spend it, reinvest it, put it into your business. It's up to you.

Let's do another deal with it, turn it once again and generate another $4,000. Then again to earn another $5,000. In fourteen to fifteen months (it could be sooner if you get called out early), we'll generate $13,500, starting with our $5,500.

And we still have our original cash. Use it to buy good stocks of your choosing, pay down your mortgage, send the kids to college. Do this in an IRA for a tax-free income and a great retirement. Pay a bigger tithe at your church. Oh, and look, even if you had used this cash to buy this same $200 stock ($20,000), and it tanked and went down half–who paid for it? You have $13,500 of someone else's money buying stocks for you.

Now is that a cool angle, or what? Don't stop now. We've only just begun to explore the power of LOCCs.

2

LOCC AND LOAD UP

Can you really get the stock market to pay for your stocks for you? Yes, and here is my plan to get your stocks for FREE. Once you own these FREE stocks, you can be completely retired in one to two years. Two years? Can it be so if you need $100,000 to live on? No. Not unless you (a) start with more money, (b) get better returns on a few of the deals and (c) are willing to spend a bit more time at this process. However, you can retire on $3,000 to $6,000 a month, starting with much less.

Also, before we go on, unless you understand the components of this Large Option Covered Call process, including (a) the high option premium and (b) the length of time we use for writing the premiums, then this chapter will be a trifle difficult. To review information on writing covered calls, please read *Volumes 1, 2* and *4* of my new *Wall Street Money Machine Series.*

Basically, the difference between traditional covered calls and LOCCs can be summarized as follows:

Traditional covered calls buy lower-priced optionable stocks with some volatility and write covered calls for the same month or next month out. These stocks are purchased on margin, if possible and if appropriate.

7

The LOCC variation is to buy higher-priced optionable stocks with higher volatility and write covered calls that expire in five to seven months.These stocks are also purchased on margin, if possible. You're choosing stocks that you feel will go up, as you definitely want to get called out. You are writing calls that are close to or at the money. We do not expect to make money on the stock. We are playing this strategy to capture the option premium.

LOCC allows the use of higher-priced stocks with lower amounts of cash tied up. For example, if you purchase 100 shares of a $90 stock on margin, you are only putting up $45 per share. If a stock is relatively volatile, the call options would be more expensive. You may be able to collect $38 on a six to seven month call option, which would give an adjusted cost basis of $52 per share ($90 – $38 = $52). The main down side is that you are giving up your upside potential on the stock.

Now, onto our LOCC Formula.

We'll start with $25,000. If you have less money, say $5,000, then work with that. Just do two of the several deals I'm showing you here. It's the strategy that matters at this point. If you have more, say $100,000 plus, then break your money down into smaller batches. Each batch could have a specific mission in life. Each could then be monitored, rated, and improved upon. Also, this would gently force you to diversify—not only into different stocks, but also into different formulas or methods of creating cash flow, growth or tax write-offs.

With $25,000, let's see if we can do about five deals. That would be convenient from a mathematical point of view, but as you will see here and in real life, the groups will not be in even $5,000 increments.

DEAL ONE

A hypothetical case: its May and we find a stock that's going for $240. With the recent sell off in the market and the extra drop in the share price, this seems like a good place to buy. We buy 100 shares. We now go looking for an option to sell. For simplicity's sake, we'll sell a close-to-the-money option. We want a big premium so we go out four to six months. The October $240 call option is going for $50. That's a huge premium. I would have a hard time buying an option at this price, but I definitely like selling for a high, fluffy price like this. We own 100 shares so we can sell one contract in a covered position. That's a whopping $5,000 that will hit our account tomorrow. It's May, and this option has an October expiration date.

It cost $24,000 to buy the stock and we've taken in this extra $5,000 premium. Our cost basis is $19,000. There are two ways of looking at this. Let's do the math without using margin. Then we'll do it again with margin.

ABC (a)	ABC (b)
Sell $240 Call	*Sell $240 Call*
October	*October*
$50	*$50*
Stock Purchase	*Stock Purchase*
$24,000	*$24,000*
No Margin	*On Margin (divide by 2)*
	$12,000
Take in (Option Premium)	*Take in (Option Premium)*
$5,000	*$5,000*
Our own cash tied up	*Our own cash tied up*
$19,000	*$7,000*
Called out	*Called out*
$240	*$240*
Total five month return	*Total five month return*
$5,000	*$5,000*
Rate of return based on $19,000	*Rate of return based on $7,000*
26%	*71%*

a. If we get called out at $240, the original option strike price, the $5,000 is a fair five month return on $24,000. It's about 20%. Not bad. But wait–is that fair to calculate the rate of return on the $24,000? As the "marketplace" gave us $5,000, we only have $19,000 of our own money on hold. This way, the rate of return is 26%. Note: From a tax point of view, the income from selling the option premium will have to be claimed when this position ends. We sell this stock for $24,000 and have $5,000 from the option premium.

b. What about margin? If this were done on a 50% marginable stock, what would it look like? Instead of $24,000 in cash, we would only have to put up $12,000. Now the $5,000 cash goes against our margin requirement, and we only have to put up

$7,000. Of course we'll still have to pay margin interest on the whole $12,000–the other side of the $24,000, or the $12,000 loan the brokerage firm lent us. Margin interest is very small in this example.

Now $7,000 to make $5,000 is one heckuva play. The rate of return is 71.4% for those five months. Also, it doesn't take a genius to figure out that once this trade is over, we can then take in another premium for four to six months and then a one to two month premium for half this amount, and we'll have taken in about $12,000–all within one year. This is cash in our account.

Do this for one more year and you could own the $240 stock for FREE. The market gave you the money. Also, keep in mind that with tweaks and accelerated plays, it could happen faster. To top it off, we still own the stock or have purchased other stock which can continue to produce income for us–either monthly or every few months by writing covered calls. We have ownership with cash flow. But, I'm getting ahead of myself. I just wanted to telegraph, ever so slightly, where we were going with this. Back to our $25,000 chunk of money.

So, $7,000 of our $25,000 is tied up for five months. Actually, tied up is not the only way of looking at it. It's working quite well. For the remainder of these examples, we'll do our transactions at 50% margin.

DEAL TWO

We find another stock for $110. One hundred shares is $11,000. On margin, that's $5,500.

a. The $110 call in November is going for $30. Again, we sell one call contract for $3,000. This $3,000 goes against our $5,500. Whoa! Look at this, we have $2,500 of our own money on hold to make $3,000. This is great! You just have to be wondering why your stockbroker never told you this. Perhaps you're wondering why you're still sitting there, not doing this. Anyway, it's another six months.

b. One side note–the $120 call is going for $25. You could move up $10 in the strike price and take just $500 less. Let's do the math. We put out the same $11,000, $5,500 if we do it on margin. We now take in $2,500 instead of $3,000. We now have

$3,000 of our own money on hold. That's still a great return. $3,000 to make $2,500 compared to $2,500 to make $3,000.

Okay, but there's an added bonus. If the stock goes up and we get called out, or sell for $120, we make an extra $1,000. We bought the stock on a dip, so we were thinking that the stock was going to go up. The $1,000 is calculated by making the extra $10 per share (the difference between $110 and $120) times 100 shares, or $1,000. Now, granted that's cash in the future, but it's only six months until $3,000 makes us $3,500.

XYZ (a)	XYZ (b)
Sell $110 Call	*Sell $120 Call*
November	*November*
$30	$25
Stock Purchase	*Stock Purchase*
$11,000	$11,000
On Margin (divide by 2)	*On Margin (divide by 2)*
$5,500	$5,500
Take in (Option Premium)	*Take in (Option Premium)*
$3,000	$2,500
Our own cash tied up	*Our own cash tied up*
$2,500	$3,000
Called out	*Called out*
$120	$120
Sold at the money	*Sold in the money*
$0	$1,000
Total five month return	*Total five month return*
$3,000	$3,500
Rate of return based on $2,500	*Rate of return based on $3,000*
120%	117%

Okay, okay. You're one step ahead of me. You're saying, "Wait a minute! Isn't $2,500 to make $3,000 (120%) better than $3,000 to make $3,500 (117%)?" If you caught this dilemma, I applaud you. You're right. But that's also why I did this exercise.

As I said before—we go shopping. We compare stock prices versus option prices at (a) different months and (b) at different strike prices. Sometimes it's better to do these slightly out of the money, but when in doubt...

RULE #1—WHEN IN DOUBT, GO FOR MORE CASH NOW.

Sell close-to-the-money or even slightly in-the-money calls. The extra cash now means you will have less cash tied up. Less cash tied up means a better return. It also means you have more cash to do other deals. So, here's the next rule:

RULE #2—THIS STRATEGY WORKS BEST (100% OF MAXIMUM PROFIT) WHEN YOU GET CALLED OUT.

Work it so you get called out of the underlying stock.

Okay, so we'll do the deal with $2,500 tied up to make $3,000. Here's our running tally. Now $9,500 of our $25,000 is tied up for four to six months and we'll make $8,000 if all goes well. That's $8,000 we can spend or apply to purchasing more of these stocks. We're about one-third of the way to our $25,000 of FREE stocks, and we've only just begun.

DEAL THREE

The next candidate is what has currently been dubbed an "old-economy stock." Funny how people give names to things so those things can be conveniently pigeon-holed. In a way they're saying, "stocks with earnings" in an attempt to denigrate "new economy stocks"–i.e., the ones who have taken the "E" out of "P/E."

With this example you must read my comments on these newer, highly volatile stocks in Chapter Five. With this volatility and added risk in mind, let's move on. A major car manufacturer sees their stock trading down around $52. This stock just a few months ago was at $65.

Again, 100 shares would be $5,200. One half for margin and our cash needed is $2,600. We have two possible deals: (a) the $50 call for November is $10, and (b) the $55 call is going for $8. Let's do the $50 strike price first. We would take in $1,000 to be applied to our $2,600. That leaves $1,600 to make or keep the $1,000. Not bad. Ostensibly, these numbers seem like a great return at 63%. Don't get me wrong, $1,000 on a $1,600 trade is wonderful in most people's books, but it's not quite this good. You see, we have to "give-back" the $2, or $200. We purchased the stock for $52 and will sell for $50. That's a $2 loss– with one hundred shares, that's a loss of $200. We use "give-back," which is just jargon–but it works. So, our return is actually 50%.

Let's go to the $55 call. Here, we take in $8 per share, or $800 total. Our own cash now becomes $1,800 instead of $2,600. This $1,800 invested to make $800 (for a pretty sure deal) is a six month 44% return. Not too shabby. But wait! We pick up an extra $300 by buying 100 shares of the stock for $52 and selling it for $55. That brings our profits to $1,100 with only $1,800 out.

CAR (a)	CAR (b)
Sell $50 Call	*Sell $55 Call*
November	*November*
$10	*$8*
Stock Purchase	*Stock Purchase*
$5,200	*$5,200*
On Margin (divide by 2)	*On Margin (divide by 2)*
$2,600	*$2,600*
Take in (Option Premium)	*Take in (Option Premium)*
$1,000	*$800*
Our own cash tied up	*Our own cash tied up*
$1,600	*$1,800*
Called out	*Called out*
$50	*$55*
Sold out of the money (Give back)	*Sold in the money*
$200	*$300*
Total five month return	*Total five month return*
$800	*$1,100*
Rate of return based on $1,600	*Rate of return based on $1,800*
50%	*61%*

Both of these trades are nice, but not great. Can we shop around and do better? Probably. So, let's keep going, after I give you rule #3.

RULE #3—SHOOT FOR 80% TO 100% FIVE TO SIX MONTH RETURNS.

DEAL FOUR

Onto our next candidate. There is a nice Internet support company that took a big dip after they made a stock split announcement. The stock, at first, shot up to $310 and then backed off to $210. This price is about where it was just before the split announcement.

The October $210 calls are currently going for $46. Let's go ahead and run the numbers, but remember the stock is coming up on a three-for-one stock split. It costs $21,000 to purchase the stock, but $10,500 on margin. We take in $4,600, which means we have $5,900 ($10,500 minus $4,600 = $5,900) on hold to make $4,600.

This stock is volatile, and while it's at a near term low, it surely is not as low as it was one year ago. It was around $60. This has been a good run-up, and yes, it could dip, but the company is also about ready to break through and start making money.

Let's move through the split. On the Wednesday before the Friday pay date (split date), the stock is at $240. It went as high as $280, then backed off with a BANG. The actual split is now imminent, and the stock price seems to be at a fairly good support level. Sure enough, the price increases into the split.

On Monday we now have 300 shares where we once had 100. The opening price is $80 ($240 ÷ 3). We also have three short call contract positions at the $70 strike price. Remember, when the stock splits, the options split. If the stock stays above $70 ($210 ÷ 3) we will get called out, but there is a long time to the expiration date.

Sure enough, as most stocks do, shortly after the split the stock backed off. It fell to $72 and briefly to $66, but rose quickly above the $70 strike price. Many things still could happen, but we don't have time here in this space to cover all of those potential moves. We'll assume it moved on and stayed above $70, and then we were called out. Remember our original premise was that we were doing this strategy to let the position run to expiration.

NET	
Sell $210 Call	
October	
$46	
Stock Purchase	*3:1 Split (300 @ $70)*
$21,000	*Called out*
On Margin (divide by 2)	*$70*
$10,500	*Total five month return*
Take in (Option Premium)	*$4,600*
$4,600	*Rate of return based on $5,900*
Our own cash tied up	*78%*
$5,900	

Also, many of these things which could go wrong also present many more cash-flow opportunities, but let's just be happy here that we've captured another premium and it's ours to have and to hold.

Okay, a quick catch up with money spent and profits made. We were at $9,500 ($7,000 + $2,500) of our $25,000 available. We'll add on this $5,900 to our total and get $15,400. Let's also tack on here $600 for commissions for those trades, totaling $16,000. Our premium profits are now $12,600 (previous $8,000 plus this new $4,600). Also, remember we have the car company trade waiting in the wings.

DEAL FIVE

A major brokerage house puts out a $700 price target (and a buy recommendation) on a $420 stock. This seems unbelievable. Unbelievable will come back into play when we check the options prices–both near term and further out. The stock opens up at $460, but within forty-five minutes it has backed off to $440. Even at that, the November $440 calls are going for $130. Unbelievable is an understatement. It verges on ridiculous. Hypothetically, this stock would have to go to $570 by expiration to just break even. Real life is different, obviously.

We know the stock. If it moved quickly to, say, $600 that could make those $440 call options worth $250 or so in a heartbeat. Wow! That would be almost a double profit deal, but remember a basic tenet of option plays is that if you're a buyer, you have a one-in-three chance of making money and in this case only if the stock goes up in a timely manner. If the stock goes down, stays the same, or only rises a little over a long time, our premium will go down. So what's a person to do? May I borrow a phrase from my real estate books–"sell."

RULE #4–WHEN IN DOUBT, BE A SELLER NOT A BUYER.

Look at these numbers as we do the math, and the word unbelievable will come back into play again.

One hundred shares at $440 is $44,000, or $22,000 on margin. We take in $13,000, which can be applied to our $22,000 hold requirement, so we only have to put up $9,000 of our own money. Spending $9,000 to make $13,000 for five months is quite nice–jolly good show.

XYZ (a)	
Sell $440 Call	
November	
$130	
Stock Purchase	*Called out at the money*
$44,000	$440
On Margin (divide by 2)	*Total five month return*
$22,000	$13,000
Take in (Option Premium)	*Rate of return based on $9,000*
$13,000	144%
Our own cash tied up	
$9,000	

Oh, and look. We've used up our $25,000. Our previous $16,000 added to this $9,000 totals $25,000. Our premium income is in our account to the blaring tune of $25,600. I repeat, $25,600!

Before we take time out to really look at what we have committed to, and what has happened with our original $25,000, let's take a deeper look at potential problems of this last transaction.

Let's say the $440 stock runs up to near $700. The company announces a four-for-one stock split at the same time it announces earnings, which weren't great. The stock shot up to $750, then backed off to $660, but over the next five weeks it climbed to near $800. It split down to four shares at $200, and immediately fell to $180, then backed down to $150.

Okay, let's jump in here. We were wisely trying to use our $25,000 to create income which would pay for $25,000 worth of stocks in two years. Nobody asked me to attempt this. It's my doing. Maybe I'm just still trying in a safe yet graphic manner to shut up my critics. Then why, you ask, use a "new economy" Internet stock for safety?

Indeed, hasn't Wade Cook been a proponent of safety, of "back to basics," and of a strong fundamental (with a hint of technical analysis) approach to trading? Yes, I have, but I'm also in the real world and sometimes the real world is a little bizarre. Some of these stocks have taken over and occupy the space of the statement, "Where the action is." In some ways it is riskier to sit on the sidelines than to get involved.

As noted businessman Peter Drucker pointed out, "There is the risk you cannot afford to take, and there is the risk you cannot afford

<u>not</u> to take." Suffice it to say, I check these stocks out. They have a story line (product, service, management, *et cetera*) that is solid. Many are candidates for mergers, takeovers and straight buyouts. Some are producing income and the revenues are increasing. Some are expanding nicely, and expanding abroad. This particular stock had a lot going for it.

Oh, you then ask, what about the 70% margin requirement? This will be an interesting lesson for many to quit tripping over pennies on their way to dollars. Come along.

The stock at $440, 100 shares at $44,000, requires a 70% hold at many brokerage houses. Point: this is the margin the stock was at when we bought it. So, ask your broker what will be on hold as the stock moves up to $700 plus.

XYZ (b)	
Sell $440 Call	
November	
$130	
Stock Purchase	*Called out*
$44,000	$440
On 70% Margin	*Total five month return*
$30,800	$13,000
Take in (Option Premium)	*Rate of return based on $17,800*
$13,000	73%
Our own cash tied up	
$17,800	

Seventy percent of $44,000 is $30,800, not the $22,000 at a 50% margin rate. Okay, so now we sell the $440 call for the $13,000 and we have $17,800 ($30,800 minus $13,000 = $17,800) on hold. This is our own money. Having $17,800 on hold to make $13,000 is still quite a good deal, I think.

However, we have now overspent our $25,000 by $8,200. What to do? Well, first of all, very few people have exactly $25,000, so if you have more you could do it. If not, you would have to substitute this play for one of the other ones.

Let's go there. Take out the first transaction and put this one in its place. Use the $24,000 stock with $7,000 on hold to make $5,000.

Take $7,000 from $25,000 and to be fair, take away the $5,000 profits for now. We have $8,400 ($2,500 + $5,900) still tied up, but now add back in the $17,800. You see, we're still over the $25,000 now at $26,200, and our profits would be $20,600. This is about as close as we're going to get to our $25,000 with these examples.

Take time out. Why would we substitute this trade for the safer trade and one which could be done at 50% margin? Usually we wouldn't. Why? It just doesn't make sense here in this book, as it usually makes no sense in real life. We would do the riskier trade in this case, simply to get at the additional cash flow–even with the added risk. But you decide.

Again, we did these trades so we wouldn't have to worry and jump back in to solve problems. We need to shop around for the best bang for our buck. This is why shopping and comparing these potential plays is so vital. Point: while you may have more or less than $25,000, you probably don't have an infinite amount of money. Each dollar must carry its weight.

Other points about this high-flying stock, before we move on. This stock did split, and then went down to $150 and started back up from there. We have a short (sold) position on the $110 calls ($440 ÷ 4 = $110). We're going to wish we had either (a) purchased the stock and left it free and clear, or (b) purchased the $440 calls for $130. These would now be the $110 calls at a price of $32.50 each (four contracts at $32.50 equals our original $13,000). We would now own four contracts. That's the right to buy 400 shares of the stock at $110. How would you like to own the right to buy 400 shares of a stock at $110 if the stock shoots up to $210? With no time value at all–only calculating intrinsic value–that would equal $40,000. Imagine $13,000 cash turning into $40,000 in three to five months. Wow!

So why do I bring this up here? Well, for one thing–a touch of reality is in order. The market may be bouncing, but let's not let our reality check bounce. Remember, in selling a call against a stock position we give away the upside movement of the stock. Let's not forget the basic rules of covered call writing as expounded on in my first four volumes of the *Wall Street Money Machine Series*. Rules are rules. Stick with them. Don't make exceptions because "this time it's different," or "this stock is an exception."

Also, in selling we limit our potential, but we also lessen our downside risk. Look at the play again. We purchased the stock for $440, but took in $130 against the price. That means our cost basis is $310. Said another way, this stock would have to fall 30% from its purchase price before we go underwater, and even at that we still own the stock. We could just hang on, or even write more calls against our position, generating more income.

Also consider—the stock ran up to $800, then post split fell back to $150, but times four. That's still a $600 pre-split price. It would have to fall to $77.50 ($310 ÷ 4) before we would temporarily enter a losing position. At its worst, it's still pretty great.

Time out! By a show of hands, how many of you wish your broker would have shown you these types of transactions? I know it's too much to ask—BUT WHERE ARE THESE GUYS? For now, this cab driver will move forward defining new ways to play the market.

"I decided to attend because my friend and client was using Wade Cook strategies in an account with me at [the brokerage where I worked]. I needed to understand better where he was coming from and what he was trying to accomplish with his trading. The Wall Street Workshop™ helped me understand the discipline encouraged and taught by the instructors and to better communicate with [my client] when he would run astray from his intended strategies. We now speak in a common jargon and can move more quickly, effectively and with tighter discipline. [My client] is making an excellent return on his accounts, I make nice commissions, and I get a great bonus—I am now using the same strategies in my own accounts far more effectively than before in my 20 years as a stockbroker."

—JOHN F., CA

"I found this [information] extremely beneficial. I am a financial planner who works primarily in mutual funds and life insurance. My practice with my clients will undoubtedly change in the future because of the results I personally have experienced."

—CHRISTOPHER M., OH

"I am a CFO of my third public company with more than 10 years experience dealing with Wall Street and over 15 years investing in stocks and I am embarrassed by what I didn't know."
                                                                    –ED J., FL

"As a former stockbroker and current commodity broker, everything I ever wanted to do to help people make money in the markets was here at the Wall Street Workshop™. This is a dream come true for me and I can never truly explain how much of an impact was made on me today."
                                                            –RICHARD M., FL

"As a former financial planner, I thought I knew a lot about securities and the market. As a current attorney, I thought I knew a lot about companies and securities. Now I know I knew nothing about companies, securities, and the market."
                                                            –MICHAEL R., WA

"An interesting thing happened at the Wall Street Workshop™. I am a licensed general securities broker, licensed insurance agent, and a CFP (certified financial planner). And compared to [the instructor], I don't know jack! It just proves that institutionalized knowledge and street knowledge is about $1,000,000+ per year difference in money making capability. Thanks for presenting difficult to understand material in an incredibly absorbable and fun way. Bravo Wade Cook strategies!"
                                                        –CHRISTOPHER K., FL

We have a pretty cool conclusion to this first go-round on writing Large Option Covered Calls, so let's finish it up.

We started with $25,000. We've taken in $25,600. On the October and November expirations we are called out. *Note: none of our positions were exercised on early. That would have been wonderful, as it would have accelerated the profits to that point, and we could have gone to work more quickly with our returned capital investment plus profits.*

All of the stocks are sold. Calculating a return of the broker-lent money we basically get back our whole $25,000. The $25,600 is also in our account. We've already figured in $600 for commissions, but let's throw in another $600 for more commissions and for margin interest. We still have a handy $25,000 profit (maybe $24,000).

Publishers Note: Commission and margin rates vary widely–from online to full service brokers. Although great effort was made to verify all transaction in this book, prudent and wise traders will use the commission schedule and margin requirements (if applicable) unique to their situation. It is highly recommended that you factor these variables into your trading (both paper and real) before you enter any individual position.

Now what do we do?

1. Go to the movies.

2. Smack your stockbroker upside the head and short of that, buy my books for him and make sure he gets to my seminars and workshops–even if you have to pay the tuition.

3. Start all over again with your original $25,000, or take the original $25,000 and actually buy $25,000 worth of optionable stocks, or $50,000 worth of good, optionable stocks on margin, and...

    a. Write more traditional calls against those positions. This cash flow should be $3,000 to $6,000 a month.

    b. Retire after successfully doing this for a few months–enough to make your spouse happy.

4. Take the $25,000 profits and...

    a. Add to the original $25,000, say $10,000, and buy more good stocks for generating cash flow by writing covered calls.

    b. Put $10,000 to work doing two to three $5 bull put spreads. This will generate another $2,000 to $4,000 per month, and be much safer. (See *Wall Street Money Machine Volume 4: Safety 1st Investing.*) In short: Retire by switching to monthly income strategies or to LOCC again for another five to six months.

c. Take $5,000 of your profits and buy stocks or options and go for extra profits in well-thought-out "position trades"– quick moves for quick profits.

BUT, did you catch it? You're now retired. You can quit your job or business. In short, you're just four to five months (maybe six) from $6,000 to $8,000 of monthly income. All this comes from working the plan. This is truly "getting your money to work harder than you work," and lets you define and work your own money machine. Oh, not enough? Then go at it one more time, take another four to six months and work it again. Use the $25,000 or the whole $50,000. You'll then have $75,000 to $100,000 at work for you. That amount writing "one month out" covered calls would produce around $20,000 a month. If you can't live on that, then you need a different seminar than mine.

Are you having fun? Well, wait until you read and study even more tricks of the trade, even if things (or a few trades) go wrong. All this takes only a few hours of shopping, studying–comparing prices. It might take more time if you want to get busier–yet then your profit potential also increases.

I truly hope this is fun for you! I know the results are worth the efforts–if these are the results you want.

3

PENCHANT FOR CASH FLOW (AND THE AMERICAN DREAM)

There is excitement in the air when we receive letters and phone calls from our students. It's wonderful and we get many every day. The stories are unique, but have a common thread. People can do what financial freedom provides. People can do wonderful things for their churches, their aging parents, their marriage and their kids.

The American Dream, however, has become a blur for so many people. They see success all around them, but it's always for someone else. When I wrote my book *Business Buy the Bible* I opened with the following statement. I'll repeat it here because it is appropriate:

WE ARE ADEQUATE TO THE TASK

> What twisted path of logic must our mind walk down to bring on fear of achieving? Life has an abundance to offer, and we are not inadequate to the task. Innate to our souls is an endless power to innervate all things around us, and to possess all good things through noble endeavor. A kind and wise God has equipped us with all that we need to find joy here and in His world. We have to think lofty ways to inspire our life. We owe Him no less, for truly, we can say He is our Father and we, His children.

–WADE B. COOK   **23**

How about you? Have you given up on seeking the good life? Is prosperity, even great wealth out of reach? And why?

It will be my humble attempt in this short chapter to help you lift up the covers and peek once again at that dream of abundance, happiness and fulfillment. Here and in succeeding chapters, I'll attempt to give you the tools to honestly make a dream gone blue become a dream come true.

But first let's go back. Did you not, while in high school or college, wish for and want the best? The nice car? The big house? Travel? To be with friends? What happened?

Oh, a job! College bills to pay. Then a marriage and the little ones. Then what? "I can't quit now. I can't live my dreams now. I've got a house to buy and car payments." Then, moving on to our forties, "Well I surely can't quit my job now. I need the income and I've got kids heading to college. I need the income. It's just too risky to _____ (fill in the blank–quit my job, travel, start my own business, start a new career, go back to school, *et cetera*.)

It's your choice. You see, the American Dream takes a back seat to all the other important things. Then our ability at making excuses really matures as we mature. I use this term "mature" loosely because maturity means making tough decisions in the face of adversity and accepting the consequences.

I can't "go for it" now because I've got more responsibilities and in fact I only have six more years until my pension kicks in. Do you know that 90% of all retirees have to substantially cut down their standard of living when they retire? The Social Security "safety net" is barely that. I should say "bearly" because so many people enter a psychological "bear market" part of their life. It's interesting that the more holes they get poked into their bodies as they enter the pin-cushion part of their lives, the more holes they poke into every great idea or plan they have. Soon the teakettle has so many holes it can't get up the steam to do anything.

"I'm too old." "I'm too tired." "It's just too late." "I can't do it–I'll just stay home and take it easy." Wow, what a downhill slide. Oh, but we get "A"s in making excuses. At that we excel.

So the next serious question. Do you want to make some small change that will have dramatic cash flow results? Do you want to have the dream rekindled and set afire?

> *One of the strongest characteristics of genius is the power of lighting its own fire.*
>
> —JOHN FOSTER

So what overcomes fear? Confidence. How do you get confidence? Gain knowledge, and use it wisely. How do you use knowledge wisely? Practice and fine-tune your skills. How do you practice the best way? Use age-old techniques and do simulation work. Will this process really work? That depends on your dedication and determination to keep learning and to keep improving and growing.

> *If you practice or study (15 minutes) every day, you'll never have to cram.*
>
> —RUSH LIMBAUGH

Rush Limbaugh said this about his skills on his radio program. It's virtually true in all other aspects of life. Another way to overcome fear is to start small; start with the "known" or little things and move step-by-step from there.

> *Practice yourself in the little things; and thence proceed to greater.*
>
> —EPICTETUS

To prove this point let me tell a story of my encounter in a hotel hallway near a bank of phones. I'll set up the scenario to make this story more meaningful.

I rarely do seminars anymore, yet it is still a passion of mine. I live near Seattle, and one day our Wall Street Workshop™ was going on in a nearby hotel. I was going to step in and address the audience for a few minutes.

Our Wall Street Workshop™ has a very unique style or method of facilitating the learning process of our students. We don't measure our effectiveness by how much we can pour into people, but by how well they perform later–what their results are. We've found that the best way to effectively accomplish this is to get our students as close to the real experience as possible.

Experience is the best teacher, but it is expensive! I think countless tens of thousands of people have realized this and have sought us out. We don't bring people in by selling anything (including investments); they come to us, asking for what we have available, and finding what they need. They come to us to help them build their skills, to show them angles and techniques for building up their monthly income through the stock market.

This process for us is our innovative Tell-Show-Do format. We teach 13 Cash Flow Formulas. We use the three-step process for seven of the 13–what we call our major formulas. The other six–or minor formulas are explained–but that's all.

So, we tell all about a particular formula–the ins and outs, the jargon and when to use it. Then we show our students "how" to do it. We get our trading department or a stockbroker overhead on the P.A. system, and get live quotes of stock and option prices.

Then, step three, is to excuse the students to get on their cell phones, web sites, hotel lobby phones and Simutrade™ (practice) or real trade–make money on paper or for real–depending on the student.

Here is where we pick up the story. I was walking toward the exit. The students were on one of their step-three work breaks. A man grabbed my arm as I walked by. He was older, say mid-seventies, and he passionately asked me, "Wade, what if you're so darn scared?"

Now, you know how, when you get into one of these situations, you have what you said, and then later what you wished you would have said? It's amazing how brilliant we can be later with time behind us to think and ponder.

Well, this happened to be one of those serendipitous occasions where exactly the right thing to say came to me at exactly the right time. I asked back, "What are you *not* afraid of?"

He said, "What do you mean?"

I continued to prod. You see, he had about $20,000 in his portfolio. Obviously, using the whole $20,000 would be tough. It was his life's savings. It was his retirement.

"Are you afraid of risking $10,000?"

"Oh no, I couldn't do that."

"How about $5,000?"

"No, that would be too much."

"How about $2,000 or $1,000?"

At $1,000 he perked up a little. I continued.

"How about $500 or $800?"

"Yes, I could risk (or lose) $800, that would be okay."

"Then go there. After you practice trade, start with $800."

End of story. Start by doing (using) that which you do not fear.

Time out.

I'd like to interject a quick thought and a challenge. I would like to kill two birds with one stone. Throughout this book I've mentioned paper trading. I want to show you what that means. At the same time, I want to challenge my critics with a $10,000 Challenge. We've put this on the Internet, in newspapers, and in the mail. I hope by putting these ideas here, that two things are accomplished in regards to you:

1. You learn how important simulation trading is before you put your hard-earned money in harm's way. Simultaneously, you learn a little of our "paper trading" system.

2. You realize you finally have someone on your team to help you gain truly functional skills for working the market.

Here's our challenge:

Dear Sir,

Owing to the many reports about our great company, and in our humble effort to set the record straight, we hereby offer the following challenge:

Stock Market Institute of Learning™ will award

$10,000

to the charity of your choice if you can find <u>one person</u> who has attended our Wall Street Workshop™, used our strategies exactly as they are taught, and then lost money.

We would like to use your findings to show the public and help people continue to learn the machinations and dangers of the market place.

Sincerely,
Wade Cook

In regards to our <u>one-time</u> $10,000 challenge, here is information so you know what we teach our students, and therefore what you're up against:

1. *Surround yourself with a good team–a knowledgeable stockbroker is a must.*

2. *Choose, study and learn one of our thirteen formulas.*

3. *Do <u>not</u> use real money until you thoroughly understand and then have paper traded (simulation trade) this strategy fifteen times, and then, only after you have paper traded this particular method ten times* successfully *in a row–again, on paper–then and only then use real money.*

4. *Use basic wisdom with help from fundamental analysis, technical analysis and trade on OMFs (Other Motivating Factors) to make better entrance points and exit points.*

5. *Diversify with the different formulas. For example, use very little money on low-cost, limited-risk options, as they are time sensitive and therefore carry an added element of risk. Specifically, if one has $100,000 to invest....*

   a. *Only $4,000 to $5,000 should be used in options.*

   b. *Then this $4,000 should be used in four different $1,000 trades, i.e. even incremental trades.*

   c. *Learn and use the "two in three chance of making money by selling" strategy.*

   d. *Put spreads in place on sell positions to limit downside risk.*

6. *Consistently learn:*

   a. *Check and evaluate results.*

   b. *Look at similar trades on WIN™ for tutorial insights.*

   c. *Continue to read and study.*

If you think you've found someone who has followed our strategies and lost money, we reserve the right to interview that person to ensure that our strategies were indeed followed.

Now back to you. What are you not afraid of? What dollar amount, what strategy can you gain skills in and then master? Go there.

Fear is an incredible protective device if it's used correctly. If fear stifles progress; if it hinders the learning process; if fear curtails and limits the "action" parts of your personality, then it is bad, and possibly dangerous to your life–especially your financial life.

If fear is a catalyst for growth and progress; if it spurs the quest for knowledge and more information; if fear can be harnessed and used appropriately, then great–you're on the right path. Fear keeps us out of trouble and hopefully points us in the right direction.

Fear is just excitement in need of an attitude adjustment.
–RUSS QUAGLIA & DOUG HALL

There is good news. Your life is about to change. I've discovered a few secrets and will share them with you. They will make all the difference in the world. Your life and your income will never be the same.

What I'm about to show you is a process. It's a wonderful way to enhance the quality of your life. It's detailed, it has a beginning, a middle, and an end (or it can keep going). It's achievable. It's not easy, but definitely worth the effort.

There are a few steps. Follow these and the results will be real. So here we go. It starts with your relationship with God.

Oh, I know you probably weren't expecting that, so I'll keep it simple and to the point. Can you find any scripture, anywhere, where it says God wants you to fail? Likewise, try to find one where He wants you to live a mediocre life—to have ordinary results and to live a lifeless life. No? Well then check these out:

Remember the scripture that says, *"The fear of the Lord is the beginning of wisdom..."* (Psalm 111:10, KJV.) Could it not also be the beginning of financial wisdom, or wisdom on developing a great family?

Fear should simply be a CALL TO ACTION. If you have doubts, if you feel anxious then consider the following: God wants us to prosper. He wants us to be successful. First, He wants us to be successful with Him. He wants us to love Him as He loves us. Find a scripture to contradict this. You can't.

I could go on and on; and I did in my books *Business Buy the Bible* and *A+*, but for here and now I want to have a go at this from a completely different angle. I know I'm going to step on a few toes, but that's okay I hope. After all, somebody's got to do it.

He wants us to put Him first. Remember the Jewish Shema. Jesus used this next scripture twice to set us straight on where our allegiance and our devotion should be. Also, the meaning of the word "might" has financial connotations, meaning possessions or wealth.

> *Hear, O Israel: The Lord our God is one Lord: And thou shalt love the Lord thy God with all thine heart, and with all thy soul, and with all thy might. And these words, which I command thee this day, shall be in thine heart:*
> –DEUTERONOMY 6:4-6 (KJV)

...Let the Lord be magnified, which hath pleasure in the prosperity of His servant.

–PSALM 35:27 (KJV)

For I know the plans I have for you, declares the Lord, plans to prosper you and not to harm you, plans to give you hope and a future.

–JEREMIAH 29:11 (NIV)

How dare we fear. What an awesome scripture. Although I've used it elsewhere, it is so appropriate here.

Now unto him that is able to do exceeding abundantly above all that we ask or think, according to the power that worketh in us...

–EPHESIANS 3:20 (KJV)

"Exceeding abundantly." I love the Bible usage of adverbs.

I ponder constantly how it is that some people do so wonderfully well in life while others struggle. How can this exist: two people sitting in my seminars–one goes home and turns $20,000 into $800,000, the other turns $20,000 into $80,000. Can you judge people by their looks? I don't think so. At least I'm not qualified to do so. Is intellect all-important? It certainly has something to do with the process, but surely not everything.

Consider this quote from J. Hawes:

Resolution is omnipotent. Determine to be something in the world, and you will be something. Aim at excellence, and excellence will be attained. This is the great secret of effort and eminence. "I cannot do it," never accomplished anything; "I will try," has wrought wonders.

–J. HAWES

Here's a good (Godly) seven-thought process to follow:

1. Do What You Do For God First

Let me tell you about this principle with a most unusual story. I've been big on teaching about the law of tithing (see *Business Buy the Bible*), but this story happened in front of an audience and brought peace and humility to my heart.

One of my students stood up, basically to confirm what I was saying. He wanted to share how totally successful he was. He said he had read about paying tithing first–serving God without doubt or reservation. He wanted to pay a tithe of $2,000 per month. So, with his first profits he paid the $2,000. He didn't wait to make $20,000, but he paid his one-tenth tithe up front in that amount. Then he said the next $18,000 was his, and he would pay 10% on everything over that. I don't remember him saying what dollar level he was up to, but it was much larger than this. He put God first.

Look at these two letters–one from a 12-year-old boy, the other prompted by that boy's actions:

Dear Mr. Cook,

My name is Zeve A., and I'm twelve. Thanks to your rolling stock strategy, I made my first (and successful) trade on Madge Networks (MADGE). I bought at six and a quarter and sold around seven. I made about $160 after commission and I'm waiting for it to come back down to six again. I have read all of your books, and I agree with your opinion about tithing, and plan to do so after each successful trade. Do you have a favorite charity where you send your donations? I hope to be going to the movies a whole lot more often using your strategies!

Yours truly,
Zeve A., CA

And then this follow-up letter:

August 22, 1997

Dear Zeve A.,

Thank you so very much for your gift of $16.00 in honor of Mr. Wade B. Cook. Your gift allows us to help homeless men and women by providing them with food, shelter, clothing, love, and compassion and a listening ear. Many homeless people we serve have given up hope for the future…they are hungry, not only for food, but for love. Because of your help, we are here 24 hours a day to tell them there is hope…that there are people who care. Thank you again for your compassion for those in need.

With God's Blessing,
Mike Edwards, President (Los Angeles Mission)

I'll take all the criticism in the world to help one 12-year-old boy learn the Law of Tithing–of putting God first. You, too, will need to steel yourself against criticism.

2. SERVE OTHERS–EVEN IN LEARNING

I've studied the learning process and one thing I've realized is that we learn better when we are teaching others, whatever the subject may be. It makes sense. The teacher always learns more than the student.

So, learn to share. Literally pick a person in your life and when you come to my workshops and seminars, come take notes–learn so you can teach it to someone else.

3. BUILD YOUR FAMILY

David O. McKay said, "No other success can compensate for failure in the home." I agree so enthusiastically. I try every day to teach concepts to develop greater family relationships. I hope you feel the same way–because life is so much better–so much more fulfilling when we're growing and sharing together.

4. DEDICATE YOURSELF TO LEARN

One evening Albert Einstein was being honored at a banquet. His young hostess, after hearing wonderful things being said about him, asked, "What is it that you do, sir?"

He said (and I'm paraphrasing), "I'm engaged in the study of physics."

She quipped back, "Oh, physics. I studied that last semester."

Look at the power of that word "engaged." Can we not be engaged in the study of all that makes our life more meaningful?

> *Efforts and courage are not enough without purpose and direction.*
> —JOHN F. KENNEDY

5. STAY OPTIMISTIC

> *Optimism is a [medicine]. Pessimism is a poison. Admittedly, every businessman must be realistic. He must gather facts, analyze them candidly and strive to draw logical conclusions, whether favorable or unfavorable. He must not view everything through rose-colored glasses. Granting this, the incontestable truth is that America has been built up by optimists. Not by pessimists, but by men willing to adventure, to shoulder risks terrifying to the timid.*
> —B.C. FORBES

6. STICK OUT—A LITTLE CRAZINESS NEVER HURT

> *No success is ever accomplished by a reasonable man.*
> —MALCOLM FORBES

> *No one can possibly achieve any real and lasting success or "get rich" in business by being a conformist.*
> —J. PAUL GETTY

7. BE PERSISTENT

Nothing in the world can take the place of persistence. Talent will not; nothing is more common than unsuccessful men with talent. Genius will not; unrewarded genius is almost a proverb. Education will not; the world is full of educated derelicts. Persistence and determination alone are omnipotent. The slogan "press on" has solved and always will solve the problems of the human race.

–CALVIN COOLIDGE

Champions keep playing until they get it right.

–BILLIE JEAN KING

I hope this seven-thought process helps you get going, keep going and find in life that which brings *true* happiness.

Our purpose in life should be to build a life of purpose.

–WADE B. COOK

4

LOCC IT DOWN

By this time, you have to be thinking–is it really this easy? Well, to be honest, it is not. There are a few things that can go wrong–or so it will seem at first. But once we learn how to deal with these few "bumps in the road" we'll have more confidence to get and keep this FREE stock program on track.

LOCC In London

The Large Option Covered Call system is easy from a "you can do it from wherever you are here and now" point of view. That's what I'd like to address. On April 17, 2000, I was in London at the Marble Arch Marriott with my family. We had gone to Paris and on the way home we missed our flight from London to Seattle. Laura and I brought the kids into town, so they could see London–even if just for an afternoon.

Now, London is eight hours ahead of Seattle, so 9:00PM there is Market Closing Time in Seattle, or 1:00PM (4:00PM Eastern). I decided to follow up on some LOCC deals. It was just about twenty minutes before market closing time, or 8:40PM London Time. The day had been long and it was a bugger to call out and dial up America. Why am I telling you all of this? To prove a point.

This process requires work, study, research. A certain element of risk–however mitigated by so many corrective methods–and a fair amount of dedication. However, the mechanics of LOCC deals are quite easy. They are definitely learnable and can be done from any-where–even on vacation.

Now, granted my stockbroker knows what I'm looking for in this type of trade. This means he can find good ones for me while I'm busy at other things. It also means he doesn't waste my time with lousy deals. We can cut to the chase. I got him on the phone and in about 15 minutes, here's what we found. I'm going to list all the stocks here that I asked about. I'll share how we explored possibilities and then picked a good batch. This time we'll use $15,000. I want you to see all of our prospects, because sometimes we can learn as much from "passed up" deals as from the deals we make.

Remember time was short. I realized I could have asked about other strike prices, *et cetera*, but for our purposes, these would suffice. The market had recovered slightly from one of the worst weeks in history. The TV pundits comments were just plain ignorant. These are the options my broker gave me:

1. **Microsoft (MSFT)**
   The stock was slightly over $75. Microsoft had been hit hard. The $75 calls for October were $11 x 11^{1}/_{2}$. We buy the stock for $7,500, but we did it on margin so we're out only $3,750. We sell the October call for $11 and take in $1,100. We have $2,650 on hold to make $1,100; a 42% rate of return. Let's see if we can do better.

MSFT
Sell $75 Call
October
$11
Stock Purchase: $7,500
On Margin (divide by 2): $3,750
Take in (Option Premium): $1,100
Our own cash tied up: $2,650
Rate of return based on $2,650
42%

2. **Intel (INTC)**
The stock was at $121, up on the day. It had seen better times. The near-term April (four days) $120 calls were going for $6 x 6^1/_8$. The further out $120 calls for October 2000 were $21 x 21^1/_2$. The January 2001 $120 calls were 25^1/_4$ x 25^3/_4$. We'll buy 100 shares for $12,100, $6,050 on margin. We'll sell the October call for $21 and collect the $2,100 permium. Put that against the $6,050 cash out for a 53% return.

INTC
Sell $120 Call
October
$21
Stock Purchase: $12,100
On Margin (divide by 2): $6,050
Take in (Option Premium): $2,100
Our own cash tied up: $3,950
Rate of return based on $3,950
53%

3. **General Motors (GM)**
General Motors was going for 85^1/_4$. The September $85 calls were 9^1/_8$ x 9^5/_8$. The January 2001 $85 calls were 12^7/_8$ x 13^3/_8$. We buy the stock for $8,500, halve it for margin, so we've got $4,250 of our own money on hold and sell the September call for $900. Only a 27% rate of return. I guess I'm spoiled. I'm looking for better returns. I know they're out there.

GM
Sell $85 Call
September
$9
Stock Purchase: $8,500
On Margin (divide by 2): $4,250
Take in (Option Premium): $900
Our own cash tied up: $3,350
Rate of return based on $3,350
27%

4. **Qualcomm (QCOM)**
The stock was at 111^5/_8$ x 111^{11}/_{16}$. The October $100 calls were $32 x 34^1/_2$. The $110 calls were 28^1/_8$ x 30^1/_8$ and the $120 calls were 24^5/_8$ x 26^5/_8$. We buy the stock for $5,600 (on margin), sell October at $28 and take in $2,800. Our own cash tied up is $2,800. A clean 100% return. That's more like it.

QCOM
Sell $110 Call
October
$28
Stock Purchase: $11,200
On Margin (divide by 2): $5,600
Take in (Option Premium): $2,800
Our own cash tied up: $2,800
Rate of return based on $2,800
100%

Now we enter a little more risky territory.

5. **Vignette (VIGN)**

A pure Internet play. The stock was up around $300 after a three-to-one stock split announcement, just a short while ago. It backed off to $140 or so, did the split and backed off even more. The downdraft in the whole market did not help. At the time of this deal, the stock was at $44^3/_8$, up $2^1/_4$ for the day. The September $45 calls were $13^1/_4$ x $14^3/_4$. This large spread between the bid

VIGN
Sell $45 Call
September
$13^1/_2$
Stock Purchase: $8,800
On Margin (divide by 2): $4,400
Take in (Option Premium): $2,700
Our own cash tied up: $1,700
Rate of return based on $1,700
159%

and the ask signifies volatility. I like this one, so let's do 200 shares for $8,800 (rounded down), divide by two for the margin, and collect $2,700 in premiums. Put that against our cost and we've got $1,700 of our own cash tied up to make $2,700. A 159% return. Very nice.

6. **Broadcom (BRCM)**

The stock was at $145^5/_8$ x $146, however, it closed a few minutes later around $150. Just to demonstrate the volatility of this stock, it had a low for the day of $114 and closed at $150. The September $145 calls were $41^3/_4$ x $43^7/_8$. The $155 calls were $38^1/_2$ x $40^1/_4$. Let's do 100 shares for $14,500, on margin that's $7,250. Sell the September $145 calls, take in $4,175, leaving $3,075 of our own money on hold. Rate of return: 136%. Let's see a mutual fund match that.

BRCM
Sell $145 Call
September
$41^3/_4$
Stock Purchase: $14,500
On Margin (divide by 2): $7,250
Take in (Option Premium): $4,175
Our own cash tied up: $3,075
Rate of return based on $3,075
136%

Let's put some dollars to all this and see what kind of moola we made. I'm going to put the transaction and commentary down the left side and a running total of our cash in and cash out, along with the individual transaction totals on the right. I'll round my numbers up and down slightly to make the formula easier to read.

Transaction & Explanation	Cash Invested	Running Total	Cash In (Profits)	Total (Profits)
1. MSFT. Buy 100 shares for $7,500. Half on margin $3,750. Sell the Oct75c for $11, or $1,100. Subtract the $1,100 from the $3,750 for a cash on hold total of $2,650. Not bad, but not great.	$2,650	$2,650	$1,100	$1,100
2. INTC. Stock costs $12,100. Margin is $6,050. Sell the Oct120c for $21, or $2,100. Subtract this from $6,050 for a total of $3,950.	$3,950	$6,600	$2,100	$3,200
3. The GM example doesn't make enough.	0	$6,600	0	$3,200
4. QCOM. We'll round up to $112. Then $11,200–$5,600 on margin. Take in $2,800 (rounded down). We have $2,800 on hold to make $2,800.	$2,800	$9,400	$2,800	$6,000
5. VIGN. Buy stock for $4,400, or $2,200 on margin. Sell the Sep45c for $1,350. $850 to make $1,350, Wow! Let's do 200 shares and sell two contracts: $1,700 to make $2,700. Note: added risk, added profit.	$1,700	$11,100	$2,700	$8,700
6. BRCM. Buy stock for $14,500, or $7,250 on margin. Sell $145 calls for $4,175. Take $4,174 from $7,250 and we've invested $3,075 to make $4,175. Again, more risk, but more profit.	$3,075	$14,175	$4,175	$12,875

Okay, we spent a little over $14,000 to make $12,875. These were real numbers. Think about it–$14,175 producing $12,915. It's probably really around $12,000 after commissions and margin interest, but it's still an impressive 85% rate of return from four to five months of having that money tied up. Remember, most of these are close to or at the money. If all goes as expected, you may lose or make a little when you get called out–but you'll still be well ahead. Remember, you're only using a small part of your portfolio for these volatile deals. Practice the strategy thoroughly before using your actual cash. Even then, with these kinds of returns, a couple of trades could sour (see Chapter 11, Stock Repair Kit for more information) and you could still come out ahead.

But tell me–where can you find actual cash profits like this with minimal risk and several back door opportunities? Follow me on W.I.N.™ at www.wadecook.com as we play out trades like these.

LESS MONEY?

What if you only have $5,000 to get started? If you're just beginning my strategies, then a rolling stock strategy may better suit you. Maybe some other safety formula would work better for you–especially if you need cash flow. You see, the nuts and bolts of LOCC are to generate income, but four to six months out. And the main purpose of this book is to help you end up with stocks–FREE and clear–stocks purchased with profits. These stocks can grow, produce income, and be sold later. If you need monthly cash flow, or just need to build up your account, look to some of the strategies with shorter time frames.

But back to the $5,000. Let's say that is all you want to use for now. Hopefully, you've been paper-trading with this amount. (See *On Track Investing* by David R. Hebert for more information on the Simutrade™ practice strategy.) We can still work with that amount.

Let's look at those London deals again with just our $5,000 account. I would probably do INTC for less risk, and the two hundred shares of VIGN for a blend. That would be $3,950 and $1,700 ($5,650) to make $2,100 and $2,700 ($4,800), for an 85% rate of return.

Or I would do the QCOM and BRCM deals, spending $2,800 to make $2,800 and $3,075 to make $4,175. The totals for these two would be $5,875 to make $6,975. Do you see the potential? That's $5,875 to make $6,975 in five months. A 118% rate of return. If you don't do this, what else will you do with your $5,875?

I know in riskier trades you could make more, but for retirement income or for stock purchases these are adequate. And just think, you could do this two or three times a year and even pile up more money to make yet even more. Ask yourself how many months you have until you retire.

I'm here to get you retired, and to get you spending more time with your kids and grand kids, giving and doing more for your church and, well, you fill in the blanks. So, whether you have a lot and want this safer-type income, or if you have a smaller sum to start with and want to build up a nice portfolio of hassle-free stocks or other investments, I think Large Option Covered Calls are relatively easy to implement. They have a beginning, middle and an end. And the end is a potential mother lode.

Let's talk about lifestyle for a moment. First we need to talk about our personalities. My life is unbelievably busy. I get up at 5:23AM, play basketball, come to work and oversee the many subsidiaries that are my responsibility. I've been doing this for seven years. All I need is a car phone or cell phone and a good stockbroker. If you're looking for the mother lode, a good stockbroker is worth his weight in gold. But that's not the point I want to make here.

I would be remiss to think that I will change my personality. Or that you will change yours. God might be able to do it, but we can't, or we won't. Our personalities are ingrained. It's the same with horses. You can't change a horse's mentality. They procreate, herd and eat. That's all they do. You may be excited about all this investment information for awhile, get three terminals, two TVs and three brokerage accounts, but after the excitement wears off, you're still left with your original personality.

The point I'm trying to make here is that you need to pick an investing strategy that fits your personality. If you're lazy, pick a lazy strategy like LEAPS® or LOCCs. If you're into extreme sports and love that adrenaline rush, then day-trade and get in and out of your plays in hours, or even minutes. Or play stock split announcements where the profit opportunities develop and disappear within days. The important thing is to study the strategies and pick one or two that fit your personal style.

Regardless of our personalities, most of us have more similarities than differences. Most of us want to quit our jobs and do more of what we love. That's what I'm about here. I will show you how within four to five months, eight to ten months, or maybe 14 to 16 months, maybe even two years, you can be retired. You will never have to work again. You can if you want to, but you won't have to.

So let's get to work and get you retired with $4,000 to $8,000 a month as a basis. Start with $25,000. Within five to 10 months from now you can retire. You can do it with less, but it will take longer, a few more turns to generate $4,000 to $8,000 a month. At this stage you need to focus on cash flow rather than assets. You want to focus on getting stocks for free. This is not complicated. Once you've mastered this strategy, you'll be able to generate $18,000 to $25,000, plus your original money.

You know, my critics crack me up. I'm one of the most controversial people in America, just a cab driver from Tacoma, Washington, but I write all these books and people buy them so they must want to know this stuff. But first I get criticized for not using real examples, then I get criticized for using real quotes. It's an amazing phenomena. Right now, I'm using real numbers for all the trades in this chapter.

Okay, just a little aside here before we get started, because we're going to be dealing with some volatile stocks. That's what the market is full of right now. But that's not a bad thing. And there will always be corrections. The recent market corrections have created sort of a Teddy Bear market, if you please. Not really a full bear market.

Last year stocks were soaring but they weren't based upon earnings. So many Internet stocks don't even have any earnings. It's like they've taken the "E" out of P/E, like the rules don't apply to them. Of the recent IPOs, only 24% are above their IPO price one year later. Yet their stocks still climb.

With all this activity everyone thinks everyone else is getting rich. This has created a great deal of volatility or speculative value in the market. An ordinary company may take two to four years to go from $60 to $110, while these volatile stocks can shoot from $18 to $110 in a very short time, some within six months.

On a quickly rising stock, the call options are also going to be very volatile and a lot larger than the options you're used to seeing. As a buyer, you might be fearful of these higher prices and go for the slower moving options that only costs $8. But I have created this wonderful new angle to writing covered calls in this volatile market. The LOCC stragety I've been showing you.

For the purposes of this strategy I want you to think about this: When it is too expensive to buy something, it is better to sell.

Got that? Okay, let's use it. Usually you write a covered call to do two things:

1. To capture the premium.

2. To sell the stock for a profit.

Let's say you own a stock. If you write a covered call, you give away the upside potential. This is an opportunity lost. So if you have a high flying stock, you don't write a covered call on it. You don't want to give away the upside. In the slower moving stock you're not giving up so much, therefore you're not going to be paid as much. If you own the fast mover, you're giving up a lot of potential. So, you can sell that option for a lot more.

When you buy a call option, you own the right to buy it at an established price. What are you hoping for? You are waiting for the stock to go up. Stock can move three ways: up, down, or sideways. When you buy a call, if the stock price stays at its current price, you lose. If stock goes down, you lose. You have a one in three chance to win. These are not good odds.

If you're writing a covered call, and the stock goes up, you make money. You get to keep the premium, plus the increase in the stock price. What if it goes down? If a stock drops down to what you paid for it, you break even and you still own the stock, plus you keep the premium. It could even drop below what you paid for it and you'd be okay. You could have a 20% to 30% drop and be okay–not lose money– because the premium could make up the difference.

Now I want to show you another reason to buy stocks and write covered calls.

3. Make the stock market buy stocks for you–stocks you choose.

That's what LOCC is about. This is a money machine like you've never seen before.

LOCC In Seattle
I want to finish this chapter with another series of deals like the London trades, where I took $25,000 to make another $25,000 in four or five months. These next trades were done during the April 19, 2000 Wall Street Workshop™ where I stepped in to demonstrate this LOCC system and talk about my seminar "Paid to Trade." What you're going to read next is a transcription from the actual event. Remember, these are real numbers, however, in a few cases I have rounded them up or down to make the formula less complicated for this book.

"Okay. For each deal we're going to buy 100 shares and sell one or two contracts against it. And I'll turn down some of these deals. I would rather want what I don't have than have what I don't want. Okay. Let's go shopping.

1. **Qualcom (QCOM)**

   Qualcom is on a major dip and trading at about $120^3/_4$. We buy 100 shares for $12,000. On margin we divide by two for $6,000 out of pocket. This amount is on hold, your risk amount. The October $120 calls are going for $28 x $29. We write (sell) one contract and collect a $2,800 premium. This leaves you with $3,200 cash out. We want to get called out for maximum potential. We could

QCOM
Sell $120 Call
October
$28
Stock Purchase: $12,000
On Margin (divide by 2): $6,000
Take in (Option Premium): $2,800
Our own cash tied up: $3,200
Rate of return based on $3,200
88%

   sell the $110 call, but we would have to give back $10 later. Let's stick with the at-the-money call. Third Friday in October we will probably get called out; it's a good calculated risk.

2. **JDS Uniphase (JDSU)**

   The stock is at $95. We buy 100 shares for $9,500. On margin that's $4,750. We sell the September $95 call for $25^3/_4$, taking a premium of $2,575 against our $4,750. That leaves $2,175 of our money invested to make $2,575 for a 118% rate of return. That's what we're looking for with LOCC. Get the idea? What if we get called out early? That would be good because all of the cash is back in the

JDSU
Sell $95 Call
September
$25^3/_4$
Stock Purchase: $9,500
On Margin (divide by 2): $4,750
Take in (Option Premium): $2,575
Our own cash tied up: $2,175
Rate of return based on $2,175
118%

   account earlier. We've paid for the stock. That hardly ever happens, but this is a great example. We want to get called out early.

3. **General Motors (GM)**

The stock is $88. We buy 100 shares for $8,800 and divide it by two for the margin, which leaves $4,400 of our own money on hold. We write the September $85 call and sell it for $11. That's $1,100 generated by selling one contract. Do the math. We spent $4,400, took in $1,100, leaving an actual out-of-pocket cost of $3,300 to make $1,100 profit. We have

GM
Sell $85 Call   *September*   *$11*
Stock Purchase: $8,800   *On Margin (divide by 2): $4,400*   *Take in (Option Premium): $1,100*   *Give back): $300*   *Our own cash tied up: $3,300*
Rate of return based on $3,300   24%

to give back $300 of the $1,100, leaving a profit of $800. That's a respectable 24% rate of return. GM is not that speculative, which means it has less risk and less return, but retirees would love even this return.

"Most of the time with LOCCs we're looking for 80 to 100% return in four to five months. Annualized that's about 15 to 20% a month. LOCC is investing for a busy lifestyle, but it's just one formula. You should diversify your formulas. Let's go to a mid-level risky stock like Microsoft (MSFT).

4. **Microsoft (MSFT)**

Microsoft is at $80, rounded up. We buy 100 shares on margin so our outlay is $4,000 of our own money. October is the next option farthest out. The October $80 call is $11³/₈ for a $1,137 premium. Subtract $1,137 from $4,000 and we used $2,863 to make $1,137. Rate of return is 40%. Not great, but okay.

MSFT
Sell $80 Call   *October*   *$11³/₈*
Stock Purchase: $8,000   *On Margin (divide by 2): $4,000*   *Take in (Option Premium): $1,137*   *Our own cash tied up: $2,863*
Rate of return based on $2,863   40%

5. **Juniper (JNPR)**
Juniper is at $195 so 100 shares cost $19,500, halved by our margin for a total of $9,750 out of pocket. We write the October $195 calls for $52 and take in $5,200. Subtract that from our outlay ($9,750–$5,200 = $4,550) for a 114% rate of return. Nice.

JNPR
Sell $195 Call
October
$52
Stock Purchase: $19,500
On Margin (divide by 2): $9,750
Take in (Option Premium): $5,200
Our own cash tied up: $4,550
Rate of return based on $4,550
114%

"What if the stock price drops to $130? Well, first of all, you won't get called out and you will still own the stock. You could sell it and redeploy the cash, or keep it and use it to generate more income using other strategies. Just do not sell or buy in a panic. Be cool, calm and collected. If real estate goes down from $240,000 to $220,000, do you sell? No, you don't move. Markets correct all the time.

"Remember, just because a stock goes down in value doesn't mean you're devoid of opportunity. Some people look at dips as a good buying opportunity. (For more information, see Chapter 11, Stock Repair Kit.) What I'm saying is you can make more money buying back and selling, but that strategy takes it out of the realm of what we're talking about. That is a busy person strategy.

6. **Broadcom (BRCM)**
This stock is at $150, rounded up. Buy your 100 shares for $15,000, halve it for the margin for $7,500 out of pocket. The August $150 calls are $33^{1}/_{2}$. November $150 calls are $40^{1}/_{4}$. Let's take those and collect a $4,025 premium. That gives us $3,475 on hold to make $4,025 for a 116% rate of return. Now we're cooking.

BRCM
Sell $150 Call
November
$40^{1}/_{4}$
Stock Purchase: $15,000
On Margin (divide by 2): $7,500
Take in (Option Premium): $4,025
Our own cash tied up: $3,475
Rate of return based on $3,475
116%

7. **Verticalnet (VERT)**
   Trading at $43 rounded down. We like this one, so we're buying 200 shares, spending $8,600, divided by two for margin for about $4,300 on hold. The October $40 calls are $14^5/_8 ($14.625). October $45 calls are $13^1/_8 ($13.125). Let's do the October $45 calls. That's a $2,625 premium for two contracts. Now subtract that from our $4,300 for a profit of $1,675 and a 157% rate of return.

VERT
Sell $45 Call
October
$13^1/_8
Stock Purchase: $8,600
On Margin (divide by 2): $4,300
Take in (Option Premium): $2,625
Our own cash tied up: $1,675
Rate of return based on $1,676
157%

"Do you love this, or what? Just for fun, let's take this trade a bit further. If the stock goes up and we get called out, we have to sell the stock for the $45, losing the $2 up side per share. That's $400 for two contracts. So, subtract that $400 from our $2,625 premium for $2,225, and we still have a solid 132% rate of return.

"But what if the price goes up and we don't get called out? We could sell and pick up that $400 giving us a whopping 180% rate of return. I can live with that. Don't forget the rules for writing covered calls. Buy on dips. Play into volatility. Let's go on to the last deal.

8. **3Com (COMS)**
   This stock is trading at around $42 rounded up. We'll buy 200 shares again for $8,400. Divided by two for margin, and we have $4,200 of our own money on hold. The October $42^1/_2 calls are $9^5/_8, or $9.625. We write that call and $1,925 dollars hits our account, a tidy little 85% rate of return.

COMS
Sell $42.50 Call
October
$9^5/_8
Stock Purchase: $8,400
On Margin (divide by 2): $4,200
Take in (Option Premium): $1,925
Our own cash tied up: $2,275
Rate of return based on $2,275
85%

"Let's take a look at what we just did.

Transaction & Explanation	Cash Invested	Running Total	Cash In (Profits)	Total (Profits)
1. QCOM. Buy 100 shares for $12,000. Half on margin $6,000. Sell the Oct120c for $28, or $2,800. Subtract the $2,800 from the $6,000 for a cash on hold total of $3,200. ROR: 88%	$3,200	$3,200	$2,800	$2,800
2. JDSU. Buy 100 shares for $9,500, half on margin. Sell Sept95c for $25.75, or $2,575. Subtract $2,575 from $4,750 for a cash on hold total of $2,175. ROR: 118%	$2,175	$5,375	$2,575	$5,375
3. GM. Buy 100 shares for $8,800, half on margin. Sell Sept85c for $11, or $1,100. Subtract the $1,100 from the $4,400 for a cash on hold total of $3,300. ROR: 33%; Respectable, but we'll pass on this deal.	$0	$5,375	$0	$5,375
4. MSFT. Buy 100 shares for $8,000, half on margin. Sell Oct80c for $11.37, or $1,137. Subtract the $1,137 from the $4,000, for a cash on hold total of $2,863. ROR: 40%; Ho hum, we'll do it anyway.	$2,863	$8,238	$1,137	$6,512
5. JNPR. Buy 100 shares for $19,500, half on margin. Sell Oct195c for $52, or $5,200. Subtract the $5,200 from the $9,750, for a cash on hold total of $4,550. ROR: 114%; That's what I like to see!	$4,550	$12,788	$5,200	$11,712
6. BRCM. Buy 100 shares for $15,000, half on margin. Sell Nov150c for $40.25, or $4,025. Subtract the $4,025 from the $7,500, for a cash on hold total of $3,475. ROR: 116%; Yes!	$3,475	$16,263	$4,025	$15,737
7. VERT. Buy 200 shares for $8,600, half on margin. Sell Oct45c for $13.12, or $2,624. Subtract the $4,025 from the $7,500, for a cash on hold total of $3,475. ROR: 116%; Yes!	$1,675	$17,938	$2,625	$18,362
8. COMS. Buy 200 shares for $8,400, half on margin. Sell Oct42.50c for $9.63, or $1,926. Subtract the $1,926 from the $4,200, for a cash on hold total of $2,274. ROR: 85%.	$2,274	**$20,212**	$1,926	**$20,288**

"And there you go. You've made about $20,000, well $19,000 after you take out $1,000 for commissions. That's $19,000 plus your original $20,000. You can take that $19,000 out of the market, reinvest it, whatever. You could do whatever you want with it. The point is, the marketplace gave you $19,000 that you didn't know was out there."

Do you wish your stockbroker would have told you about this? What if you borrowed the initial money? Could you pay most of it back now? Writing covered calls can generate 15% to 30% a month, with an average of 20%. Take the $20,000 for example. Twenty percent is $4,000. Could this allow you or your spouse to quit working, so that one of you could stay home with the kids. Could $4,000 help you live a better lifestyle?

What do people need? More cash flow, that's what. You don't need another job. You need to work less. You need to work smarter. This could be your second job. It could be your only job. This might take two hours a month to research and make your trades. You could do this in your bathrobe. Would that be a fairly good lifestyle?

Decide where you want to go in your life. Do you want to be more busy or more fulfilled? I've never heard anyone come tell me they're planning to retire soon and will need less money. I've heard that 90% of retiring Americans have to cut back their lifestyle. I want to change that. Retired people can do this LOCC strategy and help themselves immensely, because there is a world of difference between cutting back on your lifestyle and doing everything you've ever wanted when you're making $2,000, $3,000 or $4,000 a month more. You could do a version of this (without the margin) in an IRA and build it up. Study this strategy. Do it on paper perfectly until you can do it 10 times in a row, making a profit. Then do it for real.

The last thing I want to say about LOCCs in this chapter is this: If I can make $12,000 in 13 minutes on a weird phone from London, what can you do at home with all your fancy gadgets?

5

UNLOCKING IMPLIED VOLATILITY

In this chapter, I want to cover some important information on the pricing of options. Why do you need to know this? Because there is no way we can talk about writing covered calls, selling puts, or bull put spreads unless we understand what goes into the option price. When you understand how options are created, why they are priced in a certain way, and why they do or don't perform in an expected fashion, it can help you make better choices about what options to play. Does that sound like information you can use? I hope so, because that's what I'm about–giving you information you can use to help you create the lifestyle you want.

I'm going to start with some definitions, some terms, some explanations, some background so you can understand the mentality of the option market makers and the tools they use to determine the price for their securities. In order to do this, I'm going to have to speak some Greek. There are a lot of Greek names in some of the stock market investing, from beta to delta, gamma to theta to vega. Many of you may have heard of the delta formula, but probably not as many of you have heard about vega. That's where I want to take you, but to get there, you first need to understand delta.

DELTA

A delta is a relationship between a movement of an option and the movement of a stock. Sometimes we refer to the expression "tick for tick." This means for every stock movement there is a specific correlating delta movement. For example, if the stock goes up $1 and the option goes up $1, that is a 100 delta. That is tick for tick. The stock moves up $2 and the option moves up $2. When there is a one hundred percent correlation between the movement in the stock and the option price, that is a delta of 100. But there can be complications, such as time value.

You can divide an option price into "intrinsic value" and "time value." The intrinsic value is the in-the-money value of the option. The time value is what's left after you subtract the intrinsic value. If the stock price is below the option price, there is no intrinsic value. The total premium consists of time value. Once the stock price rises above the option strike price, the intrinsic value could climb or descend tick for tick. But what if at the same time, the time value is declining? Then this could have the effect of reducing the overall value of the option. So, instead of the option going up $1 for every $1 in the stock price, it might only go up 80¢. Okay. The stock goes up a dollar and the option goes up 80¢. That would be a delta of 80. What if the time value is so close to expiration it has a negative impact on the delta? Could the option price go down even if the stock price is rising? Yes. That's why it's important to understand the factors that impact the overall price.

EXAMPLE: $50 CALL OPTION			
STOCK PRICE	OPTION		
	TOTAL	INTRINSIC	TIME
$40	1	0	1
$45	$1^1/_2$	0	$1^1/_2$
$50	2	0	2
$52	$4^3/_4$	2	$2^3/_4$
$54	9	4	5
$56	14	6	8

What does this mean to you? If you're looking at an option to buy or sell, you want to find one with a high delta number. This means that it will have a bigger move for every tick of the stock symbol, and even as the time expires, the strong delta can keep the option price up.

Deltas are very important. However, many stockbrokers don't use them. Some don't even have the ability to look up deltas quickly; they either don't have the available software, or don't have a delta quote. They may not consider delta significant for the kinds of trades they do. So when you're considering whether to buy an option or sell an option, you really won't know very much about it from a delta point of view, unless your stockbroker is really up on this type of calculation.

Once again, I'll put in my plug for a good stockbroker. A living, breathing human being who happens to be a stockbroker can make you so much more money than any electronic trading program I have ever seen. Yes, the online services brag about their low commissions, but that's because they give you no service, they bring you no deals. I've seen proof of this countless times myself and my students constantly confirm it. One deal presented by a good stockbroker can make you five or six thousand dollars. That could pay for all your commissions for several months, even for a year! So, I don't want to hear about $9 trades and $18 trades online. What I want to hear is that your stockbroker called you and got you into a deal that made you $8,000. That's an exciting thing. You are relying on this person to help you make your money. You owe it to yourself to make that a quality person. And if you really think about it, can't you almost judge the quality of your life by the quality of the people you have around you?

Okay. My stockbroker is blushing. Let's move on and talk about another aspect of movement in the option prices. What I'm going to explain now is a little bit tougher to understand than delta, but as I try to work you through this, it will become clear and you'll fit another piece into the puzzle. What I want to address now is vega.

VEGA

Not Greek actually, but Roman, vega is the measure of the price change in an option divided by a percentage change in the volatility. In a practical application for options, vega would determine what the percentage increase in the volatility means in the price of the option either up or down.

Okay, I've mentioned volatility three times already so I'd better explain what I'm talking about. What does it have to do with the price of an option premium?

IMPLIED VOLATILITY

You may have heard the term implied volatility. How about speculative value? How about expected volatility? How about anticipation? The news-worthiness of an event? Coming up on news? Volatility or the "speculative value" is the amount of variation of a market or stock price. If a market or stock tends to vary often and wildly, it is said to be volatile; it has a high "speculative value."

To illustrate, one company may take two years to go from $60 to $110, while another company might go from $18 to $110 in a very short time. This latter company would very likely be classified as a volatile company. This volatility factor is directly reflected in the price of a stock option. A slower-moving company might have a particular option that sells for $8, while a volatile company's option in the same month and strike price might be $38.

When a stock has a huge premium, what that really means is that there is a lot of potential for the stock to go up, or conversely, there is a lot of potential for it to go down. The stock is erratic. It can make really dramatic moves even in one or two days. A $240 stock can go up to $280, and the next day it opens up at $230 and drops down to $210, and by the end of the day it's back to $260! Talk about erratic!

We've all seen a lot of stocks like this lately. As a matter of fact, I've almost seen a whole *market* like this. You've seen it too if you've been watching the DOW or the NASDAQ take two and three hundred point swings almost intra-day! Talk about implied volatility!

Now I'm going to give you some information that you probably don't want to hear, because it sounds exactly illogical until you really think it through. Here it is:

When a stock dips, when a stock goes down, the implied volatility goes up. Conversely, when a stock goes up (especially to new highs) the implied volatility goes down.

What does this mean? Let me say it again. When a stock goes down, say a $240 stock dips down to $200, the implied volatility goes up. Take a look at this graph, at these observable rules and features about stocks and implied volatility. It doesn't have a lot of detail, it's just a way to organize your thinking as I get into more detail.

LOW VOLATILITY	*HIGH VOLATILITY*
Stock moves up and down slower	*Fast up and down movements in stock*
Stock options less expensive	*Stock options more expensive*
Higher stability	*Unstable movement*
Less risk	*Higher risk factor*

Okay. Let's look historically at a stock and an option movement. We can track the relational option movement historically to the penny. And we know exactly what the ratios (delta) and exactly what the percentages (vega) are right now. We know what they were historically, what they were two months and eight months ago. But what about two months from right now, or a year from right now? What about the future? How do we measure a relationship between a potential movement of a stock and the option?

Well, we come up with a volatility figure again, but this time we're implying some information from it, or we're putting some sentiment into it. Now, that is what is called "implied volatility." It is a projection of the future movement and the relationship between the stock and the option price, and it is determined by the option market makers. I'll deal with them in a moment, but stick with me on these technical factors a while longer. I want to introduce you to the Black-Scholes Option Pricing Model.

BLACK-SCHOLES OPTION PRICING MODEL

The Black-Scholes computer model was developed by Fischer Black and Myron Scholes, and is used to estimate the fair market value of option contracts. It uses, among other data, interest rate levels and the price volatility of the underlying security to gauge the contracts. It is important to keep in mind that the option premiums generated by this model are only theoretical and may not reflect actual market conditions. It uses what is called a risk-free rate of return, or what the rate of return is on a T-bill. It also uses time as a factor in gauging the price of contracts, specifically, the time left before that particular option expires.

The Black-Scholes model is used by virtually every option trader, every market maker, every wholesaler in the business. These are the people who put out the bid and the ask, the people who buy and sell the options. This model was created by human beings looking at the marketplace and seeing the relationships between stocks and options and coming up with the best model that they could for establishing prices. The Black-Scholes model was created so that the options market makers would not lose money. As I mentioned briefly, there are four main things that make up the price of an option.

1. Time value. The formula that goes into making up an option price obviously has a lot to do with the time left to expiration. Time deteriorates in an orderly manner, day after day. That is measured.

2. Risk-free rate of return. To figure out a certain price of an investment like a derivative such as an option, you need a standard or a basis to compare it to. Here the computer model uses a "risk-free rate of return" based on the T-bill rate. The risk rate of return the T-bill does change, but it changes in a rather slow, orderly manner.

3. Implied volatility. This is the price volatility of the underlying security.

I want to add another factor, the human factor.

4. Market makers.

THE MARKET MAKERS

Time, risk-free rate and implied volatility are all critical in pricing options. But the final variable is a human one. Let's talk about the market makers, specifically the option market makers. They run the computers, push the buttons, change the prices, and seal the fate of the call and put options that you buy.

Behind the scenes of the stock market is a group of people who do not have to put on a good face to you. I am sad to report that these people get out of bed every morning with the sole purpose of getting your money. They cannot make their car payment, they cannot retire, and they cannot put their kids through college unless they get your money.

We are trying every way we can to preserve and protect our money and I must tell you, we are amateurs at keeping our money. These market makers are professionals at getting at our money. They know every trick in the book. With the recent downturn in the market they are finding it easier than ever before to pick off investors. Ping. Ping. Ping. Like ducks on a log. I had an options market maker basically come out of the woods and tell us here at the Stock Market Institute of Learning™ about all the things that go on behind the scenes. And believe me, option market makers all behave in a certain way. They're all going to price options a certain way.

We need to get good at knowing how the market makers work, how they think, and how they get at our money. We are at their mercy, and I seriously doubt that they have any. Basically, the option market makers are just sitting there ready for us.

HOW IMPLIED VOLATILITY AFFECTS OPTION PRICING

Now we get to the crux of this chapter. You've heard me say many times before that I believe that option market makers are a lot more in tune, a lot more into the stock market than even stock market specialists. They have to be.

When you have a $80 stock and you own a $5 call option on it, a small movement in the stock price usually means a rather large movement in the option. Well doesn't it? Isn't that what I always say? Can't it sometimes go against that? Why doesn't it always move? Why do you sometimes see a stock run up $20 and the option only go up $1 or $2? Why is that? When the stock goes up $20, and you were thinking you were going to make $12 or $13 on that option and it only goes up 50¢ or $1, it all comes down to the Black-Scholes computer model and the factor of implied volatility.

Let's break it down. What are you actually buying or selling when you buy or sell an option? You're buying the right to purchase or sell the stock at a certain price. But what makes up the premium? Say the stock is at $84 and you buy an $80 call for $9. Four dollars of that is in the money. The other $5 is the time value. What makes up this time value? I've said this before–three things:

1. The time left before expiration.

2. The risk-free related factor.

3. The implied volatility.

The options market maker directly impacts the implied volatility. They grade a stock with a numbering system. I want to give you a few market maxims, things that the option market makers know about us–the investor–in the market place. They know that:

1. Fear is pure and potent.

2. In general, when stock prices go down, the option's implied volatility goes up.

3. Conversely, when stocks go up, the option's implied volatility goes down.

4. Greed is always tempered with reality.

Now, what these option market makers can do is slow the trading down to make sure that the options and stock prices catch up to each other. They can buy a lot of stocks and dump them on the market, or buy a lot of stocks off the market to drive the price up or down. They have so many tools at their disposal to make sure that they do not lose money. Let me say this again. The Black-Scholes model was created so that the options market makers do not lose money. They want to ensure that they are selling options at the highest price that they could possibly sell them.

And you thought this was just a numbers game. Okay, so how can we psych out the option market maker? How can we know what they will do? We can't–not absolutely. But they are human after all, and if there is one thing I know about people, it is that they follow the money.

Let's rewind a minute. Let's go back to our options market makers a few years ago. A few years back the options market makers were literally having to turn off their computers, reset the perimeters for their prices and then turn them back on to post the new prices. You'd check out the options and see prices change when the stock hardly moved at all. Or you'd know that the stock had dropped $12 a few minutes before, and the options had barely budged. Then kaboom! All of a sudden the options just changed for no apparent reason.

Today that is not the case. Today computer models are so fast the options market makers don't have to turn off their computers to do the update. They can just change the implied volatility factor from 30 to 10 in a matter of seconds. What is the implied volatility factor? Let's go there.

IMPLIED VOLATILITY FACTOR

I can explain this best with an example. Let's say you have a $200 stock. The $200 stock has an implied volatility factor of 30. That 30 means 30% and it is a one-year implied volatility. What that 30 implied volatility factor means is that the options market makers are saying that this stock could go up 30%, up to $260, or conversely they are saying it could go down 30% to $140. They are saying this $200 stock could have a 120-point swing in a year. How many of you have seen stocks swing like this–20, 30, even 40 points–within a day? That's right, intra-day. Well, when the stock swings that much there is a lot of volatility built into it.

Now let me give you a real example. We did one deal just recently where the stock dropped. It was VeriSign (VRSN). The stock was at $64. We purchased a $60 call for $6. The stock dropped to $62 in about a half hour. We still owned the $60 calls, they were now $7. We finally sold them at $7.50. How can that be? In all of our seminars we say that when the stock has a small movement there is a magnified movement in the option. But here the exact opposite happened. Here the stock literally went down $2 and the option when up 1^1/_2$. It wasn't a magnified movement, it was a reverse movement. Point: When the stock dropped the implied volatility increased–the option went up in price.

Here's another example. You see a stock that just shot up to $240. You think it's going higher, you think it's going to $300 or whatever. The $240 calls are going for $40. This stock just tanks in a matter of days, from $240 to $200. And the option falls down to $30. How can $40 come out of the price of the stock and only $10 come out of the price of the option? Again, the implied volatility increased and the option premium stayed relatively high.

Last example. Vignette (VIGN) was trading at $203. We purchased the $220 calls for $18. This stock finally went up $14 dollars to $217 after about a week. The option went to $19. The stock continued to climb to $228 and the option went up to $21. How can that be? The stock rose by $25 and the option only rose $3. Remember: when the stocks rise, the implied volatility percentage goes down.

With a touch of his finger, the options market maker can change the implied volatility from a 30 to a 20. There are some stocks with an implied volatility of 90. I saw a $112 stock the other day with an implied volatility of 109. Think about that. A 109 implied volatility means it could go up 109% in this year or that it could go down 109%, which means it could go to zero in this computer model.

How do these examples make any sense? I'm asking you—I'm warning you—to *be careful*. Whenever we try to make sense of something financial, we need to ask: "Who gets what out of this deal?" Always follow the money.

Follow the Money

That little sentence has served me well. I've walked into many rooms full of people looking for investors for a deal and I don't know all the people sitting at the table and I'll always ask, "What is everybody doing here? What are you all getting out of this deal? What are you here for?" Before I go committing any money to a deal I want to know everybody who's involved in the deal and what everybody is getting out of the deal.

Apply that to options. What is everybody getting out of this deal? What is going on here?

It comes back to the options market maker. They make their living selling options. That is their job. That is how they support their family. I'll be very crass with you. They're going to sell an option for whatever someone is willing to pay for it.

You've heard that before. What is this car worth? Well, it's worth what someone is willing to pay for it. What is this house worth? It's worth what somebody is willing to pay. So let me ask you, if you could sell something for $30, why would you sell it for $10? What are you willing to sell it for? Let's look at that.

Let's say you own Stock A. Over many years it has managed to climb up to $150. It is not a fast moving stock. It could be a food stock for example, or a bank stock. It has earnings, nice steady growth and has done very nicely. A few years ago it was at $110. It's taken two years to get to $150. To get to $160 or $180 could be another year or two. You call your broker and ask what the $150 call three months out is going for. He says they're going for $10.

Okay. Look at another stock. Stock B did an IPO a little over a year ago. A year ago the stock was at $18. This stock has run up and is now also at $150. And not only has it had this meteoric climb, a financial analyst is now saying that this stock is going to $300. It's at least going to $250 says one brokerage firm. This company is about to start making money. It's getting taken over, going to merge with another company, there's all this talk about this company. They're on TV.

By the way, you want to do a good reality check on these high-flying companies before trading. Try this. Watch the ads on the Super Bowl one year and then watch the next year, see how many of those companies have come and gone. You'll see that these hot companies have so many hundreds of millions of dollars to spend on advertising right now, and they're just burning through the cash. Many won't be around to play another Super Bowl.

So here is a word to the wise. For those of you who want to get involved in these hot, high-flying Internet stocks, most of them don't even have earnings. They've taken the E out of P/E. They're saying they're at 20. Twenty what? Twenty times revenue. They're aren't even talking about earnings. Some of these are 200, 300 times sales. If you want to get good information on these companies, check how fast they're burning through their cash. It's easy to check. There are all kinds of reports coming out about this fact. You'll see that some of these companies which had $300 million dollars on an IPO are burning $20-30 million a month in advertising trying to get customers. In another seven months they'll be out of money.

Do you think the investing public will eventually get tired of funding these companies if they don't start making some money? You tell me. Check the burn rate. How fast are they burning through their cash? And you'll see that some of the most popular companies today, if they continue at the burn rate that they are at now, will burn through their cash in a year. I'm not saying they'll be out of business in a year. They could do another IPO to raise more money, a secondary offering, or they could merge with another company that has more cash, or here's a novel idea—they could merge with a company that is actually making money! They can do things to generate more cash to keep going a little longer. You will see a lot of road kill along the Internet highway. We've already seen many.

Back to my example, Stock B trading at $150. This company has all the promise in the world. Everyone is talking about this company. This is the hot one, so you call your broker and ask what's a $150 call out in three months. And your broker says it is $30 to buy an option, to buy the right to buy the stock at $150 in three months. How can this be? How can Stock A's call option for $150 be $10 and Stock B's call option for $150 be $30? Let's look at this, factoring in the volatility.

What is the volatility? Obviously if you're going to buy Stock A there's a high likelihood that it's not going to go up very much, so the option market makers cannot sell the option to you at a very high price, certainly not for $30. Why is that? Because you're just not willing to pay that much for it. You're not willing to pay $30 for an option on this company because in theory, the stock would have to go to $180 for you to even break even. Now we know in options that this is not always the case, because we know from experience that a stock could have a quick run-up and our $30 option could go to $33 in a day and we could be out. But in real life, if you really think it through, that stock has to go to $180. So, you're not willing to spend $30 because this company's track record just doesn't support that kind of run-up. Conversely, Stock B could go from $150 to $200, $250 and you'd make big money. It's probably not very educational to look at this from a purchaser's point of view.

FOLLOW THE MONEY—THINK LIKE AN OPTION MARKET MAKER

Come with me down this road—it's a little scary, but come with me anyway. Quit thinking about yourself as an investor, as a trader trying to make a living in this marketplace. Think about what the options market makers is trying to do here. Let's become him. Let's not just think we are that market maker; let's get inside his brain and become him. Let's sell that option ourselves.

Let's pretend for a moment that we're writing a covered call. Let's say that we own this stock, we bought this stock for $150 and the $150 call out three months is $30. Let's sell 10 contracts for $30,000. We are giving someone the right to buy the stock away from us at $150. What are we giving up? What is the options market maker giving up now by being a seller? You've heard before that in writing a covered call the new risk is an opportunity lost risk. But from a selling point of view we're giving up all the upside potential. We're selling everything above the $150 for cash. If there's a high potential, high implied volatility, a speculative value of a high amount then we can sell it for more money.

That's a new way of looking at writing covered calls. What are you giving up? In Stock A you're not giving up very much, therefore you're not going to get paid very much. In Stock B you're giving up a potential $100 to $150 upside, so you can charge more for that call.

Let me tell you what the scary part of this is. The options market makers can come in at any point in time, push the button on the computer, and change the implied volatility. I've just sat there and watched stocks that were $72 hardly budget at all, and the $70 call has gone from $4 to $6 and the stock hasn't even moved. How can that be? Because of implied volatility.

Of the four factors, the implied volatility changes the most. Now you can get information on implied volatility at www.cboe.com, the Chicago Board Options Exchange website. They have historical volatility. You can go in and look at the historical volatility of a stock, and compare it with the current volatility. You can look and see, for example, that a stock historically has a volatility of 28 and right now it has a 10, it has settled down. You can see historical to the current.

Another Internet site to get information is www.theoptionclub.com. This site has a lot of information. At the time of this book printing this is a free site. They may try to sell you something at the back end, but it has a lot of information; historical implied volatility compared to current implied volatility.

Another measurement you can check out are the 100 stocks which represent a major part, or a nice blending of the market, called the VIX. That will give you the implied volatility of this index, for parts of the market in general. If the VIX is at 39 and it's up 2.8 for the day, that means the whole market is down. Every time I check it, if the VIX is up, the stock market is down, and if the VIX is down, the stock market is up.

PUT VOLATILITY ON YOUR SIDE—BE A SELLER, NOT A BUYER

I have an adage that I've had since my real estate days. "When in doubt, when there's uncertainty, sell something." If you have a property, and you don't know what's going to happen to that property, get rid of it. Life is too short to have problems. And you know the old adage that I keep saying: "I'd rather want what I don't have than have what I don't want"? Well it sure is true here.

Let's give you another example of what it means to sell something. If the stock is at $240, and the option out a couple months at a $240 strike price is going for $40, and you think it's expensive to buy, why not sell it? Now, conversely, if the stock takes a dip down to, say $200, and that $240 call option is going for say $30, why not sell that? Why not sell the $240 call, even in an uncovered position; or sell the $240 call and buy the $250 or $260 call, and create a bear call spread. You would win if the stock does not go back to $240. The length of time to the expiration would determine whether I would do this trade or not.

My point is, sell something. When the options are fluffy, and the stock takes a dip, and the implied volatility is high—be a seller. As the stock rises, and continues to rise, it peaks—that's when you want to also not be a buyer, or buy back the option that you sold. Just be careful. Be on the right side of the fence—which in this example is the opposite of what you think it really should be. Our minds sometimes just don't work that logically.

If we don't master this, we're at the mercy of the market makers.

Some of you already know where I am with my life. It's to be a seller, not a buyer. When you see a stock going from $240 and taking a plunge from $240 down to $200 and the $240 calls go from $40 to $30, why not be a seller? Think this through. When stocks fall, implied volatility rises. You could buy the stock—that would be one play. Or you could sell options, both the calls and the puts. Read these sentences aloud.

The implied volatility goes up when the stocks fall. Conversely, the implied volatility goes down when the stocks rise.

When the stocks rise, this is not the time to be buying. I don't care if you're a momentum player or not. Under my way of thinking, the Wade Cook school of trading strategies, if that stock has run from $200 to $240, then climbed from $240 to $250 over the next couple of days, and hits an all time high of $260, get out of the way. That little voice in your head is telling you, or other people are telling you, that this thing could go to $300. I say get out of the way.

Why? Because the implied volatility has gone down. Which means, in theory, that the option prices are cheaper as contrasted to a high implied volatility. If you start buying there, there's just nowhere to go. I'm almost suggesting that you think backwards. Think everything you thought when you were going to be a buyer, and invert it. Be a seller.

When the whole DOW drops from 11,200 down to 10,000, call options are getting really expensive. As the stock market or a particular stock itself goes back up, the option hardly moves at all. Get that? The stock rises, but the option barely budges. Be a seller. Where you were looking to buy before, be a seller.

In this example here, you could consider doing a bear call spread. You would sell the $240 call for $30 and buy the $250 calls as your protective strategy for $25. Now, you sell 10 contracts for $30,000, you buy others for $25,000, and keep $5,000. This is a credit spread. You net $5,000 cash into your account. You have $5,000 on hold, you have a $10,000 spread, you're going to net a profit of $5,000. As long as this stock stays below $240 before the expiration date, you'll be just fine. That is a bear call spread. Learn how to be a seller, not a buyer. (Refer to my *Spread and Butter* home-study course for more on bear call spreads.)

Let me wrap up by saying that this whole discussion on implied volatility is simply meant to keep you out of trouble. Just do pretty much the opposite of what everyone else is doing. One word of warning, if you want to think this through, think like an options market maker. Price what you're willing to sell things at, and buy things at, just as if you were an options market maker. Follow the money. Follow the money. Follow the money. Do what the pros do.

6

LOCC, STOCK AND BARREL

In this chapter I want to review the basics of writing covered calls, to make sure that you're comfortable with this strategy, then talk about the difference between traditional covered calls and the LOCC variation. Then I'm going to give you some brand new important information about option cycles, open interest and how the market makers decide what options to make available for you to buy. I'll close with some ideas about places to research to find good candidates for covered calls. Let's get started.

FLYING IN THE FACE OF TRADITION

How are LOCCs different from traditional covered calls?

Traditional covered calls have you buy lower-priced optionable stocks with lower volatility and then write covered calls for the same month or the next month out. These stocks are purchased on margin, if possible.

The LOCC variation has you buy higher-priced optionable stocks with higher volatility and write covered calls that expire five to seven months out. These stocks are also purchased on margin, if possible. You are choosing stocks that you feel will go up, as you *definitely* want to get called out.

LOCC allows you to use higher-priced stocks with lower amounts of cash tied up. For example, if you purchase 100 shares of a $90 stock on margin, you are only paying $45 per share. If the stock is relatively volatile, the call options should be more expensive. You may be able to sell a six to seven month call option on that stock and collect $38, which would give you an adjusted cost basis of $52 on the stock ($90 minus the $38 premium). The main disadvantage of selling this option is that you are giving up your upside potential on the stock.

Okay, the main thing to keep in mind when writing LOCCs is that our goal in this strategy is to get called out for maximum profit. I repeat, you want to get called out. That way you get both the premium, plus you recoup part of the cost of the stock.

Now for a little refresher on options. There are two basic types of options when you talk about stock options, or any options. They are called calls and puts. A call option gives you the right to buy a stock, and a put option gives you the right to sell a stock. Whenever you talk about call options, you're talking about the right to buy.

When you buy a call option, you are hoping that the stock goes up in value. When you buy a put option, you are hoping that the stock goes down. Now you'll discover from my methods and my strategies that I am bigger into selling than I am into buying. I reinforce this point in all my courses and all my books. I learned this angle from my real estate days. Sometimes I'd get into a house and have all these horrible things go wrong. So, I have one thing, one piece of advice for anybody in real estate–sell it. I have one piece of advice for anybody in the stock market–be a seller, not a buyer.

Before I get into the nitty gritty of writing LOCCs, I want to make sure you're familiar with the basics of writing covered calls, so I'm including a list of terms and a summary of how these terms apply to writing covered calls. For some of you, this is review. For those of you who haven't attended my Wall Street Workshop™, one of my other courses, or read my books, this will be a new language. It's a language you need to understand and speak fluently in order to work the stock market.

TALKING THE TALK

ASK: The current price for which a stock or option may be bought.

AT THE MONEY: A call option is said to be at the money if the current market value of the underlying stock is the same as the exercise price of the option.

BID: The current price at which you could sell your stock or option.

CALL, OR CALL OPTION: An option contract giving the owner the right (not the obligation) to buy shares of stock at a strike price on or before an expiration date.

CALLED OUT: The option to buy the stock is exercised. When your option is exercised, this can happen on or before the expiration date, this is done randomly and electronically. For example, if you own 1,000 shares you could be called out of a portion of your shares or all of your shares. If your stock is in the money on or around expiration, you will be called out. If you get called out, you will not know about it until the Monday following expiration. Check with your broker the following Monday after expiration Friday, just to be on the safe side.

CONTRACT: An option contract controls 100 shares of the underlying stock, so 10 contracts are the equivalent of 1,000 shares.

COVERED CALL WRITER: An investor who writes (to write means to sell) a call on a stock or some other underlying asset that he/she owns, guaranteeing the ability to perform if the call is exercised.

IN THE MONEY: A call option is said to be in-the-money if the current market value of the underlying stock is above the exercise price of the option.

INTRINSIC VALUE: The amount, if any, by which an option is in the money.

MARGIN: The additional equity loaned to you by your stockbroker, based upon a percentage of the equity of your underlying assets. The underlying asset is used as collateral for the loan. Put simply, if you have 50% margin capability in your trading account, your broker will loan you the money to purchase up to the same number of shares you are buying. If you were purchasing 1,000 shares of a particular marginable stock, you would only have to put up enough cash to pay for 500 shares.

MARGIN ACCOUNT: An account in a brokerage firm, that offers additional equity as a loan based upon a percentage of the equity of your underlying assets.

OPEN INTEREST: The total number of option contracts outstanding for that specific option at the close of the market.

OPTION: The right to buy or sell a specified amount of a security (stocks, bonds, futures, contracts, etc.) at a specified price on or before a specific date (American style options).

OPTION CYCLES: The sequence of months assigned to a company's options.

OUT OF THE MONEY: If the exercise price (strike price) of a call is above the current market value of the underlying stock, the option is said to be out of the money by that amount. If the exercise price (strike price) of a put is below the current market value of the underlying stock, the option is said to be out of the money by that amount.

PREMIUM: The money you pay or the money you receive for buying or selling calls or puts.

RATE OF RETURN: The sum resulting from dividing the cash in (your cash taken in, or profits) by the cash out (your investment).

$$\frac{\text{Cash In}}{\text{Cash Out}} = \underline{\hspace{2cm}} \% \text{ Yield*}$$

The yield figure that you get does not say whether it's a monthly, an annual, or a 10-year yield. This merely tells you your rate of return.

STRIKE PRICE: The price at which the underlying security will be bought or sold if the option buyer exercises his/her rights in the contract.

TIME VALUE: The remainder of an option premium after subtracting its intrinsic value.

UNCOVERED CALL: A call option that is sold without ownership of the underlying stock. Selling an uncovered option is sometimes referred to as "going naked."

Now I'm going to use a couple of words from this list. This is just a cab driver talking. I don't know very many big words; I usually try to limit my words to five letters or four letters or less. But the word 'long'–

if you're long on a call, it means that you own a call. The word long means ownership.

The word 'short' means that you don't own something, or in fact that you have sold it. If you're considered in a short position, it means that you have sold that position. So when you sell a call, or when you sell a put, you could also be short a call, and short a put. When you buy a call or a put, you would be said to be long a call, or long a put.

You could call your stockbroker and use a sentence like, "Well, I'm long how many calls on that deal?"

And he'll say, "You're long eight." You're long eight, which means eight what? You're not going to finish all the sentences; we in America abbreviate all the time, do we not? We kind of rush through our language, and we abbreviate all the time. Long eight calls means that you have purchased eight calls and they are still owned by you.

SMALL MOVEMENT IN STOCK, MAGNIFIED MOVEMENT IN OPTION

All right, now we'll talk about the one-in-three chance compared to the two or three-in-three chance of making money when you're a seller as compared to a buyer.

Right now I want to say something that you usually can take to the bank. *When there is a small movement in the stock, there usually is a magnified movement in the option.* Did you get that? When there is small movement in the stock, either up or down, there is then a corresponding, relation-based, magnified movement in the option, up or down.

I'm going to talk about XYZ Company here, instead of a real company. In this example, the strategy is more important than the trade. The stock is at $52. You really think it's going to go up. You call your stockbroker and say, "How much is the $50 call going for?" He tells you that it is going for $4.

Let's put the stock in one column and the option beside it. Let's say that, all things being equal, there is a month or two left to the expiration date, there's a timely move in the stock and we don't get too close to expiration.

Now let me touch on a concept here that effects this idea of not getting too close to the expiration date. I'm talking about deteriorating value, or deteriorating premiums. There is a deteriorating value to options, even when the stock goes up, because the closer you get to the expiration, the less chance that the stock will or won't perform as expected, so the option value declines. Let me say it this way. *Usually* when the stock goes up, there's a magnified upward movement in the option. But there *could* be a situation where you're way away from the strike price, which we'll talk about later, where the stock could be going up, and your option could be going down. It sounds funny, but it happens in real life.

I want to illustrate a fairly ordinary relationship between the stock price and the price of the option. The stock is at $52. The $50 call option is going for $4. The stock goes up to maybe $54 dollars and the option goes to $5. My goodness. The stock goes to $56 and the option goes to $6. Actually, it has gone up more to like $6.50. Remember this is a $50 call. The stock goes to $57, the option goes to $8. Whoa! Do you see why I'm so excited about this? The stock goes up just a little and your option doubles in value!

XYZ		Stock Price: $52
Buy stock at $52	Stock Price	Option Price
Buy call at $4	$50	$4
	$54	$5
	$56	$6
	$57	$8

Let's talk about the money. Contracts are most often sold in 100 stock lots (sometimes after certain stock splits, one contract could represent 150 shares). If we had purchased one contract at $4, we'd have spent $400 and own the right to buy 100 shares of this stock at $50.

Time out. If this doesn't get your blood pumping, then how would you like to spend $4, $20 or even $30 in order to lock down the right to buy Apple Computer, or Cisco, or even a Microsoft at some price lower than the current market price? How would you like to lock down the right to buy General Motors, which is around $82 at the time of this writing, the right to buy at $80, out in six months, or out even in a year with LEAPS®. Think about that. For the next month, for a small amount of money, we have locked down the right to buy this stock at $50.

But look at our example. The stock went up to $52, $54, $56 and $57. It climbed from $52 to $57 and our option has gone from $4 to $8. The stock went up $5, about a 10% move from $52 to $57, yet the option increased 100%! *I repeat: when there's a small movement in the stock, there's a magnified movement in the option.* Now 10% is not a small movement, and 100% is pretty big. Still, it happens. Now what happened to the $400 we took in for selling that option?

Just for fun in this example, let's not do just one contract, let's do 10 contracts. In real life, you're going to do seven contracts, or 13, depending on how much money you have. But 10 contracts would give you the right to buy one thousand shares of this stock at the $50 strike price.

At your original price of $4, it's going to cost you $4,000 for 10 contracts. Now there are several things to discuss here, but let's just look at what happened. In just a matter of two or three days, this stock went from $52 to $57. You call your stockbroker and you say, "What's that $50 call going for now?" And he answers, "Eight bucks." You say, "Sell it." How long does it take to sell it?

All right, I'm going to make a point here about the liquidity of the marketplace. Because a lot of people say well, could it really sell that fast? Or what if there's nobody that wants to buy it? You don't have to worry about that. Let me say it again. Quit worrying about that. That is not a real life experience question.

Why? Because there is a behind the scenes, quasi-government agency, a corporation if you will, called the OCC. Most of you have never heard of it before, but it's the Option Clearing Corporation All through the day and every night they match up all the buy and sell orders. If there's a bid and an ask on these option prices, like 4^1/_4$ by 4^1/_2$, and you want to sell, you will sell at the bid; in this example, at 4^1/_4$, or $4.25.

Let's use our $8 example. If there's a bid and an ask–by the way, I say it that way because there could be a bid of zero. There could be a no-bid, no price at which the security could be sold, and a $$^1/_{16}$ ask, or something like that. If there's a bid and an ask, and you want to sell the option, you're going to sell it at the bid price (the lower of the two).

So let's say that at this time you're looking to sell your option at the bid, when the stock is $57 and the $50 call is $8 by 8^1/_8$ ($8.12). You want to sell it right now, get rid of this thing right now. How long does it take? Using your stockbroker or even doing it electronically, how long does it take to conduct this trade? I know all of you know this. The answer is—not very long. That's because not only do you have a very attractive product to sell because of price, you selected a security with a lot of "open interest."

Open interest is a very important factor. Before I explain about that, let me take a little detour here. Have you ever wondered why you can sometimes get one strike price, but not another? Or why you can find options for some months and not others? Let's go there. Let's kill two birds with one stone.

OPTION CYCLES AND MARKET MAKERS

When do options expire? All company options are on one of three cycles. They're on the January, the February, or the March cycle.

Any stock that is assigned to the January cycle will have options that are set for January, then you skip two months and go to April, skip two months and go to July, then skip two months and go to October.

The companies that are assigned to the February cycle will go February to May to August to November.

The stocks that are assigned to the March cycle go March, skip to June, to September and then December.

Here's a chart to show you how this works. Copy this and put it on your computer, so you don't get confused when you're shopping for options.

January		February		March
April		May		June
July		August		September
October		November		December

Okay. Every company's options are assigned to one of these three cycles. In the Wall Street Workshop™ when we get our stockbrokers or our Trading Department on the phone, we'll say, "What is an option going for out five or six months?" Now, you literally need to say that, because you can't say, "What are the October calls going for?" There may not be October calls. There may not be November calls either, depending on what? Depending on what cycle the company has been assigned.

When you get out five or six months, there's either going to be the October, the November or the December calls, depending on what cycle the company is on. If it's on the February cycle, go to the August options expiration date and strike prices, and look for a good deal. Assume you don't see any and you decide, okay, I don't want to do August. Can I do September? But your stockbroker says there are no September calls. Well, then, please let me do October. Sorry, there are no October calls. The next month out is November. You can tell what cycle your company is on by paying attention to what months have options.

This is some of the jargon of the market. If you know this you can work better with your broker. What I say to my stockbroker is, "I want to do one this year, what's the furthest month out I can go this year?" That's an easy question to ask—what's the furthest month out, without doing LEAPS®. And he'll say, "Well, we have the November options." And that's it. That's what you're going to have.

Now that I've got you all into this, let me give you the exceptions. Remember, in America, for every rule there are 10 exceptions. This is no exception: No matter what cycle the company's options have been assigned to, there will always be options written the next month out.

Let me say it again. No matter what cycle the company is on—a January, February or March cycle—when you get close to May, like right after April, on the Monday after the Friday expiration of April, they'll start writing the May options, even though there haven't been May options up to that point in time.

Did you get that? There are always the next month out options. If you're in October, even though up until October there have been no November options, as you get close to October, the options market maker will start writing the November options. By the way, they can do this any time they want, but they usually wait until the Monday after the expiration. So, in October, this might possibly be after the third Friday, depending on the options volume.

Remember, they're not stupid. What's an options market maker's job, how do they make money? Sell you options. Right? What is their inventory of trade? That's right—options. If they don't have options, the ones that you want, they're not going to sell you anything. They're going to create options for what you want.

So, let's talk about the next thing that may not be there for you. You may have a stock that's around $120, and you know it's on a January cycle. Right now in May, we have the May, but now remember, the next month out is June, so we'll have June options. We find $120 calls and they're going for $13. Well then you say we're on the January cycle, and we're here in May, so we will look at the June. There are July options, but there are no August options. Why? That's right—we're on the January cycle. What if we really want an August option or September? That's a problem. If they don't exist, they don't exist, there's just nothing there.

Another problem is this: what if you're looking at July, and you say, how much are the $140 calls going for? Well you know what? They may not be writing that $140 strike price. So you ask, "What do you have?" You broker checks and tells you, "The highest strike price for the month of July is $120. But we do have the $150s."

Excuse me? They don't have the $140s, but they have the $150s? How can that be? Because when you go out quite a ways, remember the option market maker does not need to, nor does he want to have every strike price for every month available. He doesn't need to, because if he's got a whole bunch of buyers who will buy the $150 price, he doesn't need the $130s, the $140s, the $160s and the $170s out a ways. So he may just write the $150s and the $200s. You see that? He'll write really divergent prices, because some people want options and he can pile everyone else into that price. And I like it, by the way. I like a whole bunch of people owning the same kinds of options. That means there's a lot of interest. That's called *open interest*. So now that I've brought that up again, let's go there for just a minute.

OPEN INTEREST

One of the things you don't want to do is control a market place. You know that the Securities and Exchange Commission has created all kinds of rules to govern companies that go public. What if you have a company that's going public, and there are 10 million shares issued for the public. You were the one that took it public, or helped it go public, and you have one million shares. What would happen to the stock if you all of a sudden one day decided to sell all of your shares, all one million? Out of the 10 million shares available, you're going to sell one million–10% of the company in just a matter of minutes. What could happen to the stock? With that many shares being dumped into the market place, stock prices could go from $100 down to $80 in a matter of minutes, right?

You are restricted from doing that. Even after you hold your stock for a year, you can sell it, but you can only sell so much, a percentage of the average daily volume. You may be able to sell your million shares, but it may take you a year to sell them all. You can only sell so many within any given period of time. Do you think that is a good law? I do. I think that is one *really good* law. It protects the average investor from somebody doing what is called "taking it to the window" or "dumping it on the market."

Back to the options marketplace. What if you buy three contracts of the October $150 calls, and you're the only one that owns them? And that stock just kind of hangs right around the $110 range, $120 range, and the option doesn't go anywhere, you don't make any money with it. But boy, when you go to sell it, you're the only one that owns it! Could you control an option, in effect? You bet. But you don't necessarily want to.

You want to check when you go to buy options from time to time, that there's a lot of what's called "OI" or "Open Interest." I don't check on all of these, you don't have to check on strike prices on Dell, or Microsoft or Qualcomm, right? That's because there's so much option investing going on with those companies. As a rule of thumb, you should make sure that there are several hundred contracts written on a company. Look for at least one hundred, probably more like several hundred, before you get involved in buying an option at a particular strike price.

BUYING STOCK TO WRITE CALLS ON

You can buy stocks for the sole purpose of writing covered calls to generate income. This is almost like rental real estate. Your rental property may go up and down a bit, but you still get your rent and you still own the house. When you write a covered call, you sell to someone the right to buy the stock from you at a certain price on or before a particular date. Sell is synonymous with write.

You can also write an uncovered call (going naked) which means that you do not own the stock. You do not have to own the stock in order to sell the call option, but it is risky and the only way that you could do this would be if you have a set amount of money in your account and plenty of experience. This strategy does not apply to LOCC.

When you write a covered call, you sell the option and collect the premium. You can use this cash as income, or gain, or you can use it to offset your cost in the stock. No matter what happens, whether you are called out or not, you get to keep the premium you have collected.

If you had purchased stock on July 25th and you sold the August call, you would have a one-month or four-week rate of return. Just to put things in perspective, a rate of return of 14%, based on a two-week return on investment, results in a 364% annualized rate of return! Don't forget that options clear T+1 (trading day + 1), which means the cash from selling the option premium will be in your account the next trading day following your transaction.

FINDING PROSPECTS FOR WRITING COVERED CALLS

Where is a good place to find possible candidates for writing covered calls? You can do technical and fundamental research on your own using a variety of resources, including, as many of my students do, access to the Wealth Information Network™ (W.I.N.™), which is the Stock Market Institute of Learning's™ premier Internet service and a major tool of the trade. Here is a sample update from W.I.N.™. These candidates are not recommendations, as market conditions constantly change.

MAY 10, 2000 – 7:48 AM PDT

The following list of potential covered calls has been computer generated based on a scan of the United States stock exchanges. Please note that all returns are based on margin. This list provides a starting point in our search for covered calls.

The Research/Trading Department did not research these companies before the list was posted. We suggest that you check with your own broker to discuss the risks and rewards of the covered calls candidates listed here. Be sure to do your own research as well. Remember that if you are not called out, you will continue to own the stock. So, don't buy the stock if you don't like the company.

POTENTIAL COVERED CALLS

Secure Computing Corporation (SCUR) is trading around $12^{1}/_{4}$. The May $12.50 calls are trading around $7/_{8}$. This could be a 14.29% return, and if you are called out, it could be an 18.37% return.

Athome Corporation (ATHM) is trading around $19^{1}/_{4}$. The May $20 calls are trading around $1^{7}/_{16}$. This could be a 14.94% return, and if you are called out, it could be a 22.73% return.

Sportsline.com Inc. (SPLN) is trading around $17^{1}/_{16}$. The May $17.50 calls are trading around $1^{3}/_{8}$. This could be a 16.12% return, and if you are called out, it could be a 21.25% return.

Harbinger Corporation (HRBC) is trading around $14^{13}/_{16}$. The May $15 calls are trading around $1^{3}/_{8}$. This could be an 18.57% return, and if you are called out, it could be a 21.10% return.

Aradigm Corporation (ARDM) is trading around $15. The May $15 calls are trading around $1. This could be a 13.33% return, and if you are called out, it could be a 13.33% return.

Epitope Inc. (EPTO) is trading around $9^{7}/_{8}$. The May $10 calls are trading around $5/_{8}$. This could be a 12.66% return, and if you are called out, it could be a 15.19% return.

MTI Technology Corporation (MTIC) is trading around $14^{1}/_{4}$. The June $15 calls are trading around $2^{3}/_{16}$. This could be a 30.70% return, and if you are called out, it could be a 41.23% return.

FSI International Inc. (FSII) is trading around $13^{1}/_{2}$. The June $15 calls are trading around $1^{9}/_{16}$. This could be a 23.15% return, and if you are called out, it could be a 45.37% return.

E.Spire Communications Inc. (ESPI) is trading around $4^{13}/_{16}$. The June $5 calls are trading around $^{13}/_{16}$. This could be a 33.77% return, and if you are called out, it could be a 41.56% return.

Metacreations Corporation (MCRE) is trading around $9^{1}/_{4}$. The June $10 calls are trading around $1^{7}/_{16}$. This could be a 31.08% return, and if you are called out, it could be a 47.30% return.

Parametric Technology Corporation (PMTC) is trading around $9^{25}/_{32}$. The June $10 calls are trading around $1^{7}/_{16}$. This could be a 29.39% return, and if you are called out, it could be a 33.87% return.

Geron Corporation (GERN) is trading around $22^{5}/_{16}$. The June $22.50 calls are trading around $2^{13}/_{16}$. This could be a 25.21% return, and if you are called out, it could be a 26.89% return.

If you are not already on W.I.N. please call 1-800-872-7411, and ask one of our Enrollment Representatives for a free trial.

COVERED CALLS PLACED BY OUR RESEARCH DEPARTMENT
MAY 9, 2000 – 9:39 AM PDT

The Trading Department placed a trade from Today's Covered Call List. We purchased 500 shares of Central Garden and Pet (CENT) for $12^{3}/_{8}$. We then sold five contracts of the June $12.50 calls (EQHFV) for $1^{7}/_{8}$. We placed this trade based upon the up trending chart and tradable fundamentals. The rates of return based on margin will be 30.30%, and if we are called out, will be 32.32%.

MAY 5, 2000 – 12:10 PM PDT

The Trading Department did a Long Option Covered Call (LOCC) on China.com (CHINA). We bought 100 shares at $30^{15}/_{16}$, we then sold one contract of the August $30 (UIHHF) calls for $8^{1}/_{8}$. We did this on margin to buy the 100 shares. Without margin it would have been $3,100. With margin we put up $1,550. We took in $800 on this play, giving us about a 52% return.

MAY 5, 2000 – 9:55 AM PDT

The Trading Department did a Covered Call on Imrglobal Corporation (IMRS). We bought 500 shares at $16^{1}/_{2}$. We then sold five contracts of the June $17.50 (QIQFW) calls for $1^{13}/_{16}$. We like the strength of the up trending chart, and the tradable fundamentals of this company. The rate of return is 21.96%, and if called out it would be 34.09%.

MAY 3, 2000 – 10:02 AM PDT

The Trading Department did a Covered Call on Pairgain Technologies (PAIR). We bought 500 shares at $22^{13}/_{16}$. We then sold five contracts of the June $22^{1}/_{2}$ (PQGFX) calls for $2^{5}/_{8}$. We like the strength of the up trending chart, and the tradable fundamentals of this company. The rate of return was 23.01%, and if called out it would be 20.27%. Note here that we are buying the stock above the strike price of $22^{1}/_{2}$.

EXAMPLE OF GETTING CALLED OUT

Here is an example of a deal we made with COR Therapeutics, Inc. (COR). They were trading around $15.25 per share. We bought 1,000 shares on margin and immediately sold 10 contracts of the May $15 calls for $1.50 and took in a premium of $1,500. This went against our $7,625 cash out, for an actual cash on hold of $6,125.

Stock: COR Therapeutics, Inc. (COR)
        Trading around $15^1/_4$ per share.

Purchase 1,000 shares x $15.25 =	$15,250
Divide by two (margin) =	$7,625 (cash out)
Sell 10 contracts for $1.50 ($1.50 x 1,000) =	$1,500 (cash in)
Actual cash on hold =	$6,125
Rate of return ($6,125 to make $1,500) =	24%

In this example, you have about a 24% return on your money for giving someone the right to buy this stock from you about four weeks from now. Your stock will be tied up for four weeks, but what a nice return of $1,500 in that time.

If the stock stays around $15 you may not get called out. If you do get called out, it is an in-the-money call so you will lose or give back $250. You bought the stock at $15.25 and sold the $15 call, so this would be $0.25 x 1,000 shares of stock.

Called out of 1,000 shares at $15 =	$15,000 (cash in)
You pay back the margin =	$7,625 (cash out)
Net profit =	$1,250
Adjusted Rate of return =	20%

As you can see, covered call writing is for the safety conscious investor. Remember that you can put in an order to sell the call just as you can a stock. If there is a small movement in the stock there may be a magnified movement in the option. By waiting for the stock to strengthen a bit, the call premiums might also strengthen.

"The LOCC training Wade presented allowed me to trade on [one] morning for a $2,000 profit. Thanks for the help.

–JOHN B., NV

"[Using] LOCC did RMBS. Bought 100 shares at $101^9/_{16} [and] sold November Covered Calls for $26^1/_2 the same day.

ROBERT O., MO

TIPS

- Trade on margin if possible. When we speak of 20% returns, you will not get these returns without trading on margin. IRAs won't allow margin trading.

- You are looking for stocks that are within the $5 to $28 price range.

- The stock should be mildly (that's "mildly," not "wildly") volatile.

- Buy stock in 1,000-share increments if possible. Diversify with 100 to 1,000 shares in 10 different companies.

7

LOCC – BUYBACKS AND ROLLOUTS

First let's define our terms. What is a buyback? Really, there's no such thing. I hope you understand that the term "buyback" is just stock market jargon. You could even use that term to your stockbroker, and I don't know a stockbroker out there that does not understand it, but I think you need to know the mechanics of how it works. If we want to close a position, you would say, "I want to buy back that one contract of the $200 calls for November."

Your stockbroker will buy the $200 call, in this case for $20, so your one contract will be $2,000. On his computer, he will show a short position, or a "sold" call position on the $200 strike price for November. Now that he has a purchase for the $200 strike price for November, it will literally be a wash on his computer. It will be eliminated off his screen. The trade will be eliminated, so you will not have a covered call position. You have basically, if you'll let me use a real estate term, freed up your stock. You have no liens against it. You have no positions against your stock. You own the stock.

Let's review what we've just done here. Yes I used the jargon, the term "buyback," but what you have in fact done is purchased a call, the same amount of contracts, the same expiration date, and the same strike price. You will own stock with no positions written against it.

85

Why would you do this? Why would you spend, in this example, $2,000 to free up the stock? Well, it's on a dip. You still like the stock, you think it's going to really fly. And so now, if the stock goes back up to $180 to $200 to $220, you could once again sell the November call for maybe even more money, if it's higher. But remember it's only a month or two now until November. What about selling the February $200 or the $220 call for a little bit more money?

Now I'll just make a blanket statement, and you can prove this out in the marketplace as we go. Whatever money it costs you to buy back the November $200 call, you could always sell the January or February call out two or three months further for more money.

So you could spend less money, and generate more money, if you do not want to sell the stock. Remember one of the best ways to make money at this whole process is to get rid of the stock, to have the stock taken away from you.

So, what is a rollout? It simply means that we sell an option one to several months out. It's not complicated at all, but there are a few more choices. Do we sell at the same strike price, or, as we roll out in time, do we also roll down to a lower strike price, or roll up to a higher strike price?

Again, we have to check the fundamentals; news and stock direction, and ask that all-important question: do we want to keep the stock or sell it? Once we figure that out, we go shopping for the best possible option that also reflects our trading style. The questions are, which month, which strike price, and which movie we're going to go see.

Writing covered calls is a serious way to produce income. It has too many virtues to disparage here. Its only real new risk, or additional risk, is what we call "opportunity lost risk." In other words, giving away the upside movement of the stock.

To a casual observer there might be other risks, but remember, the stock is owned. By owning the stock we have upside potential and downside risk, plus we receive any dividends the company pays out. If we sell a call, we are taking on an obligation to sell, or give up, our stock at a certain price. If the stock moves up, we do not participate in the move. Now to give away this upside we get paid. Someone else now owns the upside growth of the stock. They bought it, we sold it.

How much we received for selling the call is a function of two things and one of these two things is broken down into three parts. The first of these two things is the price at which we're agreeing to sell the stock, in relation to the time remaining for which we are committed to sell. I mentioned the second one had three parts–actually, this option premium is made up of the aforementioned time, volatility (or movement swings), and a constant (like the T-bill rate) for comparison. These prices are set by an option market maker on one or all of four exchanges. These market makers make money buying and selling these options. (Refer to Chapter 5, Implied Volatility, for more information.)

The price of an option can devolve to a cliché. The market makers will sell the option for what someone is willing to pay for it. Why all of this here? Because as a seller we want to position ourselves in the best way possible. We want to sell the option to generate income, but only if the trade is worth it. You see, this is an unusual way to look at option pricing.

As a purchaser, we look at potential. If we buy and go long on a call option, we're hoping the stock goes up. If so, the option should rise–again, it's a function of the relationship of the stock price to the strike price and the time left to expiration. The only thing that skews this pricing again is the volatility–does it exist or not, and to what degree? Let's try a different view.

As a seller of the option, we're going to take in the premium (income), big or small. If there's hardly a chance of the stock rising much, the options will be less expensive. If the stock is wild and on a tear, the option will reflect this "wildness" and be expensive. We'll return to this thought after an example.

Example
Stock A is at $110. It has gone up in a fairly consistent way, but it is pretty stable or docile. The $120 call, out two months, is $3. Stock B, also at $110, is in the hi-tech arena. It's a "dot-commer." It has gone from $18 to this $110 range in about nine months. It's not uncommon for the stock to have $5 to $15 one-to-two day swings. The $120 call, out two months, is $13. That's $10 more than Stock A.

DOCILE STOCKS

WILD STOCKS

How can this be? Again, people think Stock B is going to $150, maybe $200. People are willing to pay $13 for a $10 out-of-the-money option, because to them it's value—actually, it's potential.

Just think. If you owned a stock for the sole purpose of selling this call for income purposes, which one would you choose? Back to our previous thought of selling not buying. If we're going to give up the future potential rise in the price, how much do we want to get paid? If there is little or no upside potential, then what are we really giving up? Not much. Conversely, if we're willing to give up $40 to $90 (or more) of upside profits, we want more money for what we're giving up.

Before I go on, this scenario has become much more exaggerated of late, with the new technology sector spreading to wireless applications, broadband technology and services, and support and selling e-commerce aspects of the Internet. There are $290 stocks with three month out $300 strike price call options at $50. They seem high and they are, but high is relative. In a way, think of the play as a $29 stock with a $5 option at a $30 strike price—just divide by 10 for a relational observation.

Also, (and I feel like a broken record saying this again) when we *buy* an option, the stock has to do one thing or we're going to lose. As a purchaser of a call option, the stock has to go up, and then in a timely manner. If it goes down or stays the same, we lose on our option. Hopefully, we're out before we lose too much.

Now, if we were to *sell* that same call, we have a *two in three* chance of making money, perhaps a three in three chance. If the stock goes up we make money because we either still own the stock or it was bought away from us. Either way we get to keep the option premium. In any one of our three examples that would be $3, $13 or $50.

If the stock stays the same, depending on if we sold it in the money or out of the money, we keep or sell the stock, but either way we keep the premium.

If the stock dips, the option income reduces our cost basis and mitigates any loss. Perhaps we take in enough income even if the stock drops and we sell it anyway—the premium income offsets the drop in price of the stock—our third in three chance of making money (or at least not losing as much). Okay, Okay, OKAY. What does this have to do with LOCC, buybacks and rolls?

Let's do a deal and explore how these scenarios play out.

Our new favorite stock is at $180. It seems high, but it's actually on a dip, down from $225. The $180 call, out six months, is going for $45. It's a perfect match. One contract against our 100 shares is $4,500. Funny, because we have a $9,000 margin requirement. That means we'll have $4,500 on hold to make $4,500.

We want to get called out at $180. The stock goes up, down and all around. Near expiration the stock is only at $190. If we leave it alone, we'll get called out and all of our money will be back in the account, ready to go to work again.

Our profits are $4,500. We bought the stock at $180 and sold it at $180. Our profit is the option premium we sold six months ago. We have to claim this amount and pay taxes on it. What if we buy back the option, even if it's on Friday, the expiration date? There's no time left, so it will cost us $1,000, maybe $1,125 ($1^1/_8$). Now let's sell the $190 call out five to six months. It's going for $50, or $5,000. No, our cash for the stock purchase is not all back in, but we are taking in another $5,000. We've moved up another $10 on the strike price scale. That would be another $1,000 ($180 to $190 is $10 times one hundred shares), plus this additional $5,000 of premium income.

You see, the new option premium of $5,000 goes against our stock position which, in theory is $18,000. We have to claim and pay taxes on the first $4,500 option premium once the position has ended. Actually, our taxable profits would be $3,500, because we had $4,500 of income, minus the $1,000 we spent to buy back the option.

By still owning the stock, we can sell it at $190 ($19,000), or sell another option against that position. This tax aspect is one reason why it's so good to do these in an IRA or other tax deferred entity. Yes, we lose margin capability, but the cash income is the same–and not taxable until we take it out when we're over 70 years old.

Back to our example. We could do the opposite deal on a dip. Say the stock moves all around and is at $180 or $170. If we want to keep the stock we can buy back the option, then keep the stock or sell a different option for more income. Now, more choices, but we're in the driver's seat making more money.

Now another very simple, but powerful adage about writing covered calls is simply this: buy the stock on dip, and wait, and wait, and wait, and then sell the call on strength. I'll say it again. Buy the stock when it's low, buy the stock on dips, and then wait for the stock to strengthen, and then sell the call when the stock is at a higher price.

Now think that one through. Because now, you're selling the call for a maximum price, and you're buying the stock when it's at a weaker price. So you could buy the stock in this case here, and you would own the stock at the $160, $170 price. Then as the stock strengthens again and climbs back up to the $200 range, you can then sell the call at that point in time, even if it's for the same month.

So for example, you could buy back that call option, that $200 call, for say $20, or $2,000, and then when the stock's back up to $200 or $210, maybe that November $200 call is going for $40 again, or $30. So you spent $2,000, so that on the next rise in the stock you can sell the same call again for $3,000, or $4,000. See, that is what we call double-dipping. More about that in a little bit.

This buy back and sell again strategy, while fun, has gone way overboard on our busy-ness scale. Those of you reading who have beaucoup time on your hands might be able to do this a few times a month. It's sort of like a rolling stock (option) in reverse. We sell the call on peaks, buy back on dips and then sell again on the next run-up. Many of my students are doing this. It's just too busy for me. But if you are into this, try double dipping!

DOUBLE DIPPING – COMBINING STRATEGIES TO MAXIMIZE PROFITS
Did your mother ever tell you to never, ever, under any circumstances double dip? Well, if she was talking about chip dip, that's understandable, but in the world of option trading, it can be a very lucrative practice. Just like a double-dip ice cream cone.

Double dipping allows you to capture not only one, but two or more option premiums on the same option before it expires. First you sell the call in a covered position, then when the stock takes a dip, you buy it back. As the stock starts to strengthen again, sell the call again, possibly even farther out to gain a larger premium. Keep in mind that there are two separate transactions here. The first is writing a covered call and the next is buying a call to end your first position. Depending on your time frame, it can be a busy strategy.

Let's say you've done your homework and really like XYZ stock. It's selling for $200 a share and you purchase 100 shares. After waiting for the stock to strengthen, you sell the November $200 calls for $50. Later, the stock drops to $160 causing the November $200 calls to drop to $20. You want to buy back the same contract of the November $200 calls for $20, in this case that would be $2,000.

The broker knows exactly what you mean when you say you want to buy back the option; it's all just stock market jargon anyway. Your broker's computer will show a short position or a sold call position of the November $200 call and a purchase for the same month November $200 call strike price, which would end the position.

You own the stock because you bought it for $200 and generated $50 per share by writing the calls, creating a $150 cost basis. When you buy the call back for $20, you take the cost basis back up to $170. Now what can you do with this free and clear stock? What else? Sell another call!!

Some stocks are so erratic you can do this even intra-month, say, within a four-week period of time. You could buy a $200 stock in October and sell the November call for $14. Then the stock takes a dip and you could buy back that call option for $5. On the next rise in the stock three days later, you could sell that same strike price for $18, then the stock backs off four or five days later and the option is back down to $9, and then on the next rise you could sell the option again. You see, you sell, and then buy back. You sell, and then buy back.

One variation on this double dipping play that applies to LOCC happens when you go out and sell a covered call on a higher strike price or another month or two further out. This should capture a higher premium with the added time value.

This is such a phenomenal strategy for those who want to roll the call option before expiration. Many of our students try to see just how many times they can roll the same option before it expires. As a matter of fact, it's kind of comical to me, but a lot of my students now are doing rolling covered calls. It's kind of funny, because you've heard me talk about rolling options and rolling stock, well, they're doing rolling covered calls in that they're selling first, then buying back, and then on the next increase in the stock they're selling again, and then on the next dip they're buying back. So they're doing a rolling stock play, but in reverse. That's not just double-dipping, that's triple-dipping, or dare I say: quadruple-dipping!

8

LOCC – NEXT MONSTER: SELLING DEEP IN-THE-MONEY CALLS

Now, are you ready for monster returns, even in the face of a downturn in the stock and option price?

Okay, let's use that word "downturn" and pose a question: Do we really care if an option premium which we have sold goes down in value? In fact, isn't that a natural course; for the option to reverse if the stock stays at the same level or goes down? The time premium, if nothing else, goes down as time marches on.

What we're going to introduce here is a pretty exciting variation of Large Option Covered Call writing. Before we do, let's review the scenario: the purchase of 100 shares of a $240 stock. We spend $24,000: $12,000 of ours, $12,000 on loan from our broker. We sell the $240 call out six months for $55, or $5,500. This new cash goes against our margin requirement—we now only need $6,500 of our own money. The hope is to get called out and get our money back for selling the stock—that's a wash. But we made $5,500 on $6,500. Pretty darn good.

Now, what if the stock pretty much stays at this level? What will happen to the $55 premium? In fact, what are the determining factors for this $55 price tag? It's not intrinsic value; it's not in the money. It's all *time value*–the price is determined by the three factors that make up time value:

a. The *length of time to expiration*

b. The *risk-free rate of return*–T-Bill factor

c. The *implied volatility*, speculative, or sentimental value

The "c" point, or *implied volatility,* is high in this case, and the premium is expensive. That's why we're selling it. The *length of time* (a), and the *risk-free rate of return* (b), go down (or up) in a fairly orderly manner. The *implied volatility* can change radically.

Think of this: if the stock stays near $240 over the next six months, the time value will go down and eventually disappear. If we owned the call option, we'd be ticked off. However, we *didn't* buy the call, we *sold* it, so who cares if it goes down? We PRE-captured the fluffy premium. If other factors enter in, we can buy back, then sell, and all the other protective and additional cash flow mechanisms kick into gear.

DEEP IN-THE-MONEY

To dramatically show this deterioration, and to show a wild angle to the LOCC system, stay tuned, buckle your seat belt and hold on.

Let's sell the November $200 call. If the stock is $240, that would be $40 in-the-money. The $55 time value is usually reduced when you sell deep in-the-money calls, say to $50–all in all the premium would be $90–this time $40 is intrinsic and $50 is time value.

Let's look at our numbers. We take in $9,000 for selling just one contract against our stock position. Whoa! That's $9,000 against our $12,000 hold amount. We now have $3,000 on hold to make $9,000. That's a triple!

Oh, you ask–what about the give back amount of $4,000? Okay, let's go there in a bit–but remember, we do this on a stock we think just might go down. Let's go there first.

If the stock goes down from $240 to $220, we'd have to give back only $2,000. If the stock goes to $200 or even below, we won't get called out. We get to keep the whole $90, or $9,000.

Give back is a strange but useful term. Let's say the stock goes up. It climbs to $280. On or before the expiration date, we get called out. We sell our stock for $200. If we bought the stock for $240 or $24,000 and we sell it for $200, or $20,000, we have a $4,000 loss–or we have to give back to this deal, $4,000. What is our profit now? It's only $5,000, but we still only had $3,000 tied up to make $5,000. This is an awesome rate of return. And we have $40 of downside protection built in.

If the stock is at $220, we would theoretically still get called out at $200 with a $5,000 profit. However, we would more than likely buy back the $240 call close to the expiration date for, say, $25,000; capture $6,500 of profit, still own the stock, and sell another profitable call.

WHY AND WHEN

Remember, one risk we were trying to protect against was that of the stock seriously pulling back. The time for selling these deep in-the-money calls is when we're using highly volatile stocks as our underlying base stock; when that stock has had a tremendous runup and is expected to go higher, but you partially doubt that the price can go up much more.

Also consider selling calls into a red light period. I would be leery to own a call option with an expiration in February, May, August, or right at the end of the first two weeks of December (say, December 1st to 15th), but we're not buying–we're selling. If the premium deteriorates, so what?

SIDE BY SIDE COMPARISONS

Let's look at a comparison of three different Large Option Covered Call examples. We'll sell a deep in-the-money option, an at-the-money option and an out-of-the-money option.

We'll do these side by side with commentary.

XYZ stock is at $140. It's on a dip and should go back up. It's at a good support level, but could go down as the whole market is shaky. It's currently June. We'll keep one constant and sell the November call options for all three.

(A)	**(B)**	**(C)**
Sell $110 Call	Sell $140 Call	Sell $180 Call
November	November	November
$60	$34	$25
Stock Purchase	*Stock Purchase*	*Stock Purchase*
$14,000	$14,000	$14,000
On Margin (divide by 2)	*On Margin (divide by 2)*	*On Margin (divide by 2)*
$7,000	$7,000	$7,000
Take in (Option Premium)	*Take in (Option Premium)*	*Take in (Option Premium)*
$6,000	$3,400	$2,500
Our own cash tied up	*Our own cash tied up*	*Our own cash tied up*
$1,000	$3,600	$4,500

We have $1,000 tied up to make $6,000. Incredible return. But, if called out (stock stays at or above $110) we have to "give back" $3,000. We make $3,000 on $1,000. If stock goes below (and stays there at expiration) we keep the whole $6,000, but have a reduced value in the stock. The stock is available to sell, or keep writing yet more calls for more income. If stock dips before expiration we can buy back the calls we previously sold for $60 ($110 strike price) and a) wait for the next runup in the stock and then sell stock or more call options, or b) buy back calls and right away sell lower strike price calls with same expiration, or further out calls—with a choice of strike prices. These strategies are profitable but require more work.	We have $3,600 tied up to make $3,400. Use the cash to buy more stock, pay off credit card bills, or whatever. This strategy is designed for the very busy person. Put it in place and let the transaction run to expiration. If the stock dips, check the storyline then a) leave alone, b) get involved by buying back the option, c) buy higher strike price option—creating a bear call spread, so less cash is tied up. (See Chapter on bear call spreads in *Wall Street Money Machine, Volume 4*), d) buy back and sell calls now (lower strike price) or further out—choice of strike prices. If this dip occurs, you'll wish you had done the strategy to your left (A).	Have $4,500 on hold (so to speak) to make $2,500 —the option premium. If the stock rises and we get called out, we make an extra $4,000. That's by buying 100 shares of stock for $130 and selling it for $180. That means our $4,500 will make us $6,500, a tidy profit. The problem is that the stock has to go above and stay above $180 by the expiration date—a big if. You must be bullish on the stock to go for this one. However, you could do a longhorn spread. Buy the $110 call for $60 ($6,000) and sell the $180 for $25 ($2,500). You create a bull call spread for $3,500 with a potential profit of $7,000, or $3,500 net. You have no margin usage. You would have to be very bullish for this to work. Consider a $120/$130 bull put spread, or a deeper in-the-money bull call spread—say $120/$150. See book reference in (B) for more information.

Again, it's all about preferences and your time commitment. Yes, there are more profits in column A, but potentially more work. Less profits in B, but hardly any additional work. This comparison is fair. You'll see that, relatively speaking, I do fewer way out-of-the-money covered calls [(C) column] than in-the-money [(A) column] and at-the-money covered calls [(B) column].

DITC—A Live Example

About the time I was finishing up this section, I was in Chicago at a live seminar. The following trade came up. I'll share it here.

DITC was around $82. Let's look on the next page at the three types of trades: in-, at- and out-of-the-money covered calls.

(A)	**(B)**	**(C)**
Sell $60 Call	Sell $80 Call	Sell $100 Call
November	November	November
$34	$25	$20
Stock Purchase	*Stock Purchase*	*Stock Purchase*
$8,200	$8,200	$8,200
On Margin (divide by 2)	*On Margin (divide by 2)*	*On Margin (divide by 2)*
$4,100	$4,100	$4,100
Take in (Option Premium)	*Take in (Option Premium)*	*Take in (Option Premium)*
$3,400	$2,500	$2,000
Our own cash tied up	*Our own cash tied up*	*Our own cash tied up*
$700	$1,600	$2,100

We now have $700 tied up to make $3,400. This is a phenomenal return. But, if we're called out (the stock stays above $60) we have to "give back" $2,200. We make $1,200 on $700.

If stock goes below (and stays there at expiration) we keep the whole $3,400, but have a reduced price in the stock. Stock would be available for sale, or to keep writing more calls for more income, out a few months or so.

If the stock dips before expiration we can buy back the $60 strike price calls, and a) wait for next run up in the stock and then sell stock or more call options, or b) buy back calls and right away sell lower strike price calls with same expiration, or c) sell further out calls— with a choice of strike prices.

Again, these strategies can be profitable but to do more trades requires more work.

We have tied up $1,600 to make $2,500. Use the cash to buy more stock, pay off credit and bills, or whatever. Note: we would have to "give back" $200, because we purchased the stock for $82 and sold it for $80 (100 shares x $2 = $200), so our profit would be $2,300.

This strategy is designed for the very busy person. Put it in place and let the transaction run to expiration.

If the stock dips, check storyline then a) leave alone, b) get involved by buying back the option, c) buy higher strike price option—creating a bear call spread, so less cash is tied up. (See Chapter on bear call spreads in *Wall Street Money Machine, Volume 4*), d) buy back and sell calls now (lower strike price) or further out—choice of strike prices.

If this stock takes a serious dip, you'll wish you had done strategy (A).

Have $2,100 on hold to make $2,000—the option premium. If the stock rises and we get called out, we make an extra $1,800. That's by buying 100 shares of stock for $82 and selling for $100. That means our $2,100 will bring in a nice profit of $3,800.

Now we have our $2,100 back. The problem is that the stock has to go above and stay above $100 by the expiration date—a big *if*. You need to be really bullish on the stock in order to go for this one.

However, you could do a longhorn spread. If you buy the $60 call for $34 ($3,400) and sell the $100 call for $20 ($2,000), you will have created a bull call spread for $1,400 with a potential profit of $4,000, or $2,600 net; and you have no margin usage.

You would have to be very bullish for this to work. Consider a $75/$80 bull put spread. See book reference in (B) for more information.

A WILD VIEWPOINT

Many times before I've discussed selling in-the-money calls, and even buying in-the-money calls. Remember there are two parts to the option premiums: time value (extrinsic value) and that portion of the option premium which represents the in-the-money portion of the option price (intrinsic value).

Using our previous $140 example, let's say the stock moves to $144 and we want to buy or sell the $140 strike price calls. Remember, the option price is determined by three factors: (a) the time to expiration, (b) the risk-free rate of return (T-bill factor) and (c) the implied volatility, or speculative value. In this example, $4 of this option price is intrinsic, or in-the-money.

The stock is at $144 and the $110 call, which was previously $60, is now at $63. Why did the option price go to $63? Sometimes it just might do that, but more often than not, there is a ratio, again dictated by a computer model, which moves the difference between time value and intrinsic value in not so determinable ways. Still, think: a $4 increase in the $140 stock generated a $3 move in the $60 call option.

Let's once again sell the $110 call, now taking in $6,300, not $6,000, and look at an off-the-wall scenario to shed light on the power of selling.

If we owned the stock at $143 and saw it drop to $110, we'd be upset. If we sold a stock at $143 before it dropped to $110, we'd be elated. Right? So, let's sell the $110 call for $63, or $6,300. If the stock drops to $110, and there's still some time left to expiration, and we buy this option back for $13, or $1,300, we captured $50 ($63 – $13 = $50), or $5,000 profit.

I like selling. We capture the profits *now*. That's now as in today– the cash hits our account tomorrow. If the stock rises, we make our pre-determined profit by getting called out. If it really does drop below $110, we keep all the $6,300 and still own the stock to *write again another day*.

The point is to accomplish a sale of a portion of the stock by selling the call option. If we think the stock could go down to a support level, say $110, then pre-selling our profits down to that level is a way of "eating our cake, and having it, too."

SUMMARY

We, for this LOCC, plan to capture the premium, lower our risk by lowering our cash outlay, and put ourselves in a position for maximum profit. We have accomplished that purpose with this "Monster Return" angle to the LOCC system.

Now, you are ready for monster returns, even in the face of a downturn in the stock and option price.

9

UN-LOCC—
FOLLOW THE MONEY

Most readers know that I love to teach seminars and workshops. Showing LOCC to thousands of people has been very enlightening. I've had a chance to see people's responses and it's been a thrill. No strategy I've ever taught has generated this much excitement. No formula has brought out the passion expressed in the audience's questioning, their slight misunderstanding, and then head-nodding approval.

The questions have been intense. The graduates of our Wall Street Workshops™, Next Step™ events and SUPPORT classes are "up on it." Most get it. They know the numbers. This plan is so simple that they sometimes try to make it difficult. It's so awesome that they try to pull it down–it gives them that "too good to be true" feeling. Undaunted, I keep showing them example after example; the numbers win people over. In the LOCC system the numbers work and the money works.

WHEN DO YOU GET YOUR MONEY?
The most common questions my students ask are, "Where does the money go?" and, "How does the money get into my account?" More specifically, if you take $25,000 and generate $17,000 of income, when do you get the money? The answer is: *right away.* To see just how this works, let's do a series of fictional transactions. This system works best, I think, in groups, so let's do that. We'll call it Group A.

GROUP A – $25,000

DEAL #1

If 100 shares of stock are purchased at $140 they would cost $14,000. You put up $7,000 of your money, and your broker puts up $7,000 on margin. The broker does this to a) get a bigger trade, hence more commissions, and b) to now charge you

DEAL #A1
Sell $140 Call
$32
Stock Purchase: $14,000
On Margin (divide by 2): $7,000
Take in (Option Premium): $3,200
Our own cash tied up: $3,800

interest. You have spent $7,000. That money is out of your account and the stock shows up in your account.

The $140 call out five months is $32. You sell one contract for $3,200, agreeing to sell your stock for $140. If the stock stays above $140 you will sell it or get called out. The income from the sale pays off the $7,000 margin loan and you get back your own $7,000. Margin interest will be deducted on a regular basis from your account. The buy and sell of the stock is a wash. We sold the option close to the money to pick up the fat premium.

The $3,200 is in our account in one day. We can take it out and spend it, or leave it in the account for other purposes. We could leave it alone, but for our cash flow and growth purposes, let's use it to buy more stock.

DEAL #2

The $3,200 would allow us to buy more than 1,000 shares of a $3 stock, or 100 shares of a $32 stock. Let's go there. What if we buy the 100 shares and then sell a six-month out $30 call for $16. That would generate another $1,600. If we get called out

DEAL #A2
Sell $30 Call
$16
Stock Purchase: $3,200
On Margin (divide by 2): None
Take in (Option Premium): $1,600
Our own cash tied up: $1,600

at $30 we get $3,000 and still get to keep the $1,600. In this case, from a purely mathematical point of view, we actually get $1,400, because we lose $200 on the sale of the stock. Still, to spend $3,200 to make $1,400 is quite exciting.

DEAL #2B

Oh, and we didn't use our margin. With $3,200 we could buy 100 shares of a $64 stock, or 200 shares of this same $32 stock. Look now, $3,200 spent with the help of margin allows us to sell two contracts, not just one. Two contracts at $16 generates $3,200, or a nice 100% return.

DEAL #A2b

*Sell 2 contracts $30 Calls
$16*

*Stock Purchase: $6,400
On Margin (divide by 2): $3,200
Take in (Option Premium): $3,200
Our own cash tied up: $0*

But hold on—we have $3,200 in the account again, let's say $3,000 after commissions. We still haven't used up our $25,000, so let's keep going.

DEAL #3

We use $8,000 to buy $16,000 worth of stock. Just our luck, we find a $160 stock headed for a stock split. We buy 100 shares. The $160 calls are going for $30. We sell those calls and take in $3,000. Our $8,000 has allowed us to make another

DEAL #A3

*Sell $160 Calls
$30*

*Stock Purchase: $16,000
On Margin (divide by 2): $8,000
Take in (Option Premium): $3,000
Our own cash tied up: $5,000*

$3,000 which is ready and able to work again. Okay, we have spent $18,200 to make $9,400 so far. We keep it moving.

DEAL #4

We spend $9,000 for 100 shares of a $180 stock. We sell the $180 calls for $5,000, which leaves $4,000 of our money tied up. We spent $9,000 to generate $5,000 of cash into our account the next day.

DEAL #A4

*Sell $180 Calls
$50*

*Stock Purchase: $18,000
On Margin (divide by 2): $9,000
Take in (Option Premium): $5,000
Our own cash tied up: $4,000*

Eventually, we'll spend all or most of our $25,000. We'll also spend all of the premium income on more stocks. When the expiration arrives, it will be party time. Okay, here is a summary of what we just did.

GROUP A DEALS						
	STOCK (BUY)	CASH OUT THIS TRANSACTION	ACCUMU-LATED CASH OUT	OPTION	CASH IN (PROFITS)	ACCOUNT TOTAL (PROFITS)
1	100 shares at $140 but half on margin	$7,000	$7,000	Sell $140 call for $320	$3,200	$3,200
2	200 shares at $32 but half on margin	$3,200	$10,200	Sell $30 call for $16	$3,200	$6,400
3	100 shares at $150 but half on margin	$8,000	$18,200	Sell $160 call for $30	$3,000	$9,400
4	100 shares at $180 but half on margin	$9,000	$27,200	Sell $180 call for $50	$5,000	$14,400

Now, if we get called out of the stocks, the cash spent will be back in our account–again, a wash. We get to keep the $14,400, whether we're called out or not. Making $14,400 on $27,200 is a great return. We'll make it $13,000 after our expenses. Five months for this kind of income in cash is a short time to wait. In five months we have $40,200– probably $38,500 after commissions and margin interest.

These past four weeks have found me doing about half a dozen presentations using an initial $25,000 investment. In the first group-go-round, $22,222 generated $19,400. The percentage yield on that group of trades would be equivalent to making $21,800 on $25,000. Twice in those presentations, the option premium income exceeded our initial cash outlay.

I know you can see it coming. Let's use the $13,000 profit from Group A to do two or three more deals. Make this Group B. Now, I want you to get used to the pattern here; get this ingrained so it comes to you instantly when your broker gives you a menu of choices.

GROUP B

This next group of stocks would look so much better with these larger "real life" cash inflows, but, just so you don't get too excited, let's stick with our measly little ol' $13,000.

DEAL #1

We'll start off with 100 shares on a company going for $120. We're doing all these deals on margin, so that's $12,000 divided by two for $6,000 out of our pocket to start with. We sell a $120 at-the-money call for $40 and collect $4,000. So that's $6,000 to make $4,000.

DEAL #B1
Sell $120 Call
$40
Stock Purchase: $12,000
On Margin (divide by 2): $6,000
Take in (Option Premium): $4,000
Our own cash tied up: $2,000

DEAL #2

Next is a company trading at $30, but we're going to buy 200 shares on margin, so that's $3,000. On this one, we sell two $30 at-the-money calls for $16. Cash in is $3,200. Put that against our $3,000 and we have gotten our cash back, plus made $200. This is what I like to see.

DEAL #B2
Sell $30 Call
$16
Stock Purchase: $6,000
On Margin (divide by 2): $3,000
Take in (Option Premium): $3,200
Our own cash tied up: −$200

DEAL #3

Okay, we buy 100 shares of a $60 stock. Margin halves that to $3,000, then we sell the five-month out $60 at-the-money call for $20. We take in $2,000 against our $3,000 cash out.

DEAL #B3
Sell $60 Call
$20
Stock Purchase: $6,000
On Margin (divide by 2): $3,000
Take in (Option Premium): $2,000
Our own cash tied up: $1,000

Okay, here's a little summary of what we just did.

GROUP B DEALS						
	STOCK (BUY)	CASH OUT THIS TRANSACTION	ACCUMU-LATED CASH OUT	OPTION INCOME	CASH IN (PROFITS)	ACCOUNT TOTAL (PROFITS)
1	100 shares at $120 but half on margin	$6,000	$6,000	Sell $120 call for $40	$4,000	$4,000
2	200 shares at $30 but half on margin	$3,000	$9,000	Sell two $30 calls call for $16	$3,200	$7,200
3	100 shares at $60 but half on margin	$3,000	$12,000	Sell $60 call for $20	$2,000	$9,200

You see we have $9,200 in our account. Now what do you think we should do with that? Take that vacation you've been putting off? Get that deck built? Maybe it's earmarked for your pre-teen's school tuition. Maybe it's just begging you to play it again, Sam. Okay, let's do that. One last time. Group C. Here goes.

GROUP C – ONE DEAL

Right away I see at $180 stock that's looking like it's going to stay put. I buy 100 shares, half of it on margin, so I've spent $9,000. I sell an at-the-money call for $50 and collect $5,000 against my $9,000. That gives me $5,000 in my account. I could do another deal.

DEAL #C1
Sell $180 Call
$50
Stock Purchase: $18,000
On Margin (divide by 2): $9,000
Take in (Option Premium): $5,000
Our own cash tied up: $4,000

GROUP C DEALS						
	STOCK (BUY)	CASH OUT THIS TRANSACTION	ACCUMU-LATED CASH OUT	OPTION INCOME	CASH IN (PROFITS)	ACCOUNT TOTAL (PROFITS)
1	100 shares at $180 but half on margin	$9,000	$9,000	Sell $180 call for $50	$5,000	$5,000

You know, we still have $5,000+ in the account, but let's stop here. The process cannot go on and on. Eventually you're going to run out of money, but we could do a few more. This, however, is enough to prove the point.

It's now expiration date. We made some good choices, and we got called out of these stocks. Remember, we started with $25,000. Let's see what ends up in the account.

RESULTS AFTER EXPIRATION DATE

GROUP A

We had purchased $50,000 but used margin—so only $25,000 was used.

We sell and get back in $50,000—$25,000 goes to the broker, and $25,000 replaces (replenishes) our cash.

We generated $14,400 of option premiums.

GROUP B

We purchased $24,000 but we used margin—so only $12,000.

We were called out and have the $12,000 back in our account.

Total cash in account is $48,600.

We sold $9,200 of calls.

GROUP C

Purchased 100 shares—spent $9,000 on margin.

We are called out and get back the $9,000.

We took in $5,000 in premiums.

THIS TOTALS:

$37,600 – that's our $48,600 including the return of our $9,200 for getting called out of the $180 stock, plus the $5,000 option premium in Group C.

Without doing a small Group D, we'll end it here.

To be fair, let's subtract a large sum, say $2,000 for expenses—that's still $55,600 on our $25,000 for five months!

We sold another $50 call contract for $5,000.

Results: That's $25,000 to make $30,600 after expenses.

Reality Check

Yes, some of these trades might not work out exactly as you planned. However, we can still make more money—remember, once we acquire the income, the subsequent transactions are FREE.

Also, in this reality check section, the major reality is that $25,000 generated more in real life premiums, $21,000 to be exact, than in our fictional Group A example. As you reuse this $21,000 rather than the $12,000 from Fictional Group A, the results are spectacular.

Summary

So what does this mean? We are capturing the premium and basically that's all we get to keep if we're selling the stock at or close to the money.

When it all shakes out—the week after each expiration date—we end up with all the cash back in. With this cash we have three things happening.

1. All of our original cash is back in. If we are not called out we still have the stock to write more covered calls.

2. The broker's margin loan is paid off.

3. We have the cash from all the premiums we've sold, which were temporarily tied up in other stock purchases.

We buy stock and sell stock. The huge option premium lets us buy more stock, so we can sell more options—and so on and so on.

Eventually all the stock we've purchased is sold and the cash is back in our account. Your $25,000 could end up buying $50,000 to $60,000 of stock—if the right stock and options are chosen. Let's go to the middle—that's $55,000 of cash in five months from our $25,000. Now that's $25,000 plus of cash *that the stock market gave us*—$25,000 to buy stocks or pay down the mortgage. Or, hey! Here's an idea. Let's give it a go another four to six months and turn that $55,000 into $100,000—switch to write monthly covered calls for monthly living expenses and really live the lifestyle of our choosing. This Large Option Covered Call Strategy lets you follow the money—all the way to your bank!

The following is an excerpt from the July 10, 2000 "Paid to Trade" Seminar taught by Wade Cook at the Seattle headquarters of Stock Market Institute of Learning(tm), in which he presented the LOCC System.

All right, Here we are in July. We're going to look out to October, November, December and January and when we get called out of all these stocks we're going to see how much money we have in the account. We'll start with $25,000. Let's target to make $15,000 to $17,000. That be a nice chunk of money for four or five or six months, wouldn't it? When we're done, we'll have all of our $25,000 cash back in plus the $15,000 to $17,000 on top of that. Now, if you only have $5,000 right now to get started you can just pick a couple of these deals we're going to do. Figure you'll make one-fifth of our target profit, something like $3,000.

1. **Cisco Systems.** We'll get our trading department on the phone and I want you call out the names of the companies you want to trade. Do we have somebody on the phone from the trading department yet? Who do we have?

CSCO
Sell $65 Call
October
$6^7/8
Stock Purchase: $6,450
On Margin (divide by 2): $3,225
Take in (Option Premium): $688
Our own cash tied up: $2,537
Rate of return based on $2,537
27%

This is Barry.

Hi, Barry. Barry, we're going to do a series of Large Option Covered Calls today. Just to get the ball rolling let's take a look at Cisco. Could you get those numbers, please? Cisco will be okay to start with, but it will not be great. Cisco is making too much money. It's one of my favorite companies by the way, but it hardly ever works for LOCC. We'll still take a look at it though. So, what is Cisco going for Barry?

Cisco's currently at $64^1/2 They're down $1 for the day.

Here we go everyone. If we buy 100 shares at $64^1/2 we spend $6,450. We divide that by two for the margin, so that's $3,225 of our own cash on hold. We're going to use 50% margin for our deals today, but if you're going to do this in an IRA you won't be able to use margin. We're going to look down the road and sell the $65 calls. Okay. Barry, what are the October $65 calls?

The October $65s are $6^7/8$ to sell.

Here's what we'll do. If we sell one contract, we'll take in $688. I'm not going to do it. It's not working. Does everybody see it's not going to work? You're going to end up with $2,537 on hold to make $688. So this is not a good example to start off with. I'll put it off to the side. Don't get the wrong idea. I love Cisco for other things; but it doesn't work for the LOCC system.

2. **Juniper.** Let's try Juniper. Can you get that Barry?

    Yeah, Juniper is currently at $148 even.

    Okay, so we spend $14,800; $7,400 if we do it on margin. What are the $145 and $150 calls going for out in the fall and January?

    It looks like we've got October $145s at $26^1/2 to sell and the $150s are $24 to sell. January $145s are $36^1/4 and the $150s are $34^1/2 to sell.

JNPR
Sell $145 Call
October
$36^1/4$
Stock Purchase: $14,800
On Margin (divide by 2): $7,400
Take in (Option Premium): $3,625
Our own cash tied up: $3,775
Give Back: $300
Adjusted Profit: $3,325
Rate of return based on $3,325
88%

All right. We're going out six months on this one. I'm going to do the January $145 calls right here. You're going to get a larger premium if you sell a five or six month out call. In this case we're buying the stock at $148 and selling the $145 call. Does anybody see a problem here? We're going to lose $3 dollars per share, right? Times our 100 shares, that's $300. So we sell one contract, take in $3,625 and have $3,775 of our own cash tied up. When we get called out, we sell our 100 shares for $145, or $14,500. The stockbroker gets back his $7,500 margin loan and we keep the rest, the $7,100 against which we put that $3,775. We realize a $3,325 profit. It's not quite a 90% return, but it is a 15% return per month for a six month investment. How many of you think putting up $3,775 to get $3,325 is a pretty cool deal for six months?

You might wonder why I'm selling an in-the-money call like that. It's so I'll get called out. Our main objective is to collect those large fluffy premiums right now, cash right now. Now if you're buying Juniper at $145 or $148, you could write the $160 or the $180 calls but you would take in less cash right now. That is writing an out-of-the-money call.

I suggest that to make LOCC work best you buy a stock on a dip and sell an in-the-money or at-the-money call. If you can wait and sell the call on a little bit of strength that would be best, but I'm doing these simultaneously, in a "married position" because that's my lifestyle. If you have more time to wait for the stock to show some strength, you could make more money, right? But I'm buying the stock and selling the call almost simultaneously and what I lose in some of those extra little profits I make up in peace of mind because I don't have to be busy all the time with the process. So, I just buy the stock and sell the calls at the same time.

All right, let's go ahead and put this on our charts so we can get going on the chart. Okay, this is Juniper. We used $3,775. Our running total of cash on hold is $3,775. Our profit is $3,325. And our running total of profit is $3,325. Okay. Somebody give me another one.

DEAL #3

3. **Corning.** We have a whole bunch of people around our company who just love Corning right now. They think Corning is another JDSU because a lot of what they are doing right now is fiber optic stuff. The GLW stands for Corning Glass Works right? Corning Glassworks. It's a hot one right now and it looks like— I don't make any absolute guesses, I'm just making a guess—it's going to do a stock split. And everybody is saying a three for one or four for one.

GLW
Sell $250 Call January $46^1/_4
Stock Purchase: $24,700 On Margin (divide by 2): $12,350 Take in (Option Premium): $4,625 Our own cash tied up: $7,725
Give Back: $300 Adjusted Profit: $4,325
Rate of return based on $4,325 56%

It's coming out with earnings. All the news will come out on July 21, so, next week. Right, all the stuff's going to be happening on this one. It'll happen or not. We're going to rally into this announcement and then sell on the announcement. We're probably going to be selling every position we have on July 21. Right, just to get out of the way because can these companies come out with incredible earnings and even stock split announcements and see 'em go up $20 or $30 and crash back $50 to $80? Yes or no? What's this stock at now, Barry?

It's currently at $247 even.

Okay. Here we go. We're going to buy 100 shares. That's $24,700 or $12,350 on margin. What are the $250 calls going for?

The Januarys are written. The January $250 calls are at $46^1/_4$.

We would take in $4,625. We are spending $7,625 to make $4,625. I don't like it. It's not that good to me. It's not that good of a deal. All right, so I'm going to set that one off to the side for now.

4. **Rambus.** Every time we've traded Rambus it has worked.

Rambus is currently at $100 even.

That's a good one for math. So 100 shares are $10,000. Divide it in half, you have $5,000 cash out. What are the $100 calls for November and December?

Novembers $100s are $24^1/_4 to sell.

RMBS
Sell $100 Call *November* *$24^1/_4*
Stock Purchase: $10,000 *On Margin (divide by 2): $5,000* *Take in (Option Premium): $2,425* *Our own cash tied up: $2,575*
Rate of return based on $2,575 *94%*

If we buy Rambus at $100 and we sell the $100 calls, what are we hoping for? We're hoping it'll go above and stay above $100, right? Because we want to get called out. What if it drops down to $90 between now and November? Are we going to end up owning the stock in November if we do not get called out at $100? Yes. Could we even buy back that $100 call option and then sell it out another four or five months? Yes. We can get busier anytime we want and click into high gear, but right now this trade just has to sit in place, stay above $100 through November and we get called out. We get all of our money back in. In this case we have $2,575 of our own money to make $2,425. I like it. Let's put Rambus up here.

Let's look at our totals. We have used $6,350 of our own cash to make $6,050. Not bad. Someone with only $5,000 or $6,000 could do these two and in five or six months $6,000 would make you $5,700. Does that sound okay? I see six of you are liking this. All right. I'll try and pick off the rest you as we go. Looks like an audience I'm going to win over slowly.

5. **Ciena.** All right, what's the next one? Does somebody have a suggestion? Ciena? Barry, can you pull that up?

Ciena is currently at $176^1/_2$.

Okay. We buy 100 shares for $17,650. On margin that's $8,825 of our own money. Now, let's look at the $175 calls.

We have Octobers and Januarys $175s. October is currently at $31^3/_4$ to sell. Januarys are at $43^1/_2$.

CIEN
Sell $175 Call   *January*   *$43^1/_2$*
Stock Purchase: $17,650   *On Margin (divide by 2): $8,825*   *Take in (Option Premium): $4,350*   *Our own cash tied up: $4,475*
Give Back: $150   *Adjusted Profit: $4,200*
Rate of return based on $4,200   **94%**

Let's do January for $4,350. That leaves $4,475 to make $4,350, right? Now, time out. Do we have to give back $150? How many of you see the $150? That's the $1.50 difference between what we paid for the stock and what we'll get called out at.

We're also not figuring in interest rates on the margin part of our account and we're not figuring in commissions right now. We'll deduct a whole bunch for all those later. So, here going to have to give back $150, so we only make $4,200 on our $4,475. Okay, let's do this one.

Somebody give me another company right now so Barry can start looking it up? Microstrategy? Did you get that Barry? Okay, stick with me on the math you guys. What are our totals? We have a total of $10,825 on hold to make $9,950. Anyone else have those numbers? I'm not going to put it up here till we make sure it works. Those are good? This is working well.

6. **Microstrategy.** Okay. Barry says Microstrategy is currently at $30^7/_8$. This'll be a good trade for those of you who don't have very much money to get started. Doing these $30 and $40 stocks is pretty cool. Let's round that up to $31 and start putting a little bit of money away for interest and commissions. So let's say that we paid $31, that's $3,100. That's $1,550 on margin, correct? Okay. Now let's see the $30 call.

We have October $30s at $8^5/_8$ to sell. Januarys are at $10^7/_8$ to sell.

I'm going to show you guys something here guys. I'm going to do them both. This is going to get very exciting. We'll do the October calls first. We have $1,550 of our own money on hold. We take in $862.50 on our one contract, so we're spending $686.50 to make $862.50. Pretty cool, is it not? But we have to give back $100. We're buying the stock at $31 then selling it at $30 so we're going to give back the $100 difference. That's still over 100% return and October is only three months away.

> **MSTR(a)**
>
> *Sell $30 Call*
> *October*
> *$8^5/8*
>
> *Stock Purchase: $3,100*
> *On Margin (divide by 2): $1,550*
> *Take in (Option Premium): $862.50*
> *Our own cash tied up: $687.50*
>
> *Give Back: $100*
> *Adjusted Profit: $762.50*
>
> *Rate of return based on $762.50*
> *111%*

Now watch what happens when we go out six months to January. My goodness. Look at this. The January calls are $10^7/8. For our $1,550 we take in $1,087.50. Is that correct? For six months we have $462.50 on hold. Only we do not make $1,087.50, we make $987.50 because we still have to give back that $100. How many think the $462.50 to make $987.50 between now and January is a pretty cool deal?

Okay. Now all we need is for Microstrategy to stay above $30. How many of you think it will stay above $30? I think it will. It's a good little company. There are a lot of good promising things coming out on this company. What do you think? Now I'm getting some smiles. Look at this. I'm getting some smiles, finally. What's that? Do Octobers? Okay, let's take a vote. How many would do the Octobers? How many would do the Januarys? Again, this is

> **MSTR(b)**
>
> *Sell $30 Call*
> *January*
> *$10^7/8*
>
> *Stock Purchase: $3,100*
> *On Margin (divide by 2): $1,550*
> *Take in (Option Premium): $1087.50*
> *Our own cash tied up: $462.50*
>
> *Give Back: $100*
> *Adjusted Profit: $987.50*
>
> *Rate of return based on $762.50*
> *214%*

your lifestyle. You know, I've never done this before, but let's do this. Let's buy 1,000 shares of this stock and do five contracts of the Octobers and five of the Januarys. Somebody help me with the math now. You guys use a calculator and check my math. You got to learn this math.

We buy 1,000 shares of the stock for $31,000. On margin we actually need $15,500. Let's sell the five contracts of the October calls at $8^5/_8$ times 500 shares for $4,312.50. But we're not making $4,312.50, are we guys? When we get called out we'll need to give back the $1 per share, or $500. Our profit here is $3,812.50. Remember we don't give back that $500 until we get called out, so our cash on hold as of today is our original $15,500 minus the October premium, or $11,187.50. Do you see that? Good.

Now we're going to do the January $30 calls. They're going for $10^7/_8$. Multiply that

MSTR(c)
Part 1: Sell $30 Call *October* $8^5/_8$
Stock Purchase: $31,000 *On Margin (divide by 2): $15,500* *Take in (Option Premium): $4,312.50* *Our own cash tied up: $11,187.50*
Part 2: Sell $30 Call *January* $10^7/_8$
Take in (Option Premium): $5,437.50 *Total Premiums Collected: $9,750* *Our own cash tied up: $5,750*
Give Back: $1,000 *Adjusted Profit: $8,750*
Rate of return based on $8,750 152%

times 500 shares for $5,437.50. Again, we subtract the $500 for the give back and we have a profit of $4,937.50. Our cash on hold today for these two deals is $5,750. Even adjusting for the $1000 we will give back, we've spent $5,750 to make $8,755 on these two deals.

Let's look at where we are with all these deals. With all the adjustments for our give backs, we have spent $16,575 to make $18,700. But let's say that at $31 you're thinking that this is pretty risky. I want to show another one for October. Barry, can you give me the $25 call for October?

October $25 calls are currently at $10^1/_2$ to sell.

Now watch this. We'll just do one contract. We spend the $3,100 again; $1,550 on margin. Now if you think that this stock could go back down – now listen carefully – why not sell a deep in-the-money call? Why not pick up more cash now? If this stock has had a run-up of $22 or $24 bucks, a run-up to $30 bucks right? If we've had a run-up and you think it might back off, why don't you sell off the profits right now?

Let me ask my question in a different way. If you had a stock at $31 and you sold it, and then it went down to $24, $25 wouldn't you be kind of happy that you had sold it? Yes or no? Yes. Selling the stock would be one way to get your profits. But why not try this? Why not sell a call option that represents the profit of that stock? That's too important of a question to pass up. So important that I think you ought to write it down. Why not sell a call option that represents the last run-up of the stock, the last profit of the stock. Sell the $25 calls.

What if the stock then goes down to $25 or $24? Let's look at that. You picked up all the cash right now, did you not, from the $31 down to the $24? You're going to pick up all the intrinsic value. I say sell the intrinsic value, sell that part of the stock that represents the last run-up. Okay. Let's go there.

We have spent $1,550 of our own money. We take in $1,050 for the $25 calls at $10.50. That leaves $500 of our own money, our own cash tied up. Now, what happens if we get called out? What's the worst thing that could happen right now if this stock goes to $40 or $50 dollars? Are we going to get called out at $25? Yes or no? Yes, we will definitely get called out at $25. Whoa. Then how much do we have to give back?

MSTR(d)
Sell $25 Call *October* *$10 1/2*
Stock Purchase: $3,100 *On Margin (divide by 2): $1,550* *Take in (Option Premium): $1,050* *Our own cash tied up: $500*
Give Back: $600 *Adjusted Profit: $450*
Rate of return based on $450 **90%**

Of that $1,050 we took in, how much do we have to give back? We have to give back the $6 difference between the $31 we paid for the stock and the $25 we sold it for, or $600.

What do we have left, folks? We have $450 left for our $500 cash on hold. The worst thing that can happen between now and October, folks is you're going to almost double your money. You had $500 of your own money on hold and you made $450.

You're all staring again. Look. By selling off the profit part of this, that $25 call, you get your profit now. Okay, what if it backs off? What if backs off clear down to $24 and we don't called out. Is this a problem? We now own the stock at $24. What did we pay for it? What's the cost basis on this stock? We bought the stock for $3,100 and took in

$1,050 bucks. What did you pay everyone? You paid $2,050. Your cost basis per share is $20.50. This stock would have to back off $10 bucks BELOW what you paid for it before you start losing money. That's selling a deep in-the-money call. Don't do this when you're driving down the freeway, folks, or you'll make a new exit.

Now if you want to see something really wild, watch this. What are the January $25 calls going for, Barry?

The January $25 calls are going for $12³/₄, or $12.75.

Okay. Same thing as before. We buy the stock for $3,100, divide by our margin for $1,550. We sell one contract for $1,275. You have $275 of your own money on hold. Do you see that? Now you sell the $25 call. How much

MSTR(e)
Sell $25 Call
January
$12³/₄
Stock Purchase: $3,100
On Margin (divide by 2): $1,550
Take in (Option Premium): $1,275
Our own cash tied up: $275
Give Back: $600
Adjusted Profit: $675
Rate of return based on $675
245%

do you have to give back when you get called out – because you will get called out? That's right you have to give back $600. Out of your $1,275 you have to give back $600. You have $675 left. Your $275 just earned you a $675 profit.

But what if you did this with ten contracts, with 1,000 shares? This stock has got six months to stay above $30, or $31. Even if it does take a dip, say down to $22, the worst that can happen is that you will double, practically triple your money. Let's go there. What if you do 10 contracts? Just add the zero. How many of you like $2,750 to make $6,750? What do you do with that? You do it again! Just park your money and do it again! This is what I call my LOCC Next Monster. My whole Chapter 8 is about this. This is just a phenomenal strategy.

How many of you think that would be a pretty good rate of return for your IRA? You can't do it on margin in an IRA so you wouldn't be able to take the margin part of these deals, yet you can still apply everything else we just did against the whole $31,000 and sell a deep-in-the-money call. Those of you with only $275 bucks to get started, you can go buy that $30 stock and sell that $25 call six months out and if that stock stays above $25 you're going to make $675 minus your commissions.

How'd you like to do about five to 10 of these a day, 1,000 shares? Some of you are plunking down $10,000 or $15,000 for call options, so here's a way to punk down $2,750 to make $6,750. How many of you wish your brokers had told you about this? Why did you have to learn this from a cab driver instead of your financial professions? I'm more into basketball than I am into stocks. If didn't have anything else to do all day but think about stocks, I 'd really be dangerous. Let's do one more? Barry, what are the January $20 call options going for?

The January $20 calls are $15.

We spend our $3,100, or $1,550 on margin. We take in $1,500 for the January $20 calls so we have $50 of our own money on hold. We have to give back $11 per share, so of this money we've taken in we have to give back $1,100. We have $400 left. Our $50 turns into $400 doing the January $20 calls. Let's do 100 contracts, or 10,000 shares. Your $5,000 will turn into 40,000!

MSTR(f)
Sell $20 Call
January
$15
Stock Purchase: $3,100
On Margin (divide by 2): $1,550
Take in (Option Premium): $1,500
Our own cash tied up: $50
Give Back: $1,100
Adjusted Profit: $400
Rate of return based on $400
800%

You like that one? That $50 deal? By the way, all you have to do is have this stock stay above $20, and it probably will, and you've got $11 of padding in here. Your $50 makes $400. The LOCC Next Monster–just a nice little deep-in-the-money covered call.

7. **Intel.** This won't work, but I'll show you why. Barry says the stock is at $138^1/_2$. Okay. We'll get 100 shares for $13,850, half on margin for $6,925. The January $140s are $19^1/_2$, but see that? We're out six months and we're only going to take in $1,950. You have $4,975 of your cash tied up just to make $1,950.

You see why that won't work? You have a big huge company,

INTC
Sell $140 Call
January
$19^1/_2$
Stock Purchase: $13,850
On Margin (divide by 2): $6,925
Take in (Option Premium): $1,950
Our own cash tied up: $4,975
Gains: $150
Adjusted Profit: $2,100
Rate of return based on $4,975
42%

but they have those little $8 and $10 options on a $100 stock. They're nice and wonderful for other things, but they just don't work for this stuff. I'm looking for a better return if I'm tying up my cash for that long. That's why we have to go shopping every day. I suggest you pick out your top 20 companies, get to know them inside out and use them over and over, pick the $120 call one month, the $140 calls the next month, *et cetera.*

8. **Broadvision.** Broadvision is going for $41^1/_2$. We buy 100 shares for $4,150, $2,075 on margin. There's nothing for fall, so let's do the December $40s for $11^3/_4$. We subtract $1,175 from our $2,075 and get $900 on hold. That's $900 to make $1,175. We have to give back $1^1/_2$ per share when we get called out? Subtract $150 and we make $1,025. Five months for $900 to make $1,025 minus commissions. Will that work for you? It works for me.

BVSN
Sell $40 Call
December
$11^3/_4$
Stock Purchase: $3,100
On Margin (divide by 2): $1,550
Take in (Option Premium): $1,500
Our own cash tied up: $50
Give Back: $1,100
Adjusted Profit: $400
Rate of return based on $400
800%

How are we doing spending our money? Let's do 200 of these, so just double up everything. We spend $8,300, $4,150 on margin. We take in $2,350. Subtract that from our cash on hold for $1,800 on hold. We give back $300 for a total cash in of $2,050. Our $1,800 makes $2,050 in five months. I like it.

9. **Dell.** Dell will not work, but some of these are working so well let's throw a boring one in here. What's Dell going for, Barry?

Dell is at $50. The fall $50 calls are $6.

Oh, how boring. But okay, I'm going to use it guys, because some of you criticize me for using all these high flying ones,

DELL
Sell $50 Call
Fall
$6
Stock Purchase: $5,000
On Margin (divide by 2): $2,500
Take in (Option Premium): $600
Our own cash tied up: $1,900
Rate of return based on $1,900
32%

so I'm going to use one of these ones that are boring as boring can be. We'll buy 100 at $50. Good. That's $5,000; $2,500 on margin. That's $1,900 to make $600. Okay. I'll take it.

What do we have so far? We were at $19,200, plus this $1,900 so we've got a total of $21,100 on hold. Over here, add the $600 for $22,875. So far we have $21,100 on hold to make $22,875. Are you with me on that? Okay.

10. **Ericsson.** Barry what do you have on Ericsson?

Ericsson is at $21^1/_2$. I have October and January $20s and $22^1/_2s.

Let's do the Januarys.

The $20s are at $4^1/_2$ to sell, the $22^1/_2$ calls are $3^1/_2$ to sell.

It's not going to work and show you why. We buy 100 for $2,150. Margin is $1,075. The $22^1/_2$ calls would be $350.

> **ERICY**
>
> *Sell $22^1/_2 Call*
> *January*
> *$3^1/_2*
>
> *Stock Purchase: $2,150*
> *On Margin (divide by 2): $1,075*
> *Take in (Option Premium): $350*
> *Our own cash tied up: $725*
>
> *Gains: $100*
> *Adjusted Profit: $450*
>
> *Rate of return based on $450*
> **62%**

Subtract that and you have $725 on hold to make $350. You'll make another dollar when you get called out, see that? You buy at $21^1/_2 and sell at $22^1/_2, so you could add on another $100 for $450 cash in, but it still isn't great.

11. **Vitesse Semiconductor.** Give me another one. VTSS? That's Vitesse Semiconductor. What's VTSS at, Barry?

VTSS is currently at $74^1/_2. The $75 October calls are $17^3/_4 to sell.

We take in $1,775 to make $1,950 and we're all going to ignore the $50 give back. Okay. Let's do this one, just one contract. We could double up on

> **VTSS**
>
> *Sell $75 Call*
> *January*
> *$17^3/_4*
>
> *Stock Purchase: $7,450*
> *On Margin (divide by 2): $3,725*
> *Take in (Option Premium): $1,775*
> *Our own cash tied up: $1,950*
>
> *Give Back: $50*
> *Adjusted Profit: $1,725*
>
> *Rate of return based on $1,725*
> **88%**

this but I'm not going to. I want to show you what to do with some of this money.

Let's look at our tally on the next page. We're up to $23,050. A couple of these deals are a little riskier than I would like. If I'm doing deals that are riskier than I usually like, I will do them a little bit more in the money. Let me say that again. When in doubt, sell an in-the-money call. If you're looking at buying a $78 stock and selling the $75 or the $80, a lot of times you'll want to sell the $80 because you want to pick up that extra money and you expect the stock to go up. I say no. That's just me, but we want to be called out, so I say sell an in-the-money call, pick up the cash now and give it back later. Does that make sense to you?

Now in this example we spent $23,050. I'm going to not spend the entire $25,000 because if we have a margin call, we'll want those few thousand dollars available. If this really is your only $25,000, we want to protect it. Now we really haven't accounted for margin interest and commissions so I'm going to knock off about 10% for those. That's a lot, but it's an easy number to work with for now. So that's $23,000 plus change making $22,000 plus change. I've never done a presentation that came out that close. I've done a couple where we've taken $15,000 to make $17,000, taken $25,000 to make $27,000. Today we made $22,000 with $23,000.

Transaction and Explanation	Cash Out (Hold)	Running Total	Cash In (Profits)	Today's Profits	Call Out (adjusted profits)	Total (Profits)
1. CSCO We passed on this example.	$0	**$0**	$0	$0	$0	**$0**
2. JNPR Buy 100 shares for $14,800, half on margin. Sell Jan145c for 36\frac{1}{4}$. Subtract premium from cash out for $3,775 on hold. ROR: 88% after call out.	$3,775	**$3,775**	$3,625	$3,625	$3,325	**$3,325**
3. GLW We passed on this example.	0	**$3,375**	$0	$3,625	$0	**$3,325**
4. RMBS Buy 100 shares for $10,000, half on margin. Sell Nov100c for 24\frac{1}{4}$. Subtract premium from cash out for $2,575 on hold. ROR: 94%.	$2,575	**$6,350**	$2,425	$6,050	$2,425	**$5,750**
5. CIEN Buy 100 shares for $17,650, half on margin. Sell Jan175c for 43\frac{1}{2}$. Subtract premium from cash out for $4,475 on hold. ROR: 94% after call out.	$4,475	**$10,825**	$4,350	$10,400	$4,200	**$9,950**
6c. MSTR Buy 1,000 shares for $31,000, half on margin. Sell 500 Oct30c for $4,315. Sell 500 Jan30c for $5,440. Subtract premiums from cash out for $5,750 on hold. ROR: 152% after call out.	$5,750	**$16,575**	$9,750	$20,150	$8,750	**$18,700**
6d. MSTR Buy 100 shares for $3,100, half on margin. Sell Oct25c for 10\frac{1}{2}$ for $500 on hold. $450 profit. ROR: 90% after call out.	$500	**$17,075**	$1,050	$21,200	$450	**$19,150**
6e. MSTR Buy 100 shares for $3,100, half on margin. Sell Jan25c for 12\frac{3}{4}$ for $275 on hold. $675 profit. ROR: 245% after call out.	$275	**$17,350**	$1,275	$22,475	$675	**$19,825**
6f. MSTR Buy 100 shares for $3,100, half on margin. Sell Jan20c for $15 for $50 on hold. $400 profit. ROR: 800% after call out.	$50	**$17,400**	$1,500	$23,975	$400	**$20,225**
7. INTC We passed on this example.	$0	**$17,400**	$0	$23,975	$0	**$20,225**
8. BVSN Buy 200 shares for $8,300, half on margin. Sell Dec40c for 11\frac{3}{4}$ for $1,800 on hold. ROR: 113% after giving back $300.	$1,800	**$19,200**	$2,350	$26,325	$2,050	**$22,275**
9. DELL Buy 100 shares for $5,000, half on margin. Sell Fall50c for $6 for $1,900 on hold. ROR: 32% after call out. Not great, but we'll take it.	$1,900	**$21,100**	$600	$26,925	$600	**$22,875**
10. ERICY We passed on this example.	$0	**$21,000**	$0	$26,925	$0	**$22,875**
11. VTSS Buy 100 shares for $7,450, half on margin. Sell Jan75c for 17\frac{3}{4}$ for $1,950 on hold. ROR: 88% after call out.	$1,950	**$23,050**	$1,775	$28,700	$1,725	**$24,600**
Totals	$0	**$23,050**	$0	$28,700	$0	**$24,600**

Less 10% Commissions and Interest $2,460

Net Profit $22,140

10

MAKING LOCC WORK BETTER

There are a good many extra aspects to Large Option Covered Calls, or what you would call "techniques within the formula," that just don't seem to fit anywhere specifically in this book. So, this chapter is a potpourri of these add-on angles to bring in more cash flow, protect yourself and make your LOCC plan work even better.

Just because there is no central theme to this chapter does not minimize its importance. In fact, some of these ideas are truly dynamic.

CREATE A TAX ENTITY

Do the LOCC system in a tax-free entity. I've spent many years showing people how to take a legal entity, like an IRA, SEP-IRA, or Corporate Pension Plan (my favorite) and turn taxable profits into tax free investments.

We have so many students doing so well with their realized gains (gains made by selling for a profit), that April 15th of each year became a real eye opener. Sometimes it's quite painful. Then they rush back to my "Asset Protection–Tax Reduction" seminar to breathe in the same information they learned one or two years ago. We tried to warn them to get set up now, not to wait to properly structure their affairs. But, often to no avail.

All of our coaching did no good, until that moment when they realized, "Hey, I *need* this!" "When the student is ready, the teacher appears."

Most people have heard of tax-free investments, like municipal bonds, but are turned off by their 5% to $7^1/_2\%$ <u>annual</u> returns. My students get used to 10% to 20% monthly cash-flow returns. So, I've contended that the best shelter is to make more money. Yes. Make hundreds of thousands of dollars and take the consequences–but what if you could have both? What if you could have incredible profits, keep it all working tax free until you turn 70, and then at that time only pay taxes as you pull out small parts of your new fortune? And just think, what if you could get a tax deduction on your contribution, or on the money you put aside?

Read the following testimonials, see the huge profits other people have made and then we'll talk.

"Recently, I've been following a stock, IDC (Inter Digital Communication) [that] you've traded on W.I.N. I started buying options this fall when the stock was about $6 a share. My investment in November 1999 of $30,000 in various IDC options grew to $2,421,000. A second account went from $18,489 to $385,363 [in] only a two-week time frame. On my single best day the account values went from $1,028,000 to $2,323,969. This was an increase of $1,295,969 in one day. On December 30th [I had] a return of 954% in two days. I was ecstatic with these results. I want to thank you for your techniques, which gave me the knowledge and confidence to use your strategies. Without your videotapes I would not have these outstanding profits. Thank you."

–GLENN M., IL

"Currently today I'm up $94,600 net profit to a total net profit in my account of $1,273,931.43. WOW. Interestingly enough, in the last six straight business days I've increased $512,323.86 and that doesn't even include any Internet stocks (well, I did play YHOO for one day and made $13,751.81) but other than that it was strictly DELL and MSFT. This sure is fun. I'm planning on

retiring this Friday for good and spending more time with family, friends and doing fun things while I'm still relatively young. Here is a "scan" of my January 1999 brokerage account report. As you can see, it shows the amount last period ($318,170) compared to this period ($1,057,048)...by the way, yesterday my portfolio was up $80,830 and today it was up another $84,306. Not bad for an old guy like me."

–MYKE L., WA

"I have done very well with Wade's strategies. I had $36,000 as of September 30, 1999 and turned it into $460,000 [by] January 10, 2000. That was on one account. Then in another I took $100,000 and turned it into $400,000 in four weeks, and then took another from $120,000 to $150,000 in one week for a total of $960,000."

–JOHN T., OK

These are exceptional profits. Not all of our students make this level of profits. I'm not implying here that you will make this kind of money–they couldn't believe it either–but they successfully put my cash-flow formulas to work.

I've used these testimonials in other places, usually to prove the point that you can't expect to give your money to a mutual fund, or any other professional asset manager, give up your control, and then expect these kinds of results. Show me one fund that has taken $30,000 and turned it into $2,421,000, or taken $36,000 and turned it into $460,000 like the testimonials above. You can't. So my point is–we want to show you the tools and help you develop the skills to use them so *you*, not someone else, can make a dramatic difference in your financial life.

Now I want these testimonials to tell a different story. Get ready. Set up a tax free entity and get going. (Note: we have contracted with a law firm to establish Corporate Pension entities, as well as the other entities. Call 1-800-872-7411 for their number.)

Now pension trust plans allow for options trading, but even in a single IRA, you can buy stock and sell calls against that position. Did you get that? Virtually everything in this book can be done tax free. Okay, tax deferred until you pull it out in 30 years. What about now and the asset and income build up over the next several years? Simple question to drive this home: How fast can your money grow, this LOCC way, if you don't have to pull out 20% to 40% each April 15th and pay taxes?

REINVESTMENT PROGRAMS

Most brokerage firms have dividend reinvestment programs. If you own stocks which pay dividends they will use the incoming cash to purchase fractional shares of the stock. This is how you end up with 101.824 shares of stock in a few months when you had only purchased 100 shares.

In most cases, I do this on all stocks the broker can put into the system. It's sort of a forced savings plan. Over the years this can add up to an extra bonus–especially if those stocks continue to grow in value.

However, if you have a need for more cash flow, you may just want to have the dividend hit your account as cash. Let's think it through. If you own 101.824 shares of one stock and 204.635 shares of another stock, and you write one contract against the 100 shares and two contracts against the 200 shares, and then subsequently get called out, you would have 1.824 shares of one and 4.635 shares of the other. This is awkward to carry on the books and relatively costly to sell these small share amounts.

On LOCC stocks I just want cash in for the dividends.

GAINS AND TAXES

Now, let me address an issue that should be near and dear to our hearts: how and when we pay taxes on option premiums. We'll try to kill two birds with one stone, addressing the issue of long-term capital gains, and the secondary issue of when this premium income becomes taxable income to us.

Let's say we own a stock for three months, and at that time decide to write a covered call on the stock. At first glance, we are taking the premium income in against the stock position. But as long as they are married together, the offset of the stock for the premium is taxable to us, when the position has ended. For example, let's say we write a covered call against the stock position, and then do not get called out. When the position expires–which is more than likely a particular "third Friday" expiration date–*that* is the time the premium income for selling the option would become a taxable event.

At the same time, we must understand that by writing a call against our stock position, we have basically suspended the time that the stock needs to become a long-term hold. Again, our example is that we own the stock for three months, and we write a one-month out covered call, and we do not get called out. We would have to own the stock another nine months from the date of expiration to qualify for the full twelve months, which is necessary for the time period to be considered long term. We have actually owned the stock for thirteen months. But if we write a covered call for one month, or for three months, or for six months, the time that there was a position written against the stock, is the suspended time.

Another timing factor that may become very important would be the time of year we own the stock and write the call, in relation to what time of year the option expires or we are called out. For instance, say we owned stock in November, and then wrote a covered call for a January expiration date. You see, whether the stock is a long-term hold (12 months) or short term (any time under twelve months), the income hits our account in November, but does not become taxable to us until the expiration date, or the position has ended. The position could end in advance of the expiration date if we were called out on the stock. We would then have a capital gain on the stock, and have to claim the option premium as income at that point in time.

Writing a covered call near the end of the year may put off a taxable event until the beginning of the next year, even though cash comes into our account in the current year.

A STOCK SUBSTITUTE – BULL CALL SPREAD

As a substitute to the stock purchase, you could buy a call on the stock and then sell a higher strike price call against that position, reducing your cost basis and generating income.

I talked about using this strategy in the previous chapter, because it's a good strategy to recover a deal that isn't doing what you expected, but it's a good strategy on its own merit too. You don't own the stock, you own the right to buy the stock. By selling the higher call option, you do cap your upside potential, just like in selling a call on a stock position. But, you sell the call to reduce your cash outlay for the purchased call. You've created a bull call spread. It's a covered call, but with an option instead of stock. (For more information, read my book *Wall Street Money Machine, Volume 4: Safety 1st Investing*.) Two examples will help you see how this works.

A stock is at $110. It's slightly volatile, meaning the option premiums are higher. The $100 call is going for $18. The $110 call is $11. We usually do these close spreads for the next month out. Sometimes this means it's only one to three weeks to expiration. Let's do 10 contracts, and only then if we're really bullish on the stock and feel it will go above and stay above $110. We also would usually try to do twenty contracts at a time, but for the ease of the mathematics, let's do 10.

We buy 10 contracts of the $100 call for $18,000. We sell the $110 call for $11,000. We spend $18,000, but take in $11,000 for a net cost (credit) of $7,000. We get called out of the $110 (the trading desk uses SDS, or same day substitution), and exercise the $100 call. The results are the same as buying $100,000 and selling it for $110,000. There is a $10,000 gross profit, but we spent $7,000 to do this. That's a $3,000 profit, less our transaction costs.

Oh, you think, LOCC is better. Here a $7,000 cost to make $3,000 is not as good as other examples found in this book. True, but this was a one month deal. Using $7,000 to produce $3,000 each month for five to six months is nice indeed. A lot more work, but nice, fairly safe profits.

LONGHORN COVERED CALLS

Let's do a bigger spread and have it run longer. In my new home study course "Paid to Trade" I call these longhorn covered calls because of the wide spread amount. This is one of my preferred strategies. For an example we'll use a high-tech stock with a lot of talk going on. The stock is at $240. Rumors abound of a stock split. The news just came out that they're going to ask the shareholders for approval for more shares—a fairly good likelihood of a stock split announcement. Earnings are good, and improving.

The $220 calls, out three months, are going for $62. Remember, a $220 strike price is $20 in the money. The $260 calls are still going for

$41. This creates a $40 spread. Ideally, we want the stock to go above $260 and get called out.

Let's first see what it costs. We spend $62,000, but simultaneously take in $41,000. That means we have $21,000 cash invested and at risk. What is our upside? Again, substitute in your brain the stock, and then we'll go back to the options. $220,000 purchase price and $260,000 sell price–a $40,000 profit–but then we subtract our cost of $21,000 and get a $19,000 profit.

With options we don't have to put up all the cost of the stock. Again you ask–isn't LOCC better? We have examples of $21,000 producing $19,000 everywhere. Yes, they are, but again consider, this was for three months, not five or six months. We could do this twice in the same time period.

We have, by being in this wide spread, limited our down side risk, but have also given the stock time to run up (so we can make $19,000), and have also limited our upside potential–we're not simply long on the $220 calls. We did this on 1,000 shares (ten contracts), not 100 shares of a stock. The point is, the similarities can only go so far.

Just remember in a Large Option Covered Call position your stock can go down, and may take awhile to recover, or earn profits back, by writing subsequent covered calls. In short, bull call spreads work many times and give you a shot at more near-term profits. (Also see my *Spread & Butter* all-day video course for more on this type of trading.)

DO BULL PUT SPREADS FOR MONTHLY PROFITS

A Large Option Covered Call has a similar risk/reward relationship as selling naked puts. No time here for a long explanation, but I like an aspect of naked puts–the incredible bull put spread, which I've repeated, is my favorite monthly cash flow strategy. Indeed, my favorite by far. That's why I've spent so much time creating my *Spread & Butter* and *Paid To Trade* seminars and video sets.

BEAR CALL SPREADS

Now, this is a pretty exciting strategy. If you don't understand this, I invite you to get my book *Wall Street Money Machine, Volume 4: Safety 1st Investing*. I have a whole section on bear call spreads which is one of my absolute favorite strategies. Now I can't give you all the mechanics here of a spread, but I'll tell you the simple basic strategies.

In an up and down marketplace, I use bull put spreads (which is a credit spread and you have only one set of commissions) when the stocks are going up. I use a bear call spread (which is also a credit spread, which means it generates cash into your account) when the stocks are coming down, or at least are not going to go much higher.

Get that? A bull put spread when the stocks are going up. A bear call spread when the stocks are coming down, or you think they won't go much higher.

Let's say that the stock is around $200, and you really don't think it's going to go anywhere–it's really peaked out. You would sell a call for $220. Even if you don't own the stock, you can sell an uncovered, or naked, call.

Now a lot of your stock brokers won't let you do that, and if they do they're going to require 30% to 50% on margin anyway, even if you don't own the stock. Why? Because, it's risky. You've sold an option to someone, and you have the obligation now to deliver the stock at $220.

Well what's the risk here? If you don't own the stock, if you're uncovered, if you're in a naked position, then that stock could run to $240, $260 or to $280 and you could be forced to buy the stock at $280 in order to deliver it to someone who is only paying you $220. So yes, selling uncovered calls has an added element of risk. But wait.

Someone paid you $20 premium for that $220 call. Before you could start losing money, the stock would have to go up over $240. Because you could buy it at $240, deliver it at $220 and have a break-even situation. Do you see that?

Sold naked $220 call for $20	+ 20
Option exercised on buy share	− 240
You sell share	+ 220
Balance	0
If the stock rose over $240, you would be in a losing position.	

But what about this? Let's say you sold the $220 call, and remember the risk now is that the stock is going to run up. But you protect your upside by buying the $230 call, say for $17. So let's look what you've done.

You've sold the $220 call for $20 and taken in $2,000. Only, let's use 10 contracts instead of one, so that would be $20,000 you've received. Now what we're going to do here is buy 10 contracts of the $230 call for $17. Those 10 contracts would cost you $17,000. You've taken in $20,000 and spent $17,000. You now have a net credit–actual cash hitting your account–of $3,000.

Now your amount of hold doesn't become 30% or 50% of the stock price. Your hold now becomes the amount of the spread, minus the cash that you received. Stay with me here. The spread is a $10 dollar spread between the $220 and $230 call, times 10 contracts, that's $10,000. You have a net credit of $3,000. So you in fact now have on hold, at risk, $7,000 in order to make $3,000 for the next four or five weeks. That is called a bear call spread. Here's a picture.

Sold $220 call for $20, 1000 shares	*$20,000*
Buy $230 call for $17	*– $17,000*
Net credit	*$3,000*
Spread between 230 and 220	*$10,000*
Minus net credit	*– $3,000*
Your cash on hold	*$7,000*

Now this is a *powerful* strategy. Let me give you the definition of bear here, because that'll make some sense when I show you how this is going to apply now to our Large Option Covered Call strategy. I want to slow down and explain it so that you get this one.

You would use a bear call spread with this new definition of the word bear, or bearish. A bearish strategy in this case is not necessarily a stock that goes down, it is a stock that *stays* down below a certain strike price. So if you have a stock that's at $200, $205 or $206 and you really don't think it's going to go to $220, you could sell the $220 call and buy the $230 call and create a bear call spread. As long as that stock stays under $220, you're going to make $3,000. You have paid

$7,000 and have it on hold to make three grand. If you didn't get that, reread it until you do. Do the math.

Now do you see where you can use this in a bearish situation? That you can use it when you are not necessarily thinking that the stock is going to go down, but that it's going to stay down below the $220 strike price? That is a bear call spread. It is a credit spread. If the stock does stay below $220 it will just expire on the expiration date, and you'll be able to keep that $3,000 minus commissions in your account.

So once again, we use a bear call strategy when we *think* that the stock is going to go down or stay down below a particular strike price.

USING A BEAR CALL SPREAD IN LOCC

Now what does all this have to do with LOCC? When would you use this strategy? Let me show you how it's used.

Let's use an example of where we sell the $200 call option on a stock we own for $50 and generate $5,000 by selling one contract. That's $5,000 cash into your account. This stock is now in a position where it has taken a few dips and is down to the $160 range.

SCENARIO A

We can now buy *back* the $200 call for $20. A lot of the time has gone out of the premium, so the price is only $20.

Premium	*$5,000*
Buyback	*– $2,000*
Net	*$3,000*

SCENARIO B

We could do that, but let's not stop there. Let's look at another scenario. Look at that $200 call for $20, but let's also look at the $210 and the $220 calls. The $210 call is going for $15 and the $220 call is going for $10. Let's not buy back the $200 call, let's buy the $220 call for $10 instead.

Why would we do this? Because it costs us $1,000 to buy the $220 call and create a bear call spread, as compared to spending $2,000 to buy back the $200 call for $20.

Premium	*$5,000*
Buy $220	*– $1,000*
Net	*$4,000*

What's the ultimate effect of buying the $220 call? We have a stock that is freed up. You now have three positions to create two strategies: You own this stock and a bear call spread (buy $220 call; sell $200 call) and we've made $4,000. As long as the stock stays below $200, these options will most likely expire worthless.

Our stock's down around $160. We could sell the $180 calls, or if it dips down to $150, we could sell the $160 calls. On the next rise, say the stock goes to $180, we could sell the $200 or $220 calls.

We bought the stock at $200. The stock is currently at $160. Here our choices:

SCENARIO A

Sold $200 @ $50	*$5,000*
Buy back $200 call @ $20	*– $2,000*
Net credit	*$3,000*

SCENARIO B

Sold $200 @ $50	*$5,000*
Buy back $220 call @ $10	*– $1,000*
Net credit	*$4,000*

This creates at $200/$220 bear call spread.

The reason you would do this is the $1,000 difference, and you have freed up your stock for other trades.

Here's the point. If you really don't think this stock is going to go back up above a certain strike price, in this example the $200 strike price, then instead of buying back the $200 strike price, you could buy the $210, or the $220, and create a bear call spread.

Now there's a certain element of risk there, so you need to really pencil this out, paper trade a couple of these, and then *only* use this strategy in a bearish mode where we think that the stock is either going to go down, or stay down below a certain strike price, in this example the $200 strike price.

Again, it's a buy back situation, but we're buying back a different strike price and creating a bear call spread for the sole purpose of spending less money, so we have more cash in our account to work with.

This is a testimonial that came in from one of our students.

"I attended a $5,000 seminar from another company for two days, and I didn't get it. Your seminar provides all the support one needs to be successful. I thank you so much for all the training. It's one of the best-kept secrets in wealth creation seminars we have around. You are the best. I made my year's salary in two and a half months."

–TINA D., CA

In one of my videos, I told the following story about being in Regina, Saskatchewan, Canada, for the Royal Red Arabian Horse Show. I told about having our hotel clear on the other side of town from the fair grounds where the Arabian horse show was going on. I was trying to get over there as fast as I could because we had to drive back and forth several times a day. My kids were in different classes, and they had to change into different outfits and all that. It was hot. It was in the middle of August. When I first got there, it was taking me 25 minutes to get across town, and boy I figured out the little freeway system. You could zip down here, jump on this road at this angle, and you could get over here. (Remember I'm an ex-cab driver.) I worked the route and I got it down to 18 minutes, then down to 14 minutes, and finally I got it down to 12 minutes. Was I proud of myself. I'd shaved my time in half.

Then I was kind of bragging. I mean, here I am from the Seattle area, and I was bragging to this one guy who was from Regina, and I said, "Now I've got this thing down to 12 minutes." And he asked, "Where are you staying?" I told him where I was staying, and he said, "Well, why don't you just go here and do this and do this?" And I said, "Oh, man!" I looked at the map and next drive, it took me eight minutes to get across town.

Now, I had it down from 24 minutes down to 12, and I thought I was pretty cool. But then I talked to somebody who was in the know, somebody who lived in the area, someone with the inside scoop, and there was an amazing difference in the amount of time it took, in how my performance improved. The reason I'm telling you this is because as you get good at something, you too will learn to fine-tune it, you'll get better and better at it. We all do. As long as we keep an open mind and keep seeking new knowledge.

Here at the Stock Market Institute of Learning™, we have literally done hundreds and hundreds of these covered call trades–thousands of other trades. We've traded all kinds of companies–big companies, small companies, high-flying Internet companies and more stodgy old economy companies. We've sold short-term calls. We've sold long-term calls, and we have a lot of experience, which we hope we can share with you.

So I invite you to keep learning. Keep coming to my Stock Market Institute of Learning seminars. Keep getting our home study courses and keep studying our books. And get involved in our SUPPORT programs. It's all good.

Get creative and increase your powers of observation. Gain knowledge, understand that knowledge, and then apply that knowledge. It's a never-ending cycle that you can move through repeatedly, each time enhancing your skills to improve your wealth and grow your cash flow.

11

STOCK REPAIR KIT

I live in a very beautiful area of Washington state, in the foothills of the Cascades, and there seem to be an incredible number of bicyclists around our place on the weekends. Bikers are just everywhere. We finally found out it's because this is one of the most highly written-up locations in almost every bicycle magazine in Washington. So bikers are always going by our house, following the trails in their maps and magazines.

Now, there is a little bicycle repair shop nearby, so if they have something wrong with their bike, they can get it fixed. But what if they are 13 miles from the repair shop? How helpless would you feel, out in the middle of nowhere, with a flat tire and no alternatives for getting down the mountain? Well, I've noticed another thing—the diehards always carry a repair kit. Almost every weekend we'll see someone off to the side of the road with their bicycle taken apart and their little repair kit spread out. They can fix almost anything, any time, any place. They don't leave home without that kit.

What about the stock market? Do we put ourselves in danger trading without a repair kit? This is what I want to introduce—a "stock repair kit" you can use if your stocks or strategies break down. It won't fix everything, but it will help you grasp this simple fact: *just because something goes wrong does not mean you're devoid of opportunity.* As a matter of fact, in many cases when things go wrong, it gives you *more* opportunity to profit. This seems backwards–how can something go wrong, yet still put more money in your pocket? Well, to be cliché, we're going to take lemons and make lemonade. It's that simple.

What If The Stock Dips?

When I teach this LOCC strategy, this is always the first and most pervasive question and concern. What if the stock dips? I want to put this in perspective. Let's use an example. You purchased one hundred shares of XYZ Company at $260. You spent $26,000. You then sold the $260 calls, five months out, for $60, or $6,000. This $6,000 goes against your margin of $13,000 ($1/2$ of $26,000). You have $7,000 of your own money on hold to make $6,000, minus your commissions.

Writing Short-Term Calls

Okay, the stock goes up, but on expiration it has dipped down again to $240. This situation is simple, and by the way, it's not that uncommon. You won't get called out. On the Monday after the third Friday, you will still own the stock. Now, you probably already have in mind what you can do. You could:

1. *Sell the stock.* Just think, you are still $40 profitable, or $4,000. How's that, you ask? Remember the $60 option premium goes against your cost of $260 leaving a cost basis of $200 ($260 – $60 = $200). If the sock is at $240, you are $40 profitable. You would sell the stock if you are tired of it and think your money could be deployed better elsewhere.

2. *Write another covered call,* either out another five to six months, or write a shorter-term call, say next month.

The choice here is once again based on where you are with your own life and time availability. If you're still really busy and have no time for monthly management of these positions, then:

3. Shop around for a good premium out several months.

Again, you have three choices:

1. *Which month?* It's October now. The January $240 calls are $30, and the April $240 calls are $40. There are no February or

March calls yet. In this case, I'd probably take the $30 ($3,000) in January. The extra $10 ($1,000) to tie up the stock for three more months does not seem worth it.

2. *Which strike price?* If you really think the stock has bottomed out, or is on a temporary dip, you have the same choices (depending on availability of strike prices as all strike prices are not available in each month's listed options). You can sell the $220, $230, $240, $250 or $260 calls. If you want more cash now, sell the $220s. You'll pick up a fat premium. If you want to tap into the bounce or near-term price increase, sell the $260s. You'd get less premium now, but maybe capture the rise in price.

3. *Wait to sell.* If you expect an upward move, you could wait. If the stock goes back up to $260, maybe you could get $50 out of the April $260 calls. Think of this. You'll have another $5,000 hit your account just for agreeing to sell the stock at the exact price where you paid for it, at $260!

Added point: your real cost is now $150. We subtract from the original $260 cost the $60 premium, and this new $50 premium. The stock would almost have to dip in half before we go underwater.

Good choices, all. It's a matter of style and preference. If you want to step up your involvement and be a little more active, switch to monthly call writing. Here we go. The same $260 stock is on an even bigger dip. Keep this in mind. Dips are dips. Sometimes they last only days. It bottomed at $220 and it's on its way back up. Again, it's October. The November $240 calls are $10. The $250 calls are $7 and the $260 are still going for $5. Choices, choices. Take more cash now and get called out, or less cash now and possibly live to fight another day. A few thoughts:

1. If you really do want to get called out–perhaps put your money to work in a different deal, then sell the $230 call for $15. That's $1,500 additional income. At least sell the $240 and take in the $1,000 ($10 times one contract). If you want to just get rid of the stock, wait for a nice rise and just sell it. That was our original choice.

2. If you hear good things, you may just want to hold on. Let's say a firm puts a $340 price target on this $260 stock. Wow! Do your homework. These are usually one year out price targets. Many things can happen and this is, after all, far away. That's two LOCC style premiums, and/or even 12 monthly covered call premiums. This decision has to be based on whether you need money now or not and how busy you want to be.

3. If you like this stock and want to generate more income as you ride it up, then sell the more out-of-the-money options. Remember the rules, good at least until the week of expiration.

Sell on increases (or spike-ups) in the stock price.

For example, the stock hit the $230 range and lulled around there for a few days. You've been trying to get $8 out of the $260 calls. Then, whammo! One day the stock spikes up to $252. You get filled at $9. Yes, you had a limit order in at $8, but brokers must do their best to get you the best price they can. Oh, and after the fill, the stock went to $254. You could have gotten $10, but you're already filled at $9. Oh well, be happy. Within hours, the stock is back at $244 and the option is back at $5. Your higher limited order worked well.

But what if you don't get filled and we're coming up on expiration—in this example, November? The stock is at $248, and the $260 call is now only $4. Most of the time premium is gone. To sell would be $400—why not take it? If not, start looking out to the next month.

Another rule:

The next month will always be there.
Take the cash now and live to fight another day.

Another day, in this case, is next Monday or so, after this Friday's expiration. Remember that $260 stock we wrote a $260 call on? We sold the call for $9, or $900, and then the stock dipped to $240. The call dropped in value to $4, at $400. Just think, if there is high volatility, we could buy it back—spend the $400 and free up our stock to write the $250 or $260 call on the next increase or run-up, maybe generating another $900 or $1,000.

But what if, shortly after we've taken this $260 stock and sold the five month out $260 call, the stock really drops, say to $220, or even $180? Obviously, one choice would be to be patient and stick it out. We knew there was volatility and some rough edges in some of these stocks. If we want that, that's all we do. We have decisions to make in five months or so, when we find out if we get called out or not.

If we want to buy back that $50 ($5,000) call for say, $10 ($1,000), we can pocket $4,000 and then look at the stock market in general, and the company in particular, and make other trades. Again, when we own the stock, we have the benefit of ownership:

1. We can hold on. We used the covered call formula as a way to buy wholesale.

2. We can sell the stock.

3. We can write short-term calls to generate income.

4. We can wait (as in #1) but then on an increase, sell short-term or further out calls.

You see, even when the stock falls out of bed, we're not devoid of opportunities. We should not sell in a panic, nor buy in a panic. Remember, we choose the formula to fit our trading lifestyle and our own personality. Those two things did not change just because the stock is in a lull.

Stay true to the system. It will work. You see, it's easy for me to give this noble, level-headed advice, because this just hasn't happened that many times. Oh, it's happened, and has been somewhat painful, but if we do our homework, from a Fundamental/Technical approach, then we'll lessen our chances of having this happen. Buy on dips. Check support levels. Buy on major dips. Check the storyline news and did I say, *"Buy on Dips?"*

If you want to increase your activity level, there will be many times to sell the call, then buy it back, then sell it again–probably about once a month. You'll make more money that way than in a "buy-stock/sell-call-and-wait" scenario, but you'll deserve the extra money as you'll have to work harder.

BULL CALL SPREAD

Let's do another example using a different strategy. Say we buy 1,000 shares of a stock on a dip at $18. We wait for it to go up a little, then write a covered call on it, selling a $20 call for $2 a share, or $2,000. Now what happens if we don't get called out sometime before the expiration date? What if right after the expiration date the stock heads into one of those "no news" times—a red light period—and the stock tanks? Now we're sitting there with stock we bought at $18, expecting it would go to $21 or $22, even in the short term. Not only did it not go to $22, it went *down* to $16. Does that sound like a breakdown to you?

I'm going to show you what to do with that stock. We did this one cautiously, but wisely on margin, because this stock had every indication it was going back up. We bought 1,000 shares at $18 to equal $18,000. At 50% margin, we have $9,000 of our own money tied up.

Now we have two problems. First of all, we could get a margin call and have to bring in more cash because there is no more collateral in the account. The second problem is common when we write covered calls: we wind up selling the winners and keeping the losers. By selling a covered call, we're giving away the upside—in this case, the upside sell didn't pan out, we didn't get called out, and we now hold a losing stock.

Let's take care of the margin requirement first. When we purchased this stock for $18 and later sold the $20 calls for $2, we took in $2,000 of premium. That $2,000 premium is in our account and can be used to cover the extra margin. Our covered call became a kind of preventative strategy for this situation.

Now we'll address the issue of owning a losing stock. We really have *four choices*:

1. We can continue to hold the stock.

2. If we really like the stock, we can buy more.

3. We could sell calls against it to bring in more cash for next month.

4. We could write a bull call spread.

Option four is what I want to share with you now. Here is a way of capturing some upside and mitigating your losses. Remember, the stock dipped to $16 and we had to use our $2,000 in premium to cover the margin, so we are breaking even right now. Here's how we recoup some of our losses: sell double the amount of contracts that we originally sold, and buy the number of contracts to match the stock we currently own. In this case, sell twenty and buy ten contracts. Sell double, buy single.

Let me explain what I mean. With 1,000 shares of stock at $16, we're going to sell twenty contracts of the $20 calls–double the amount of contracts we originally sold. We'll set the strike price out about three months; since this is May, we'll sell contracts that expire in July. With the stock on a dip, these go for about $4 each. Selling twenty contracts brings in $8,000 cash.

For the same month, we'll buy ten contracts of the July $17.50 calls at $6 each. We own 1,000 shares, so we're going to buy ten contracts to cover the rest of the calls we sold. That will cost us $6,000. We sold double, bought single.

Now let's explore what we have accomplished by doing this. First, our hope here is to break even. Even if we spend $8,000 to buy the lower strike price calls, that would be all right. In this case, we netted a small profit, about $1,500 after commissions. We've generated some cash by selling the same strike price out a little bit further. What else have we done? If you look, we have now created a ten contract bull call spread.

Let's look at another option. What if the $15 calls were going for $8? Now we would break even. We took in $8,000 to sell twenty contracts, and we could spend $8,000 to buy ten contracts. What do we get out of this deal? Look at what we've done: we have created a $15-$20 bull call spread. Let's stick with the stock for a minute, and then we'll go back to the options to see if this makes sense.

If we purchase a thousand shares of the stock for $15,000, and we sell it for $20,000, we would have $5,000 profit. In a typical bull call spread, we would have the amount of money that we spent to put it in place and the amount of money we took in. So, we would have a net debit to our account. Well, if we do the $15 strike price and the $20 strike price, what is our net debit in this example? We took in $8,000, and we spent $8,000. How much does it cost us to do this? Zero. Now if that stock goes above $20, and we get called out at $20, we're going to make an extra $5,000.

Let's analyze our total income from this transaction. First of all, remember we bought the original stock for $18. We took in $2,000, so there's $2,000 profit. Then the stock dipped to $16, we were not called out, we used our $2,000 profit to cover the margin, and we sold the $20 call. The second time we sold the $20 call, we netted zero (remember, we took in $8,000, but we spent $8,000). Now, when the stock rallies up to the $20 range, we get called out of the stock for an additional $2,000 in capital gains. Plus, if the bull call spread works, we pick up another $5,000.

So with an initial $9,000 out-of-pocket investment on a stock that took a major dip, we have not only recovered all of our $9,000, but now have a $7,000 profit! The $2,000 first premium which then held our margin was a wash, but we also made the $2,000 capital gains on buying stock at $18 and selling it at $20, and the $5,000 from the $15-$20 bull call spread. We took what could have been a fatally wounded market position, added three or four months of recovery time, and turned it into a healthy 78% profit!

By the way, if you don't make anything on the bull call spread, it didn't cost you anything. So what if it expires in July or August worthless? You can just do this again. Sell a higher strike price call and buy the lower strike price call, creating another bull call spread to generate more cash, because eventually, hopefully, you will get called out of the stock. It just may take a while to materialize.

So there is your repair kit for covered calls. Buy the stock, sell the call, and if it doesn't work, double up. Sell twice as many of the original strike price calls, and buy the same amount of calls as the amount of stock you own. Try to break even on that transaction to create a bull call spread, and pull in extra profits when the stock turns around and starts working for you.

You may never need your "stock repair kit", but keep it handy just in case!

12

LOCC— ACHIEVING DREAMS

Before I get into the meat of this chapter, look at the following stories and then begin dreaming…

Dear Wade,

I went to my first Wall Street Workshop™ in November of 1998. I spent two months just paper trading because our instructor… suggested it. Well, by the end of January 1999 I was trading with on and off success. I went to two more Wall Street Workshops™, a Day Trader Seminar, a Semper Financial [Seminar], and Fortify Your Income™ (FYI). By the end of February I was making on average $1,500 each day using the concepts and strategies in your seminars. My wife and I have dissolved a very successful cellular company since then and now enjoy the complete freedom the stock market has to offer. We are also planning on building a ranch for my parents and purchasing some horse property for my wife's mother.

To be honest Wade, the greatest thing I have to say about meeting you and taking your seminars is how close I've come to know God.

Through your seeds my family has started tithing, attending church, and Bible study. If nothing else, your seminars have given us more time to serve and to discover what our ministry will be. I thank God for your courses and for you!

My one suggestion to anyone thinking of starting in this challenging business is this: After your Wall Street Workshop™ take another one, then the Next Step™, then the Trader's Forge. Don't stop your education short of success!

YOURS TRULY,
M.S., TX

Trading has allowed me to quit my profession and stay home and care for my handicapped wife...

–RALPH D., CO

...Started with $25,000, added $75,000 in last six months–portfolio now at $421,295...

–CHERIE L., FL

I've made $100,000+ in five months starting with $5,000.

–RICKY I., CA

I am so inspired when I read these kinds of things. These people put their drive behind their dreams. They said, "I can do this." They took the time, made the commitment and did the work, and they now are on the way to having the lives they've dreamed of.

You see, helping people find and employ an appropriate strategy to help them on their way has been what my educational career has been about. Now that you have your $50,000 or $500,000 in free stocks, what are you going to do?

With all this, let's not forget one simple thing I have talked and written about since my earlier teaching days in Real Estate: the process is about retiring. Yes, you may forget this, but I won't. My whole educational life and mission is to help people live a fuller, happier life. That is why I use Biblical systems and ideas–they truly help us build a grand and noble life.

I sincerely hope you obtained my S.A.I.L. (Scriptural Applications In Life) course. I tell the following story there, and have told this story in many places. You see, I've been really big on the question, "To whom are you listening? Where are you going for advice?"

When I ask the question, "How many of you would like to make over $100,000 a year?" many people raise their hands. Then, in an effort to prove my point and to really get people thinking, I continue with this question, "Then why are you listening to anyone making less than $100,000 a year?" Do you see the logic of this? People who make only $40,000, and who don't understand how to make more, and don't know what it takes to build up this kind of income, will shoot down big ideas.

Keep away from people who try to belittle your ambitions. Small people always do that, but the really great make you feel that you, too, can become great.

—Mark Twain

We must be careful whom we go to for advice. We must, I repeat we *must*, really watch out for and guard against who we allow to have access to our brain—to our soul. There have been many times in my life when I needed to follow the advice: "Physician, heal thyself."

Many years ago, I was making fairly good money—several hundred thousands of dollars a year. I knew I was worth more. I knew I could do so much more with my life. I went looking for people with real wealth and real income. I found a few, but then I realized the truly wealthy people lived long ago. I started studying Abraham, Isaac, Jacob and Job. I've written extensively on my findings in *Business Buy the Bible*. Suffice it to say, I found the answer and will put it here to help you understand why these words are so important to me.

Thus saith the Lord, thy Redeemer, the Holy One of Israel; I am the Lord thy God which teacheth thee to profit, which leadeth thee by the way that thou shouldest go.

—Isaiah 48:17

God will teach us. Why go anywhere else to learn these important topics? God wants us to profit. Think about it. It's right there in the

Bible for all to observe. My attempts in books and seminars have been to help in this process, and always to put God first.

As I've mentioned before, my mission has been to get people retired. To help people become more of who they want to be. What does that mean? Well, for one it means stopping all the busy-ness and having time and money to do the more quality things of life.

I have been involved for years with thousands of people who are facing retirement. I generally see two types of situations. One, the people have huge assets but no income, or two, they have a lot of income–work, pensions–but not much in the way of assets.

At this point in your life, look at what you need. The goal is to have the assets produce the income so you won't have to. Your concentration should be on income (cash flow) instead of assets. As you work your investment strategies, the assets will come. That is what this book has been about: building up a grouping of assets that will produce the right level of monthly income. It can be accomplished by people in their 30s as well as people in their 60s. It's a "cash-flow" mindset, not a "wealth for wealth's sake" mindset.

Retirement is an elusive dream for so many. Some of you will never retire–you'll just switch careers. Some of you have people to visit, places to go, and things to see and do. Others have families, churches, causes that you want to be engaged in with more vigor.

Most of you have more in common than you have differences. Most of you would like to quit your job, and we can show you how. Some will be retired in four to five months, some in eight to 10 months, while still others may be 14 to 16 months. If you have $25,000 to start with, you could be retired in five to 10 months, earning between $4,000 to $8,000 per month.

Whatever the case may be, it will help if you know your direction and your passion, so you can know how much continuous monthly income you'll need to generate. Once you know this amount, the level of activity, indeed, the exact strategy or formula can be determined. Find the strategy that fits your personality. Everyone is different, so to say or even think that there is one trading strategy that is just right for everyone is ludiricous. You need to decide what type of trader you are and then match a strategy with your temperament or situation. If you are really busy or really lazy, we have a strategy for you. If you are a person who likes high-tech trading, then we have what you need. No matter what type of trader you are, we have the right strategy for you. Here are some other ideas to help stimulate the thinking process.

ONGOING FINANCIAL MANAGEMENT

1. You may want to keep employing LOCC (especially in an IRA type account) to build up yet additional assets.

2. You could pull out small amounts for various things.

3. You also could put aside say, $10,000 (the annual gift amount to others with no tax consequences) for children or grandchildren, and then if possible, show them how you work it. It is a "teach a man to fish" concept.

4. You definitely should start using a Charitable Remainder Trust for deductions, later on cash flow, tax free (deferred) growth, and bequeathment.

5. If you need more monthly income consider (a) rolling stock or options (b) one month out covered call writing or (c) bull put spreads and bear call spreads. You should have learned a lot about the workings of the market and somewhat about these particular strategies.

6. You should keep educating yourself and hanging around people who are the "movers and shakers." Treat your brain like a muscle and do not let it atrophy. Exercise it regularly and vigorously.

7. Set new targets. New amounts and new deadlines.

Retirement is not a destination, but a new level of life with a whole set of new choices and possibilities. Your $50,000 will pretty consistently generate $8,000 to $12,000 per month. Using $500,000 will boost the amount up to $80,000 to $120,000 per month. These amounts give you the freedom of choice so few Americans have. This liberty is such a dynamic power–we should learn and grow in our use of this power to be all that God wants us to be.

A1

1-2-3
READY, SET, GO

Q. *Is the stock market the answer to your income needs?*

A. Probably not if you use it the old-fashioned way. (more inside)

Q. *What does the stock market need?*

A. Wade Cook's safe monthly income strategies.

I've made $1,338,081.43 net profit in $11^1/_2$ months. I originally started with $36,000... – Myke L., WA

WADE COOK WANTS TO GIVE YOU A FIGHTING CHANCE TO MAKE THIS KIND OF MONEY.

I started trading on 10-19-95 with $2,900...I recently took an account from $16,000 to $330,000 in 2 weeks, and $35,000 to $2,484,000 in 6 weeks. I made $1.25 million in one day.

– Glenn M., IL

I am a financial planner who works primarily in mutual funds and life insurance. Any financial professional who criticizes Wade's strategies is simply speaking <u>out of ignorance</u>.

– Christopher M., OH

**The Stock Market Institute of Learning, Inc.™,
is here to help you AVOID boring,
old-fashioned RISKY investments.**

There are three reasons for investing: cash flow, tax write-offs, and growth. What do you need? For most, especially those looking at quitting their job or retiring, the answer is cash flow. If you have more income than you can spend, then you can invest in all the boring investments for tax write-offs or growth that you want. Building up cash flow is an elusive endeavor–many people have given up on the American dream. They have resigned themselves to the 'ol 9 to 5 and we think that is sad.

Can the stock market be the answer to your income needs? We submit to you that the answer is "no" if you look at investing the old fashioned way. Very few financial professionals know how to really "work" the market. Look at just four testimonials made about Wade Cook and his strategies.

I have a background as a stockbroker and have been investing for about 15 years. I thought I knew how to make money in the market, but I wasn't even close!...

–Neil W., PA

I am a licensed general securities broker, licensed insurance agent, and a CFP (certified financial planner). And compared to (the instructor), I don't know jack! It just proves that institutionalized knowledge and street knowledge is about a $1,000,000 plus per year difference in money making capability. Bravo Wade Cook strategies!

–Christopher K., FL

I wish to take this opportunity to advise you how impressed I was with the learning experience. I have 25 years experience as a broker with 3 major firms, and I was convinced I had nothing to learn from Wade Cook. How wrong I was! It was the most professional, dynamic and thoroughly enjoyable series of meetings I have ever attended. I plan to write my clients and advise them to seriously consider attending. Once again, it was a profoundly educational seminar.

–Carl G., CO

As a former financial planner, I thought I knew a lot about securities and the market. As a current attorney, I thought I knew a lot about companies and securities. Now I know I knew nothing about companies, securities, and the market.

–MICHAEL R., WA

So, just who is this Wade Cook, and why should you get to know him and what he teaches?

Wade Cook is an educator, dare we say the most effective instructor in the country. He has taught tens of thousands of people and has sold millions of his books–many selling because of word of mouth. He started as a cab driver in Tacoma, Washington, and there learned and developed his now famous "meter-drop" system.

He first applied this strategy to real estate and even today his books *Real Estate Money Machine, Real Estate for Real People,* and *101 Ways to Buy Real Estate Without Cash* continue to sell and help people do better at their real estate investing. Robert Bruss, of the Tribune Media Services said, "On my scale of one to 10, this excellent book rates 10" about *Real Estate for Real People.*

> **DISCLAIMERS**
> *AND WHY WE USE TESTIMONIALS*
>
> We use student testimonials throughout this book. We have thousands more. Some show "big bucks" being made. Some show "steady monthly income." Others show "how LITTLE start-up money" was needed. Still others are from wise financial professionals who are also our students. These professionals have put aside their stodgy "get-the-commission-at-all-costs" training, as they learned our cash-flow methods. We applaud them, as they truly serve their clients better.
> Obviously, these results are particular to these students' experiences. You should not expect the same results. Your trades and your results will vary. We hope your make more and we want to teach you how to do so!

In the 90s he took his keen sense of cash flow development and applied it to the stock and options market. Soon, hundreds of thousands of people were flooding into his seminars so they could find out how the stock market really works. Not long after that, three of his books, *Wall Street Money Machine, Wall Street Money Machine, Volume 2,* and *Business Buy the Bible* hit virtually every best seller list that exists.

Currently, Wade continues to write and develop seminars and workshops, and manage Wade Cook Financial Corporation–a publicly traded company (OTCBB: WADE). He lives with his wife Laura and their children on a beautiful Arabian Horse farm.

A subsidiary of the parent company is the Stock Market Institute of Learning, Inc.™ (SMILe). This company promotes knowledge and education about ways to cash flow the market that many people know little about. It is to this end that we introduce to you our **1-2-3** collection of seminars, video and audio recordings and reports, to help you learn and implement ways to build up your income.

We wonder–Wade has best selling books. He makes millions without the help of self-proclaimed professionals. He's helped tens of thousands learn how the market really works. Is it any wonder why he's so controversial? It is said best by Albert Einstein, "Great Spirits have always had violent opposition from mediocre minds."

If you want boring old stodgy information then call your stockbroker, you don't need us. If you want to buy mutual funds then we can't help you. If you want someone else to manage your money and control your financial destiny, then what we teach and share will probably rub you the wrong way.

We are pure educators. We get nothing out of what you do. Look at four testimonials which show the "big bucks" that people have actually made. Obviously, these results are particular to these people. We hope you make more and we'll show you how.

I had $36,000 and turned it into $460,000 in less than 3 months. In another account, I took $100,000 and turned it into $400,000 in 4 weeks, and in another, I made $30,000 in one week for a total (account balance) of $960,000.

–JOHN T., OK

I turned $200,000 approximately into $1,200,000 in 6 months.

–LARRY G., CA

I've made $1,338,081.43 net profit in $11^{1}/_{2}$ months. I originally started with $36,000...

–MYKE L., WA

I started trading on 10-19-95 with $2,900...I recently took an account from $16,000 to $330,000 in 2 weeks, and $35,000 to $2,484,000 in 6 weeks. I made $1.25 million in one day.
—GLENN M., IL

Now, when you read this, what are you thinking? We hope you're thinking, "WOW, I finally have someone on my team; who gets nothing out of what I do; who is not trying to hustle me on their next deal—their next 'stock du jour.'" Read the following testimonial from David S., who is a stockbroker who really sees the difference between us and "them."

This seminar and Wade's books filled in the gaps in my stockbroker education. As a stockbroker, I learned how the markets work but not how to personally make money. The firms I have worked for focus on selling and on customer service...not on learning strategies beyond buy and hold. Thanks for showing me what I was missing.
—DAVID S., TX

Read again the results: $960,000, $1,200,000, $1,338,081, $2,484,000, and ask yourself—"Where do I go to learn how to make this kind of money?" For example—go to your stockbroker and tell them you want to put in $36,000 and in $11^1/_2$ months have $1,338,081. Tell them: Wade Cook can show me how—why can't you? After they criticize, point out that Wade Cook and Team Wallstreet™ (including the Trading Department) of a publicly traded company put all of their trades on an Internet site for the whole world to see. If they want to criticize, we'll give them the truth and ammunition they need.

So again, what does this mean to you? It means you are aligning with a company that walks the walk. It means you can learn these strategies, practice them and get good at them. It means that your cash flow results can be so much better.

Is that important to you? Think: more steady income. Why not pay off bills or your mortgage? Retire early and/or better. What would you do with an extra $4,000 to $9,000 per month? One of our greatest benefits as a company is seeing what others do with this extra (new-earned) money.

You are not here merely to make a living. You are here to enable the world to live more amply, with greater vision, with a finer spirit of hope and achievement. You are here to enrich the world, but will lessen yourself if you forget the errand.

—Woodrow Wilson

I committed myself to getting all of the education I could. I LOVE THIS STUFF! The best part of this is the fact that I have been able to help my Mom and Dad retire in comfort (and lots of it) and I have been able to not worry about finances AT ALL! I plan on retiring in about 6 months, but probably sooner.

—Jason A., UT

I have increased my faith promise to $1,000 per month for missions, and have been able to help some others whose needs were being challenged.

—Doug C., FL

Bought new home and now financing the upcoming birth of triplets.

—William S., GA

Have become a full time artist while simultaneously trading!

—Dallas M., NM

We are going to send our son, who has severe dyslexia, to a private school starting in September. Thanks!

—Patricia D., FL

I am excited about my future. I am 72 yrs old and have a new burst of energy. I have made over $250,000 in just three months selling covered calls and have definite plans to realize all my life's unfulfilled goals. What a rush!!

—Dwight H., CA

Our purpose in life should be to build a life of purpose.
–Wade Cook

What wonderful things can you do with your life? What good things can you do? Then ask yourself again: "Do I know any people investing in boring investments or mutual funds that are able to generate cash flow to do those things?" Again—is the stock market the answer to your cash flow needs? *Yes!* is the unequivocal answer if you use Wade Cook's safe, time-tested cash flow strategies. Look at the chart comparison on page 162. We realize you may get angry at your stockbroker or other financial professional for not showing you these things, but remember, that's not their job. Their job is to sell you things. Our job is to educate you. That's why so many "in-the-know" financial professionals recommend our books and send their clients to our workshops.

Our **1-2-3** (Ready, Set, Go) program will get you started and headed in the right direction—the direction of more cash flow in numerous "small chunks."

Do you need a lot of money to get started? Well, if you have thousands of dollars that would be nice, but look at the following testimonials. The first is from Jodi L. Her words are touching and we want you to see her letter in her own words.

I attended a Wall Street Workshop™ in July of 1998. I didn't have any more money to start an account with, so I paper traded for six months.

As a single mom finishing a degree, I finally found an on-line firm who would accept me with no required minimum balance. I started in February 1999 with $200... My first trade on a stock (VTRL) netted me $9. Not a lot, but with more time than money, I studied hard and really concentrated on technicals.

...I had turned that $200 into $6,200. (I added $500 tax return in May.) As of August 1st to Semper Financial (September 8th), I've increased that to $9,000 doing rolling stock and some covered calls since July 1.

–Jodi L.

I just wanted to let you know that I was able to play one (rolling) stock over a three week period, seven times, and was able to realize a $7,000 profit from a $500 investment.

–THOM A., TX

Hold it! Did you catch that? $500 to $7,000 in three weeks. Can your stockbroker help you do that? Call and get your **1-2-3** Start-up Kit today.

Just getting started in the last six months. Started with $600 in an online account, trading calls. At present, I have $6,000 in this account. Thank you for the continuing education!

–CLARK R., FL

Within two weeks after the workshop, I have made four successful trades using the rolling stock strategy. I don't have much to start with but I've made over $550 so far and that's a blessing.

–TOM C., NY

I love this seminar. I've learned a lot. I've made $100,000 + in five months, starting with $5,000.

–RICKY I., CA

Bought Jan 1 $220 LEAP at $47 approximately on 5/4/99. Bought and sold Jan 01 LEAPs at varying strike prices through splits and run-ups. Ended up on Jan 3, 2000 with approximately 20 LEAPs at approximately $100 – Turned $4,700 into $200,000 in eight months.

–RALPH A., WA

Now, you would think that all financial professionals must assume everyone has $1,000,000 to $5,000,000. Seriously–they're into things like "asset allocation" and the completely ignorant concept of "dollar cost averaging." I guess we'd be the same if people attracted to Wade's books had those net worths, but what about the people with $200, $2,000, $20,000–the butchers, bakers, and candlestick makers? For those who need more income, we say, "Formula Allocation." Pick a formula; learn it, practice it, get good at it, and retire off of it.

You see, we get excited about our students who make millions, but we also love hearing from the ones who literally start with very small amounts. We want you to know that our theme is "monthly cash flow." Rolling stocks, writing covered calls, bull put spreads, even options on stock splits are designed to generate monthly income.

Here's what our students say about monthly income:

I am now a retired chiropractor at age 37... Averaging about $30,000 a month.

–ALAN P., AZ

I currently make $8,000 to $15,000 per month. Thanks for changing my life.

–KATHIE L., CA

I've made $7,000 to $10,000 per month since January 1, 1999.

–STEPHAN H., CA

Before any Wade Cook info, I was trading with about 7-10% profit. Now I have increased that to 100-150% with a holding period of 5-7 working days.

–JONATHAN P., WA

Can we help you? We've helped tens of thousands and we have drawers (huge drawers) full of testimonials that speak to our effectiveness. Can you afford to listen to these "so called professionals?" Use them for placing orders but *you* need to control your financial destiny– not some commission based, hardly trained financial pro. Come, walk the walk with us.

Here's our offer: $123 gets you....

DYNAMIC DOLLARS SEMINAR ON VIDEO

Number 1 is a very exciting video presentation (about 90 minutes) called *Dynamic Dollars.* You get to see Wade in action. You learn about the power of formulas–including a presentation about rolling stocks, writing covered calls, low-cost, limited-risk options and stock splits–

the five times to get involved and uninvolved. You'll get an introduction to the incredible Wall Street Workshop™. Do not go near the stock market until you watch this video. Share it with your stockbroker. Get your family involved.

This is a professional video demonstration. It is literally worth $10,000–many times over. You'll use this information to change the way you look at every trade. Look at what Henry Clasing wrote about our seminar.

Dear Wade,

I had the pleasure of attending your introductory seminar in New York this past Saturday. I was impressed. Given I have spent more than 30 years in the financial field, I have never seen such a well thought out, orchestrated, practical and successful approach to trading. Your "meter drop," setting reasonable targets and stop-out points, is already turning my financial world around.

To add some credibility to these observations, I operated a top quality futures fund, Group Veritas, in the Middle East during the early 90s. My books on trading options are in many investing libraries. The co-authored book with Dr. Andrew Rudd on Modern Portfolio Theory was required reading for many top quality MBA programs.

–Henry Clasing

123 DAYS OF W.I.N.™

The second component is 123 days of W.I.N.–yes that's right–123 days of W.I.N. You can subscribe for $3,600 per year. This is our subscription based tutorial Internet site. You can see the archives at www.wadecook.com.

Where else can you see tens of thousands of dollars traded every day? You get lists of rolling stock candidates, potential covered call stocks, upcoming stock splits–not to mention the awesome actual trades section. The site was chosen by readers of Security Trader's Handbook

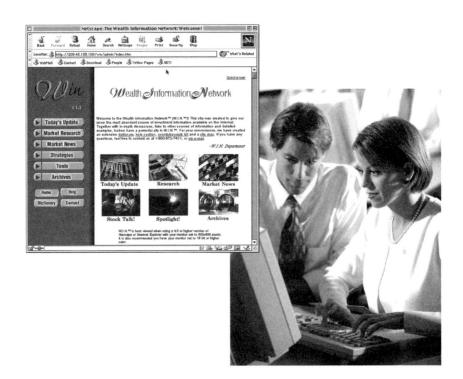

as the web site "with the most new ideas." The following comments about W.I.N. are from our students:

I have made $10,000 the last five weeks writing covered calls off W.I.N.

−GARY O., AR

I purchased the January $150 calls of GE for $4³/₈ and sold them for $9¹/₂, for a total profit of $3,450. (after commissions.) This was done on Stock Split Strategy #1, that I received and reviewed on W.I.N.

−VINCENT V., CT

I made 42% on a rolling stock mentioned on W.I.N. (It took two days!)

−JOHN M., OH

I purchased AOL (approximately $10,000 worth) because it appeared on W.I.N. as a stock split candidate. The day of their board meeting (about three days later) AOL declared a stock split. Phenomenal!

−LIONEL M., NY

BASEBALL, THE STOCK MARKET AND YOU

Plus you'll receive an information packet special report called, "Baseball, the Stock Market and You." This is about making small repeatable profits. It's about cash flow. It's 32 full size pages ($8^1/_2$ X 11) with dynamic knowledge, examples and quotes. Also, to go along with this report is a seminar presentation called "Hitting Singles and Doubles in the Stock Market." It's a wonderful compliment to the special report.

Again: A fabulous Video Presentation–*Dynamic Dollars*, 123 Days of our incredible Internet site W.I.N.–where you can watch over the shoulders of Team Wall Street as they make money–hard, spendable cash, and the Special Report and CD for solid functional knowledge to get you going the right way–the cash flow way in the market.

We promise you that this will be the best $123 you'll ever spend. Consider it an investment in your own brain power. Just one trade of $1,230–and you'll potentially have hundreds like this, or more–will mean you're just paying one-tenth with this $123. Not to mention the bonuses.

Time out. Do you really need bonuses? Don't you see the value of knowledge skills with this basic package?

> *If a man empties his purse into his head, no one can take it from him. An investment in knowledge always pays the best interest.*
> —BENJAMIN FRANKLIN

Read our own results on page 164. Read in charts 1 and 2 (pages 162-3) what we do. Study again the difference in what we do as compared to the others. Review our students' testimonials and then look at the price of $123. Now ask about the cost: One lost trade of $10,000 costs you $10,000. Learning how to make an extra $500 to $1,000 a month on a trade can add up to hundreds of thousands of dollars a year.

Oh, we love bonuses too, after all, everyone wants quality and value, but bonuses, or Freebies, are usually meant to entice or to derive action from the potential customer. If that is a by-product of this offer then great–we are so very proud of our educational materials and know you will benefit greatly with more cash flow results.

BUT, that is not the reason for these bonuses. We want to prove a different point. We want you to know who we are and that we can really make a difference in your life. We want to give so much more value than you would ever expect. And we want to be the company that will stick with you until you make it.

Consider these bonuses as you determine the value. (Hint–it's way over $100,000.)

When you order the incredible **1-2-3** you'll also receive, absolutely FREE:

BONUS #1

OUTRAGEOUS RETURNS™–STOCK SPLIT SEMINAR ON CD

This demonstration CD is jam packed with stock split information, including the five times to get in and out.

1) Pre-announcement: One of the best ways and easy to master.

2) On the Announcement: (BEWARE!) This is the most dangerous play (Fully explained in the seminar).

3) Between Announcement and Actual Split: These stocks spike up, pull back, and often form rolling patterns.

4A) Rally into the split: Amazing formula for two to three day profits.

4B) On Split to Ex-Dividend Date–what happens is predictable but unexpected by most.

5) A week or so after the split: slower ways to capture profits.

This information alone could be worth $10,000 PLUS dollars a month. It's a lively seminar. ($26.95)

BONUS #2

UNCOMMON STOCK MARKET WISDOM™ CD

You will also receive a complimentary seminar CD called Uncommon Stock Market Wisdom™. Whether your dream is to buy a new home, send your kids to college and still retire early, or give more to your family, church or community, the key is knowledge. This seminar will show you how to make dreams gone blue become dreams come true. ($59.95)

Experience is a hard teacher because she gives the test first, the lesson after.

—VERNON LAW

And just when you thought that was enough, we pile it on. Here's BONUS #3. Yes, it's FREE!

BONUS #3

180° DEGREE CASH FLOW TURNAROUND SEMINAR™ – VIDEO

A major plus for your educational tool bag is a video-taped seminar that we are extremely proud of, which we call "the 180 Degree Cash Flow Turnaround" video, or "180°" for short. This video captures Wade in front of a live audience, doing what he knows and loves best–educating. You will learn some of the most powerful stock market principles to ever hit the trading floor; information that is not only extremely profitable but simple to comprehend. ($59.95)

BONUS #4

SPECIAL REPORT
HOW TO TRADE INTERNET STOCKS

How to Trade Internet Stocks touches on the opportunities and dangers of trading on one of the newest stock market frontiers–hi-tech, high volatility Internet stocks. Trading these highly volatile power-punched stocks calls for serious consideration, coupled with excess caution! Wade has brought to light some informative guidelines and actual trading strategies that can help boost your profits to new highs, as well as cut short some of the potential losses inherent in trading Internet stocks. ($29.95)

BONUS #5

INTRODUCTION TO RED LIGHT-GREEN LIGHT™

Wade Cook is president and CEO of a publicly traded company and as America's premier financial educator exposes and explains the quarterly "news–no news" cycle. Don't be fooled. This is powerful information and will change virtually everything you do in the market. The ultimate question: "What compelling reason does a stock or option have to go up?" is answered in a concise way–you'll make better entrance and exit points. ($34.95)

BONUS #6

SPECIAL REPORT
DAY TRADING IS DANGEROUS, DANGEROUS, DANGEROUS™

A Special Report revealing some of the less well-known aspects of S.O.E.S. (Small Order Execution System) level two trading that are dangerous enough to humble even the most experienced of stock market traders. This enlightening special report challenges the long established myth of "high-risk" options versus the outright purchase of stock. These penetrating criticisms can open the door to unrealized profits, which can gain even the average investor an unprecedented advantage in the stock market arena. ($29.95)

Bonus #7

Wall Street Money Machine, Volume 4

We want you to have one of Wade's hard bound books. You'll receive with your **1-2-3** knowledge package, *Wall Street Money Machine, Volume 4: Safety 1st Investing.* This book is all about generating monthly income with super safe strategies. The first four chapters are great for beginners, then it picks up to a slightly intermediate level. We'll leave the advanced (risky) stuff alone. This book sells in stores for $26.95.

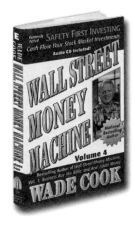

Bonus #8

Behind Closed Doors™ CD

Another "unheard" presentation on CD. Literally go "Behind Closed Doors" as Wade teaches his instructors. This seminar is a "must listen to," as Wade exposes and explores the fallacies in the market. You'll love what he teaches about–you. Yes, about you. You'll hear his passion for knowledge, the formulas that work and how he can make a huge financial difference in your life. ($32.95)

Bonus #9

Special Report
Simutrade™ To Success by David Hebert

Simulation Trading: Profit on paper before you use real cash. This informational report explores ways for you to practice Wade's awesome strategies while safeguarding your cash–then trade with confidence and expertise. ($29)

BONUS #10

SPECIAL REPORT
TRADING ON COMPANY NEWS™

Trading on Company News™ focuses on utilizing the pile driver behind most major stock moves: company news. Wade Cook is CEO of a publicly traded company with SEC reports, *et cetera*. His insights will astound you as he discusses various connections in the stock market that many people miss. You will learn how to become a better monthly cash flow trader, getting better fills (entrance and exit points). ($29.95)

BONUS #11

CD SEMINAR
ONE HUNDRED FOLD RETURN™

Wade loves the Bible. This wonderful seminar explores these ancient words of wisdom in a dynamic presentation. Wade Cook is the author of *Business Buy the Bible, Don't Set Goals*, and *A+*—all based on the Bible. These books, plus *Wade Cook's Power Quotes* are available in fine bookstores.

This powerful CD will teach you the principles behind the 100-Fold Return and is free with **1-2-3**! ($26.95)

And the best is just beginning. As a cherished customer of the Stock Market Institute of Learning, Inc., you will be prepared, taught, surprised, helped—in any way we can.

The best comes when you put to use these income producing methods.

Bonus #12

CD Seminar
Introduction to LOCC™

This incredible seminar will show you "How to get the stock market to pay for your stocks." There's a little secret and seldom used strategy which will help you get your stocks for free. YES, FREE. Build assets, increase cash flow, retire in 10 to 12 months. This LOCC (Large Option Covered Calls) is a great formula. ($29.95)

Bonus #13

Two Tickets to Wade Cook's 2½ to 3 Hour Financial Clinic.

You will receive free admission to a live stock market seminar that we call the "Financial Clinic." We travel to various cities across the United States, teaching time-tested principles of wealth enhancement to information-hungry students of all demographic levels. You have only to call to ascertain the class nearest you. In fact, you may even register for a Financial Clinic while ordering this extraordinary package! Call 1-800-872-7411 for seminar schedule–offered on a regional basis. ($33 x 2)

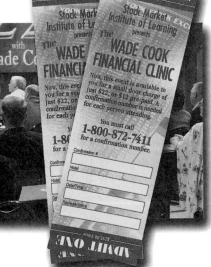

BONUS #14

CURRENT LIST OF ROLLING STOCKS

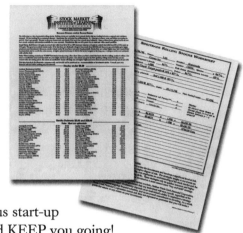

Rolling Stocks – Wade's first cash flow love is a great three to five week cash flow machine–maybe more. With your 1-2-3 package you'll also receive, for FREE, a list, including ROLL RANGES (buy and sell points). ($Invaluable!)

We offer you this fabulous start-up package to get you going and KEEP you going!

Did we prove our point?

The bonuses give you added:

- Depth
- Techniques
- Strategies
- Methods
- Knowledge
- Formulas
- Pitfalls to Avoid
- Hints, Tips, Concerns

Yes, a whole new level of EXPERTISE few people (including most Financial Professionals) know anything about.

YES–Wade shares a Wealth of Information. It's all yours for $123. (Plus $12.30 Shipping and Handling–no extra Shipping and Handling Charges for bonuses–that too is free.)

YES – Ordering is as easy as 1 -2- 3.

1. Decide how many sets you want. Just think–this is a perfect gift for dad, grad, sis, mom or grandparents, anyone who needs to make more money. Now save on additional sets as follows:

    1st Set: $123 + S&H ($12.30)

    2nd Set: $112 + S&H X 2

    3rd Set: $99   + S&H X 3

    4th Set: $84   + S&H X 4

2. Call 1-800-872-7411 with credit card handy, or fax in the order form on page 165. Copies are okay. Or mail to:

    Stock Market Institute of Learning, Inc.
    14675 Interurban Avenue South
    Seattle, Washington 98168-4664

3. Wait–But while you do, check out the W.I.N. archives at www.wadecook.com and get to your bookstores to buy *Wall Street Money Machine, Volumes 1, 2 and 3*. (These three volumes are not included with this package–Volume 4 is. However ask about our "while you're on the phone" special Jump Start Package.)

chart 1

YES, WE ARE DIFFERENT...

The following shows the major difference between Stock Market Institute of Learning and all the other financial professionals.

STOCKBROKERS AND FINANCIAL PROFESSIONALS	STOCK MARKET INSTITUTE OF LEARNING™
1. They receive commissions for selling investments, regardless of returns to client.	1. We sell no investments. We get nothing out of what our students do.
2. They advise clients on specific investments.	2. We explain formulas, methods, and techniques to work the market. Stocks are mentioned as working examples. No specific advice is given.
3. Many financial professionals get paid a percentage of the asset base they manage, whether assets increase or decrease.	3. We teach. The students learn and earn. They work the formulas, after paper or Simutrading, and keep all the profits.
4. They sometimes get investors involved in risky investments.	4. We show students how to avoid and minimize risk with a dedication to knowledge and specific tools like low-cost options, spreads, and writing covered calls.
5. They preach "asset allocation" placing portions of investor's money in harm's way.	5. We teach "formula allocation" for cash flow, tax write-offs, and growth. We help students learn to find certain stocks/options that fit the formulas.
6. They constantly sell investors the new "investment du jour."	6. We teach and show investors how to work the formulas, spread out risk, avoid losses and not get caught up in erratic and fad investments.
7. Most do not show their trading results, they surely do not publicize their personal trades.	7. We tell all, show all. All trades are listed on our award winning Internet site at wadecook.com.

chart 2

THE REST OF THE GUYS	THE WADE COOK WAY
1. Long-term hold.	1. Rolling Stocks: Buy and sell on repeated and predictable patterns (highs and lows).
	2. Options: Proxy investing–low-cost, limited-risk options for safety investing.
	3. Writing Covered Calls: Generate income monthly on stocks you own.
	4. Stock Splits: (and other news) There are five strategies to enter and exit stocks or options doing splits.
	5. Sell Puts: Generate income–get paid now.
	6. Bull Put Spreads: Generate income, limit risk, lessen margin.
	7. Bull Call Spreads: Writing covered calls by covering with options.
	8. Bargain Hunting: Bottom fishing for long-term hold or quick pops.
Note: We realize this is embarrassing to financial professionals, so we keep inviting them to our seminars. They definitely need this 1-2-3 package. (Buy an extra one for your stockbroker.)	9. Spin-offs: Capture the stock–buy options on stock.
	10. IPOs: If not at first, wait, get in and get out. Use 25-day IPO rule.
	11. Turnarounds: Catch the wave up and do stocks or proxy investing.
Note: In the 1-2-3 informational package you will learn about all 13 cash-flow strategies.	12. Slams and Peaks: (Really two strategies.) Catch the turn on one- to five-day plays.
	13. Long-term hold of Blue Chip Stocks.

chart 3

WADE COOK FINANCIAL CORPORATION
ALL BROKERAGE ACCOUNTS

YEAR ENDED 12/31/99 AUDITED
RATE OF RETURN RESULTS
WADE COOK FINANCIAL CORP.   127.59%
*includes all realized & unrealized gains/losses

AVERAGE IN BROKERAGE ACCOUNTS   (MONTHLY)
WADE COOK FINANCIAL CORP. $2,917,816

REALIZED/UNREALIZED GAINS
WADE COOK FINANCIAL CORP. $3,722,950
Realized Gains $3,255,760
Unrealized Gains $467,190

WADE COOK FINANCIAL CORPORATION
VS. THE MARKETS – Year End 12/31/99

Return on S&P 500   19.53 %
Return on DOW   25.22 %
Return on NASDAQ   85.59 %
WADE COOK FINANCIAL CORPORATION   127.59 %

NOW LOOK AT POTENTIAL RESULTS

IF YOU STARTED WITH $10,000
ON JANUARY 1st, 1999
                                              value on 12/31/99

S&P 500 $11,953
DOW $12,522
NASDAQ $18,559
WADE COOK FINANCIAL CORPORATION $22,759
                    Your results will vary

$123

READY, SET, GO . . .
HERE'S WHAT YOU GET

This awesome Start-up Knowledge Kit:

1. Video: Dynamic Dollars–a cash flow presentation ($59.95)

2. WIN: 123 Days of our tutorial internet site (Wealth Information Network) ($1,213) @ wadecook.com

3. Special Report: Baseball, the Stock Market & You ($29)–and Hitting Singles & Doubles in the Stock Market–a CD seminar. ($24.95)

PLUS—14 BONUSES
ABSOLUTELY FREE

1. Outrageous Returns 2: seminar on CD
2. Uncommon Stock Market Wisdom: seminar on CD
3. 180° Cash Flow Turnaround Seminar: video
4. Trading in Internet Stocks: special report
5. Intro to Red Light-Green Light: seminar on CD
6. Day Trading is Dangerous: special report
7. Wall Street Money Machine, Vol. 4: book plus bonus CD
8. Behind Closed Doors: training CD
9. Simulation Trading: special report
10. Trading on Company News: special report
11. One Hundred Fold Return: seminar on CD
12. Intro to LOCC: seminar on CD
13. Two tickets to a Financial Clinic
14. Updated List of Rolling Stocks

Call and ask for
Offer Code OTT-2248:

1-800-872-7411

or Fax:

206-901-3006

or Mail to:

Stock Market Institute of Learning, Inc.™
14675 Interurban Ave. South
Seattle, WA 98168-4664

☑ YES, I Want:

☐ 1st Set:	$123	=	_____
☐ 2nd Set:	$112	=	_____
☐ 3rd Set:	$99	=	_____
☐ 4th Set:	$84	=	_____

☐ _____ additional sets (beyond 4) each: $84 = _____

WA residents add tax (%)   = _____

Shipping and Handling: $12.30 ea. x ( )   = _____

Total = _____

Offer OTT-2248

Customer Name: _____

Address: _____

City: _____ State _____ ZIP _____

Phone #: _____

Email: _____

Method of payment: ☐ money order ☐ check ☐ credit card

check # _____ credit card: ☐ VISA ☐ M/C ☐ AMEX

credit card # _____ exp: _____

signature: _____

printed name: _____

print billing address if different from shipping:

_____

_____

Copies are O.K.

A2

KNOWLEDGE IS "CASH FLOW" POTENTIAL

To say that this special report is unique would be an understatement... way under. I'm going to throw everything at you but the kitchen sink. I'm going to show you really cool stock market angles. I'm going to reason with you. I'll try to uplift, inspire, elucidate and do all I can to help you make the only logical conclusion that these words are meant to accomplish: to get you to financially commit to coming to my Wall Street Workshop.

Oh, you'll have to do your part. You know the old adage... "you get out of something what you put into it." Nothing you've ever read will be like this. Nothing I've ever written has been like this. It's a brief

---

Testimonial Disclaimer: Because this special report is also a marketing piece, we need to put this disclaimer up front about the student testimonials we use herein: the results they have achieved are personal to them. This does not reflect the results of their entire account or trading experience, and your results will vary. Using testimonials in a Special Report may seem strange, but when we teach a formula or strategy, we want to show that real people do these real deals and get real results, and are able to make real changes in the quality of their lives. Investing in the stock and options markets involves significant risk. The Stock Market Institute of Learning does not guarantee that you will achieve the rate of return demonstrated here, or any return.

journey through words, sentences and paragraphs—all designed to help you on the greatest journey of your life.

> *Somewhere, something incredible is waiting to be known.*
> —CARL SAGAN

I hope you enjoy this marketing piece, hidden in this special report.

TIME OUT! Yes, even before the game gets going, we have a DELAY OF GAME. But oh, so worth it! I offer here a few powerful insights that will hopefully make this report more meaningful, so dear reader, spend a few pages with me before the actual special report begins.

Okay, right up front, let me give you the punch line: if you want to kick some major fanny in the stock market, you need to attend the Wall Street Workshop, learn (by doing) my strategies, and build more income. Now that I've cleared the air by telling you the results I want this Special Report/Marketing Piece to achieve, let me share a dilemma with you.

You bring with you into every situation the culmination of your experiences (good or bad), your opinions (whether they're on target or off target); your dreams (both active and dormant); your attempts (both successes and failures) and your prejudices (both helpful and hurtful). For me to convince you to do anything is a major accomplishment. To say the least, it's an uphill struggle.

However, I have hundreds of thousands of people who have benefited greatly because I refuse to give up on them. I am who I am and I want to be the very best, the #1 financial educator in the country. To many, I've made it, but probably not to you....

A message from Wade's staff:

"We're Wade's staff and from time to time in this special report, we're going to put in our 'two cents' worth. We think our perspective will help you make great choices. You'll hear from us later."

So, let me tell you straight away, I know I can help you achieve a success beyond your wildest dreams if you'll just give me a chance. I positively know I can make a *small, great, HUGE* difference in your life. You choose. I've helped people who are in no way as smart as you. I've made a difference in people's lives who have much less money than you have. I've definitely helped people with less luck than you have. In this uphill battle to sell you something and do good in your life, I have a three-way challenge. I must convince you of three things:

1. *YOU CAN DO IT.* You can. I know you can. You can get rich–whatever that means to you. You can quit your job shortly. You can pay off your bills. You can pay a large tithe to your church, etc., etc. But how? I'm glad you asked. The stock market can make a perfect part-time business. All you need is a phone. No computers, no gadgets. You don't need all the usual expenses of a regular business. *Trading* (not *investing*) has entrance and exit points (usually three to five weeks). Buy wholesale to sell retail. There are learnable, workable formulas that are really cool–because the extra cash flow lets you accomplish so much.

   These systems are not easy, but by knowledge, by practice and by a clear understanding of the components, you can work with your money and it can (YES, it will) replace your day job. Again, I'm confident you can qualify yourself for admittance back into the American Dream. I won't give up on you. If you become one of our students, you deserve the best fighting chance to kick your life into high gear.

2. *YOU CAN DO IT HERE.* (where you are) In your back bedroom, in your car, on a coffee break, you are minutes a day from stirring up more cash flow than you can spend.

   Yes, it may be tough at first as you go through the learning curve, but believe me the results are worth it. Just imagine having hundreds of thousands of dollars waiting for your retirement. Look at the words of just a few of my students.

   My first option trade was four days after Microsoft announced a stock split. $11^{1}/_{2}$ months after my first option trade, I've made $1,338,081.43 net profit. I originally started with $36,000 so that makes it a 3,716.89% actual increase on my investment. WOW!!

   –MYKE L., WA

I started trading on 10-19-95 with $2,900...I recently took an account from $16,000 to $330,000 in 2 weeks, and $35,000 to $2,484,000 in 6 weeks. I made $1.25 million in one day.

–GLENN M., IL

I had $36,000 and turned it into $460,000 in less than $3^1/_2$ months. In another account, I took $100,000 and turned it into $400,000 in 4 weeks, and then, in another, I made $30,000 in one week for a total (account balance) of $960,000.

–JOHN T., OK

They did it, you can too. Just imagine, a free and clear house, no debts, a new car, great vacations, helping others. Where would these people be if they had listened to the average stockbroker? If you keep doing what you've been doing, why would you ever expect different results? Isn't that the definition of insanity? If you want this great life, it's yours for the taking. And...just imagine doing all of this in your pajamas.

3. *YOU CAN DO IT NOW.* Yes, now–in this crazy volatile market. Actually, most successful stock market traders love volatility and learn to use it to their advantage. You play the market at hand. Don't be fooled–the energy flows are real. There are fortunes being made all around you. You don't need luck, you need expertise. There is no such thing as negative energy, but you can sure do things to block positive energy. Stop it.

Get in the flow. You can't get rich on a mental desert island. Surround yourself with achievers. Lose the losers. May I humbly ask that you consider, as an alternative to the old rut you're in, a new place to go and a new group to hang out with–yes, me and my "Team Wall Street.™" We're not perfect, but we're students first, educators second. We are doing what we teach and teaching what we do. We are always improving and all this is to your benefit.

I've always enjoyed a good sales presentation. I appreciate honesty and integrity. My personal style of selling has been to get people excited with knowledge. That is a constant theme of our marketing efforts. I'll share, you learn and try my strategies. You decide. "Don't trust me, test me," is a quote in many of my books and seminars. I'll not back off this style here in this special report, but I will apply it with a slight twist. I won't try to sell you on me and my seminars, but I'll try to sell you on you: that you can make a big financial difference in your life with the application of small methods for cash flow—my infamous "meter drop™."

That you, the old dog, not just everyone else can learn new tricks.

It's amazing what ordinary people can do if they set out without preconceived notions.

–CHARLES F. KETTERING

The attempt and achievement are worth the effort. One of my students, a successful but bored Real Estate broker, said, "When the pain (of staying the same) is worse than the pain of change, people will change." He, like thousands of others, has found that the decision to change may have been slightly painful, but our educational process to effectively and quickly get you through the learning curve can be quite enjoyable.

I am excited about my future. I am 72 years old and have a new burst of energy. I have made over $250,000 in just three months selling covered calls and have definite plans to realize all my life's unfulfilled goals. What a rush!!

–DWIGHT H., CA

I am a retired attorney, real estate broker, and financial planner who was looking for a new direction; something lucrative, but fun. I came (to the Wall Street Workshop™) with great interest and am leaving a ball of fire. Is this fun or what!

–GEORGE R., ID

Three words: Vision, Scope and Perspective. I thought I had had all three before. I realize now I've been trading in the dark–(the instructor) turned on the lights! I'll be back.

–ROD M., UT

If you'll do for a few years what most people won't do, you'll be able to do for the rest of your life what most people can't do.

—WADE B. COOK

Now, as I said before, you bring a lot of baggage on this trip. To get off the ground, we need to discard much of it. Misplaced skepticism never accomplished anything. Again, test, don't trust. I'm coming up on a major (earth/mental moving) challenge, but first this quote by Patrick James, one of the Stock Market Institute of Learning's instructors. "The person with a theory is always at the mercy of a person with an experience."

I want you excited again! Oh, not so much excited by what we teach as by what you'll be able to <u>DO</u>. The American Dream is alive and well. We're here to help you live that dream to its fullest.

And while I have this brief time out I'd like to interject these comments by Carol Floco who writes for *Lifestyles* Magazine. She came to our Wall Street Workshop™, like many, to find fault. She was as impressed as you will be:

"Again, great care was taken to caution the class that buying and selling options can be risky business. While the idea of a substantially smaller investment turning potentially sizable returns is extremely appealing, the novice trader can get himself or herself into a negative cash position quite quickly. We were tutored in the common mistakes that are made due to a lack of experience and urged to begin with paper trades and continue the practice until eight out of ten of those trades turned a profit.

"Cook has assembled and trained a top-notch team of facilitators and support technicians to teach, uplift, and encourage all who participate in his programs.

"RISK was the first order of business. I was deeply impressed by the fact that Cook wants his students to fully understand–before getting caught up in the excitement of the learning curve–the risk of loss associated with investing in the stock market.

"No rookie to the motivation and self-improvement workshop circuit, I have had the opportunity to make the rounds and acquaintance of a number of engaging public speakers and idea entrepreneurs. From Zig to Tony, I have listened, laughed, learned, and, on occasion, come away disenchanted.

"Wade Cook is the first person to step up and say that he doesn't have all the answers, nor is he promising a miracle. He has made his share of mistakes, and even gone broke. Critics have accused him of motivating followers to make rash, ill-informed investments. I disagree, feeling rather that I now have the incentive and confidence to take control of my own financial future. I left the Wall Street Workshop™ feeling that I had been given the gift of a new skill—one that could potentially change my life. It is now up to me to hone that skill and put it to practical use."

I have no investments for sale. I share useful knowledge. I get nothing out of what my students do. They learn and earn.

Right now, I must convince you to put aside all of the mental games you play that serve you not. Read on in this special report. You'll learn a little about the stock market, BUT you'll learn a lot about you. I don't really need to convince you about the stock market, but I do need to convince you that "you're the one."

I feel that you need to find again that "better you". That you can do so much more. That you can make such a difference in other people's lives if you have the tools. I humbly ask that you consider me: my Zero to Zillions™ home study course, my tutorial service on the Internet (WIN™–Wealth Information Network™), and my powerful two-day Wall Street Workshop and one day B.E.S.T.™ (Business Entity Skills Training) seminars.

Respectfully: you can do so much more with me on your team. I pledge you my support, my continued quest for "cash flow" knowledge, my ongoing desire to keep improving and my faith in God and his desires of Abundance for us. Our lives can and will be so much better when we put Him first.

> **Time out: Here we are, the staff.**
>
> You will find "you" within this report. Yes, you'll learn somewhat about the stock market, but you'll learn and discern things about you that will frankly "make or break" you financially.
>
> That's the tough part. Oh, Wade makes a case for choosing him and us to help you. That's your decision. We want you to know that most of us did not know Wade's strategies, nor his personality and characteristics before we came to work here. We stand by, ready to help. That's it! That's who we are!

> *Inherently each one of us has the substance within to achieve whatever our goals and dreams define. What is missing from each of us is the training, education, knowledge and insight to utilize what we already have.*
>
> –MARK TWAIN

Do you see how tough my task is? So I pose this question: if you do not believe in your own ability to succeed, will you test me to the point that you'll believe in the systems I've developed? I say trust no one (but God), test everyone. Later you'll read our actual results; you'll read heartfelt testimonials; you'll be asked to think, consider and decide.

> *Knowledge is of two kinds. We know a subject ourselves, or we know where we can find information upon it.*
>
> –SAMUEL JOHNSON

Herein lie the tools to help you decide. This is an important decision. The consequences of your choice will affect your life and your family's life for generations to come, or your decision will leave you alone–where you are. If where you are is where you want to be, that's great, but if where you want to be is a small or great distance from where you are and you need a sturdy vehicle to help you get there–all of us at the Stock Market Institute of Learning, Inc.™ invite you on the journey. We're glad we can be a part. Bon Journee.

NOW, ON TO THE ACTUAL SPECIAL REPORT.

I honestly think the last thing you need is more useless information. I also feel that the last thing you need in relation to the stock market is real time trades, and ignorant strategies, which get even the best traders in trouble...

> *It is important that students bring a certain ragamuffin, barefoot, irreverence to their studies; they are not here to worship what is known, but to question it.*
> —JACOB CHANOWSKI

In addition to this, I have seen people follow stockbroker's advice into risky and even boring investments with disastrous results—setting their wealth process (nest egg) back years.

I have learned by sad experience that people who use "asset allocation" as their primary strategy suffer immensely. They need "formula allocation," which only the Stock Market Institute of Learning, Inc. shares. All of us need to be careful of the "get-the-commission-at-any-cost" financial professional.

> *This seminar and Wade's books have filled in the gaps in my stockbroker education. As a stockbroker, I learned how the markets work but not how to personally make money. The firms I have worked for focus on selling (creating commission) and on customer service...not on learning strategies beyond buy and hold. Thanks for showing me what I was missing.*
> —DAVID S., TX

> *As a former stockbroker and current commodity broker, everything I ever wanted to do to help people make money in the markets was here at the Wall Street Workshop™. This is a dream come true for me and I can never truly explain how much of an impact was made on me today.*
> —RICHARD M., FL

> *I have 25 years experience as a broker with three major firms, and I was convinced I had nothing to learn from Wade Cook. How wrong I was! It was the most professional, dynamic and*

thoroughly enjoyable series of meetings I have ever attended. I plan to write my clients and advise them to seriously consider attending the next Wall Street Workshop the next time one is scheduled. Once again, it was a profoundly educational seminar.

—CARL G., CO

I am a financial planner who works primarily in mutual funds and life insurance. Any financial professional who criticizes Wade's strategies is simply speaking out of ignorance. My practice with my clients will undoubtedly change in the future because of the results I <u>personally</u> have experienced.

—CHRISTOPHER M., OH

You just read four comments made about us. I use tried and tested safe cash flow strategies. Indeed I think that the stock market makes a wonderful full or part-time business–<u>if</u> you treat it like a business. Many people wonder what that means. First of all, I am absolutely against day trading–defined as level two, or S.O.E.S. (Small Order Execution System). Investor carcasses now dot.com the landscape. I am into positrading, or position trading. Yes, call this home trading, or call it phone trading if you will, but it is built on cash flow/business principles.

I use certain formulas for generating cash flow–actual cash money each month to pay the bills, get out of debt, retire and live a valuable lifestyle. I show how to know your exit before going in the entrance– and don't go in if you are unsure of the exit (profits). I use simple to understand fundamental, technical, or OMFs (Other Motivating Factors) like stock splits (five times to get in and out), earnings, share buy backs, mergers, acquisitions, etc., to sharply increase our skills at entrance and exit points. Just two to five trades a month can generate $5,000 to $15,000 per month of cash flow.

... my portfolio has increased $50,000 - $60,000 per month...

—ALDEN F., CA

I have left my full-time job, and continue to make large amounts of money each month. Thank you for helping me fulfill my dreams!!

—J.S., CO

"Mr. Binky, I quit!" ...Will go to Europe in March & May and play in a golf tourney in April. Single parent (of) 22 years, daughter just graduated from college and got engaged. I'll be able to pay for her wedding and college all on my own and I'm happy about that!

–NANCY H., TX

I also know you are really cheating your bottom line (and brokerage/bank account) by not having this knowledge. These trading skills are easy to master with the right facilitators. Quit expecting your commission/fee based financial pro to teach you. That is not what they do. They educate only to sell you things. We educate to protect you.

Wrote Covered Calls and made an average 17% per month return. Gave control to my broker and now I'm broker. As soon as I violate Wade's rules and strategies, I start losing in the market. Now we are back on track! Thank you.

–DON G., CA

Before you invest in stocks and bonds, take stock in knowledge and bond with us.

So, what is the difference between someone making $50,000 a year, and someone making $250,000 per year? And $2,500,000 per year? The answer is the effective use of specialized knowledge.

That's where I come in. The stock market isn't for everyone, but for those who look to the market to find answers to their financial needs I am here to truly help them see and work the alternatives. Working formulas for cash flow—actual income on a monthly basis—is what I do, and what we help our students gain. Here are several testimonials that speak to our effectiveness. This is monthly cash flow that these people *would be living without* had they not learned and applied our unique, powerful, yet very safe "income formulas." Please read the paragraphs following these people's personal experiences to get a good comparison of Stock Market Institute of Learning, Inc., vs. the other financial professionals.

Since I attended the Wall Street Workshop in October 1998, I have done Covered Calls and I am averaging between 25% to 35% monthly returns.

–JOHN B., NY

We're making our living by trading now. Each event fine-tunes our trades and helps us see more clearly where we need to improve and where we're succeeding.

–RENITA S., WY

I have been a (Wealth U) person since September 1999. I am averaging $30,000/month...

–EDWARD A., HI

In 1999, (I'm) averaging about $5,000 per day.

–NEAL L., MA

Quit my job and am making twice as much as I was there in the stock market. Will end the year with 5X the income I otherwise would have had. The best part is being more available to my family.

–JANET S., ID

Virtually every financial advisor in this country is trained in a certain way. The focus or methods from one to the other are different, but all of them sell people things for the future–their future retirement, estate, etc. This is a noble endeavor, and while we disagree with some of their methods and most often with their fad products, that is not the point here.

We show, tell, educate, facilitate for the *here and now*. People need more income. They need to get out of debt. They have dreams and plans–like putting kids through college, buying a bigger house and traveling to visit the grandkids. We believe that if a person learns how to get their money to work harder–yes, even to the point of generating "pay the bills" income, they can live better now and the future will take care of itself. In fact, here's a shift: we want to help you get more money now so you can fix your lifestyle, and then spend all your extra profits buying these other people's investments.

So look at the following two lists, and realize for yourself how we are widely and wildly different from others, and then we'll help you figure out what this means to you.

The following shows the major difference between Stock Market Institute of Learning™, Inc. and the other financial professionals:

THEM	US
They receive commissions for selling investments, regardless of returns to client.	We sell no investments. We get nothing out of what our students do.
They advise clients on specific investments.	We explain formulas, methods, and techniques to work the market. Stocks are mentioned as working examples. No specific advice is given.
Many financial professionals get paid a percentage of the asset base they manage, whether assets increase or decrease.	We teach. The students learn and earn. They work the formulas, after paper or Simutrading™, and keep all the profits.
They sometimes get investors involved in risky investments.	We show students how to avoid and minimize risk with a dedication to knowledge and specific tools like low-cost options, spreads, and writing covered calls.
They preach "asset allocation" —placing portions of investor's money in harm's way.	We teach "formula allocation" for cash flow, tax write-offs, and growth. We help students learn to find certain stocks/options that fit the formulas.
They constantly sell investors the new "investment du jour."	We teach and show investors how to work the formulas, spread out risk, avoid losses and not get caught up in erratic and fad investments.
Most do not show their trading results. They surely do not publicize their personal trades.	We tell all, show all. All trades are listed on our award winning Internet site at www.wadecook.com.

EVERYONE ELSE	WADE COOK'S STRATEGIES FOR CASH FLOW	
LONG-TERM HOLD	1.	LONG-TERM HOLD
	2.	ROLLING STOCKS™
	3.	OPTIONS (CALLS & PUTS)
	4.	WRITING COVERED CALLS
	5.	STOCK SPLITS (AND OTHER NEWS)
	6.	SELLING PUTS
	7.	BULL CALL SPREADS
	8.	BULL PUT SPREADS
	9.	ROLLING OPTIONS™
	10.	BARGAIN HUNTING/TURNAROUNDS
	11.	RANGE RIDERS
	12.	IPOS
	13.	SPIN-OFFS

(Beginning on page 181 you will find more detailed information on our 13 strategies.)

Notice the first one on our list. We like great stocks also and we know we have the greater methods to elucidate this arena—indeed, to keep you out of trouble and away from risky investments promoted by people who usually don't even buy these same investments.

Also, notice if you didn't catch it that we have 13 formulas that are street-tested ways to put your money to work. Check this out: even in our own accounts, the one strategy that causes us the most concern is the buy and hold—be out of control—formula. The other twelve are methods to help you quit your job. *We want to help you quit your job.*

I do many radio and TV talk shows. Many hosts ask me the difference between me and everyone else. The obvious answer is that they sell investments, I educate. They have stodgy old methods, which more often than not produce bad bottom lines. I share formulas for cash flow. I put the emphasis on selling, on meter-drop income (consistent predictable cash profits), on rational, logical ways to use the stock market as a business—a business that will support people and their families so they can get on with their lives.

Even within this educational process, everyone needs to realize that each of my thirteen strategies are different.

1. They have their own beginning, middle and end–entrance points and exit points.

2. Each has its own set of rules or factors which make it work.

3. Each has a specific time to be used and only works or works best at that time–or market occurrence.

So, coming up will be the strategy, a brief definition or explanation, when it is to be used and who should use it. Remember, the "why" is usually more important than the "how."

STRATEGY #1: BLUE CHIPS (LONG-TERM HOLD)

WHAT: Use fundamentals and technical analysis to find great stocks in companies with likelihood of going up for your future. May be used for Writing Covered Calls. Sold when profitable for extra cash. Many of these may pay dividends.

WHEN: Anytime. My other strategies are more income generation oriented, so you can pay off debt, pay the bills and then invest in these nice (safe?) stocks. Don't be afraid to clean house. Build your own "Mutual Fund."

WHO: Start young. Add to positions as you go. Monitor account to make sure you have the best. Great for gifts and gifting and donations to your church.

STRATEGY #2: ROLLING STOCKS™

WHAT: A system of buying and selling less expensive stocks–trading in a sideways pattern–buy at $2 (support) sell at $3 (resistance) in repeated waves. See the charts on page 182 for examples.

WHEN: In a flat market, or sideways moving stock. Even in good markets, many stocks move in rolling patterns.

WHO: Beginners. Those who want little risk, and not huge, but consistent profits.

STRATEGY #3: OPTIONS

WHAT: Use small amounts of money on low-cost, limited risk options to control large blocks of stocks. A movement in stock from $84 to $88 could see the $80 call option move from $6 to $8, i.e., $6,000 to

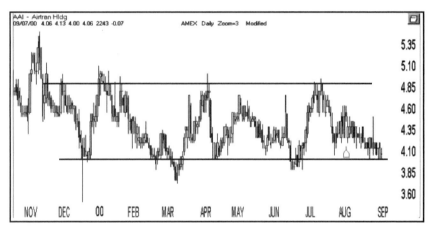

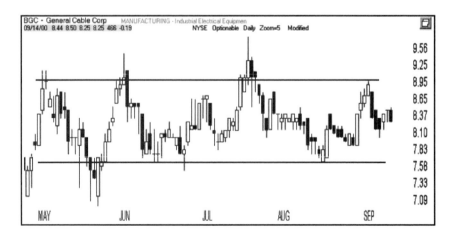

Charts courtesy TC2000® and Worden Brothers, Inc.

$8,000 in hours, days or weeks. Upside potential is huge, loss limited to premium paid.

WHEN: Use calls on up movements, puts on down movements. Risky, should be practice traded. Huge profit potential–available and workable in all markets. Added risk: options expiration dates.

WHO: People who do research, understand connections and power of news and potential news (rumors). People who want large, quick profits. Note: only use small "risk" capital.

STRATEGY #4: WRITING COVERED CALLS

WHAT: Sell options (generate income in one day) against your stock positions–agreeing to sell stock at predetermined price (profits). Nice monthly cash flow machine–10% to 15% cash income–per month. More, if stock is on margin.

WHEN: Used on large stocks–with options. Used anytime to pick up cash and then sell stock or keep it depending on the strike price– "Do you really want to sell the stock?"

WHO: People who want income. $100,000 in stocks will produce $10,000 to $15,000 of extra income. Many beginners buy stock just to sell calls.

STRATEGY #5: STOCK SPLITS

WHAT: Many companies split their stocks when they get pricey. If good, company stocks have tendency to go back up to or above price before split. Sometimes in two to five years. Sometimes in three to nine months. See the charts on Page 184 for examples of Stock Splits.

WHEN: Five times to get in and out. Build a portfolio of these stocks with limits of doing splits or quick-turns. Options trading on these enhances potential and reduces risk.

WHO: Anyone needing profits. Easy to practice on and master before using real money. Many one to three day trades available.

STRATEGY #6: SELLING PUTS

WHAT: Generate income by agreeing to have a stock sold to you at a price you like–on a company you like. Nice income, plus potential to

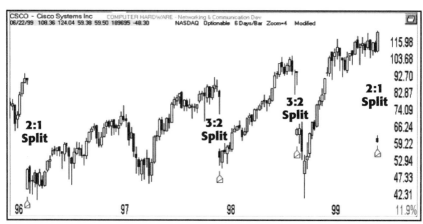

Charts courtesy TC2000® and Worden Brothers, Inc.

buy stock wholesale. Seems risky to naïve stockbrokers, who, ironically, will sell you risky stocks in a heartbeat.

WHEN: Use in bullish situations. Stay above strike price and consider your margin requirements. Note: a variation of this is the Bull Put Spread to eliminate much of the risk and lower margin.

WHO: People who want cash flow. Can be as safe as someone wants, depending on stock choices and option strike prices.

STRATEGY #7: BULL CALL SPREADS

WHAT: Similar to Writing Covered Calls, but use purchase of call option (much less money) rather than stock. Limits risk, and by selling upper calls you limit profits. Spreads are created when you buy a call and sell a call on the same stock at different strike prices.

WHEN: Can be done repetitiously. Good in any market–works best with uptrending stock. Huge profits (more risk) in high flying stocks.

WHO: Good for cautious people. Could generate 15% to 30% cash, three to four week returns.

STRATEGY #8: BULL PUT SPREADS

WHAT: This is my favorite. It's a credit spread which means you get paid to put it in place. You sell a put (income) and buy a put (outgo) below the price of the stock on a Bullish stock. Stock stays above strike price, and you keep the cash.

WHEN: New definition of Bullish: the stock goes up, or at least stays up above a certain strike price. Used when stocks hit support, or on bounce (dip). Note: use a Bear Call Spread on opposite–downtrends

WHO: People who want monthly income. 20% to 40% two to four week actual cash returns are very common.

STRATEGY #9: ROLLING OPTIONS™

WHAT: Same as rolling stock, but on more expensive stocks. As a stock hits support and starts up, buy a call, then at its peak buy a put; or do bull put spreads on upswings and bear call spreads on downturns.

WHEN: These are available everyday. You must grasp option volatility and pricing. You need at least $5 to $10 swings in the stock.

WHO: People who have extra time to monitor positions, or get adept at placing sell orders. Good money-maker.

STRATEGY #10: BARGAIN HUNTING, TURNAROUNDS AND BOTTOM FISHING

WHAT: Buying low priced stocks on serious dips, check fundamentals and buy stock or options on stock. Try for doubles and practice, practice, practice. Use extreme caution with penny stocks.

WHEN: When stocks fall out of favor, and take on new management, company comes up with new products, ends lawsuits, or is a takeover candidate.

WHO: People should use limited money here—profits are spectacular, but few and far between. Expertise can be developed.

STRATEGY #11: RANGE RIDERS

WHAT: Similar to Rolling Stocks, but with upward trend. Use trend lines (and/or support lines) for entrance points. Place sell orders to exit trades with 20% to 40% profits. Use stop loss to minimize losses (risk).

WHEN: Many stocks follow this pattern. Can be played with stock or options. Spreads are also effective here. Reverse range riders can be used when stock moves in opposite (down) patterns.

WHO: People with time to monitor positions. Nice two to three day trades available. Also, trader should subscribe to charting service for support lines, trend lines and moving averages.

STRATEGY #12: INITIAL PUBLIC OFFERINGS (IPOs)

WHAT: Invest in stocks in a PRE, on OPEN, or POST IPO formula. Each has concerns and definite exit points. Tough to do on open—consider 25 day IPO rules (quiet period) and jump in there. These stocks are highly volatile. There are probably better times.

WHEN: Obviously, when a company is ready to, or is going public. Watch local newspaper. Many times to get in. Don't let ads (fads) on TV affect you. Difficult to make money with IPOs.

WHO: People who like a challenge and added risk—must do extra homework and be above the hype.

STRATEGY #13: SPIN-OFFS

WHAT: Good opportunity to get in on a company with a market niche, good management with a lot to prove. Great examples abound. Best play is on the company being spun-off (BABY), not the parent (unless parent is generating a lot of cash).

WHEN: This is a rarely-used strategy because there just aren't that many available, but great when available. Buy stocks, options, or do spreads.

WHO: People who like a lot of safety–even then, one must be careful. There are many ways to play these. Often options aren't available for several months.

There you have it. A complete package. What do you need? Income? Safety? Monthly Cash Flow? Growth? Bigger Profits?

Again, we share–you learn and earn.

I've pretty much offended every stockbroker and financial professional in the country. Most of these people, who you think would be up on these cash flow methods, know little about them. When this cab driver took on Wall Street, I had no idea what a commotion I'd cause. I'll apologize to them in advance, and invite them to attend the Wall Street Workshop. We should charge them double to pay for all the anguish they've caused people. Profits are waiting. All you have to do is grasp the knowledge, gain an understanding, and apply it for profits.

Consider what everyone gets out of this. Brokers get commissions. I get book royalties. You get profits today and more profits tomorrow. You actually take control of your financial destiny. You. You and only you. No one will learn and understand your financial situation like you.

You have choices. One is to keep trading your time for money; the other is to put your knowledge to work and get your money to work as hard as you do–even harder. Expect more from your money, learn what it takes and then get more from your money.

Coming up is a matrix. Find yourself–your risk/reward tolerance, cash flow needs, safety requirements and future growth needs; then look at market conditions and movement and see what it takes to gain an expertise so you get the results you want.

MARKET CONDITION	Zero to Zillions Home Study Course	Blue Chip Trading	Rolling Stock	Options (Calls & Puts)	Stock Splits	Writing Covered Calls	Selling Puts	Bull Put Spreads	Bull Ca II Spreads	Bargain Hunting/Turnarounds	Wall Street Workshop	IPOs	Spin Offs	Rolling Options	Range Riders	W.I.N. – Internet Tutorial Service
Whole Market Bullish	•	•	•	•	•	•	•	•	•	•	•	•	•	•	•	•
Whole Market Bearish	•			•							•		•	•		•
Sector Moves	•	•		•	•	•	•	•	•		•		•	•	•	•
Hi-Tech Trades	•	•		•	•	•	•	•			•	•		•	•	•
Low-Tech Trades	•	•	•	•			•	•	•	•	•	•		•	•	•
Stock – going up	•	•		•	•		•	•	•		•			•	•	•
Stock – going down	•			•			•		•		•	•		•		•
Stock – going sideways	•		•	•			•		•	•	•			•		•
YOUR CONDITION																
I need cash	•		•		•						•	•				•
I need steady income	•		•		•						•					•
I need growth	•	•			•	•				•	•	•	•			•
More safety	•	•	•			•					•		•			•
More risk, more profits	•			•			•			•	•	•		•	•	•
Little time to trade	•	•	•			•		•			•					•
Quick Turn Profits	•		•	•	•			•	•		•	•	•	•		•
Retirement income	•	•	•	•		•		•	•		•			•		•

SO JUST WHO IS ATTRACTED TO US?

Our strategies are not for everyone. People who like a lot of risk (yes, the returns could be higher) don't like our safe "calm-down" multiple small profits methods. People who like someone else spending their money probably should put their investments with money managers. People who are contented with 8% to 12% annual returns (even the worst money managers can do this) should put their money in mutual funds. Time out: if this is you, at least find a *good* index and put your money in that fund. I, Wade Cook, with some of my "hold" money, park it in Spiders (SPDRs–Standard and Poors Depository Receipts). Have your money person check out SPY, MDY, DIA and QQQ. You can create your own so-called mutual fund.

To continue. If you don't need more income, or you don't have anyone in your life (kids, friends, parents) who needs more income, then you probably don't need us. Now, we still think you do for even more safety in your out-of-control buy and hold trades. We could go on–literally forever–and give you testimonials, reasons, strategies for why you need to align yourself with us, but first, what is it that you need?

We're about results. Do you need better results from your financial activities?

We're about effective training. Do you need to learn skills that could possibly make you millions?

I turned $200,000 approximately into $1.2 million in 6 months.
–LARRY G., CA

(This class) sharpened my knowledge and confidence to avoid making past mistakes. Using Wade's strategies has made me a millionaire.
–FRANK A., CA

BUILDING YOUR TEAM

Once in a seminar I asked who they thought was the hottest basketball player in the country. Michael Jordan was the overwhelming response. I then asked, who the worst team at that time was. The Dallas Mavericks (though they are so much better now) was the answer.

Then I asked, "Who would win in a game between the Dallas Mavericks and Michael Jordan?" Though it was debatable at that time, the audience finally agreed the team would beat the one, single player. Now, I've seen Michael play. He seems to defy gravity. He has an incredible work ethic—he is willing to pay the price. His attitude is a powerful force. Michael once said, "I've always tried to lead by example. I never really tried to motivate by talking, because I don't think words ever mean as much as action." But still, five on one would be too much, even for him.

The team. The players. Who can you pass the ball to? Who is your go-to guy? Who protects you? Who helps you be better and get better? Our whole company exists to be a team player for our students. Yes, sometimes we're the coach, oftentimes we're on the floor, playing defense, offense, and making plays. We want to be the lead dog (pardon changing the metaphor) but....

> *If you aren't the lead dog, the view never changes.*
> —LEWIS GRIZZARD

Back to basketball. Bill Walton summarized it this way, "In basketball, you can be the greatest individual player in the world and still lose every game, because a team will always beat an individual."

Choose your team wisely.

> *It is impossible to estimate how many good ideas are abandoned every day as a result of difficult-to-manage relationships.*
> —JOHN P. KOTTER

• We have a passion for helping people. Do you need someone on your team who is in-the-trenches every day working wonders and has a mission to help you better your precision that results in profits?

Note: Passion, Precision, Profits, the three Ps, cornerstones to successful achievement. They go together—you hardly can have one without the others. Point. So many people focus on the prize, not on the price. They want to win without learning and working the process. *And there is a process.* We'll show it to you in our awesome "TELL-SHOW-DO" format.

- We show our results. We lead the way. Do you need someone to talk the talk or to *WALK the WALK*? Who else do you know who puts their trades (win, lose or draw) on an Internet site as a tutorial service for the whole world to see?

Staff Here – TIMEOUT

We can't go on without sharing with you one of the greatest financial tools ever ever ever put forth. Wade Cook, the developer of the awesome and results-oriented Wall Street Workshop, had numerous requests by his students to share what he was doing, what he was learning, and to teach about his actual trades. He thought of more books, a monthly newsletter, even a 900 number wherein people could call in–but none of these ideas worked. Obviously, when he does a trade, that particular trade is past tense, even in seconds. But thousands can grasp the method and look for similar or peripheral trades.

The award-winning <u>W</u>ealth <u>I</u>nformation <u>N</u>etwork, or WIN, was born.

> *Up my confidence level – one trade just days before class made $3,663, after commissions, using WIN – Rolling Stock.*
> –ROGER M., OK

> *I actually have made almost the tuition cost before the class with the assistance of WIN.*   –DAVID D., NY

Just think: what results could you achieve if you could look over the shoulder of a millionaire and his trading department and instructors (Team Wall Street™)? Many millionaires won't even talk to you. Many made their money in such ways that they are not able to be duplicated by the average person. Not Wade. He shares. He teaches. He understands many "connect-the-dot" situations and has a passion for teaching. This passion is even stronger than his passion for making money. It's what drives him. He shares so much because he cares so much. Just look at some of the books he's written.

You can see these trades on WIN at www.wadecook.com. Keep asking yourself: so what? What does this mean to me?

> *Knowledge is of two kinds. We know a subject ourselves, or we know where we can find information upon it.*
> —SAMUEL JOHNSON

Remember: Cash Flow (Being Rich) Success comes from the effective application of specific knowledge. Many trades on WIN are put forth in a unique way. It's a process—once again, totally to help our students make more money in less time with less risk.

Step 1: The scenario. What's going on with that stock, sector, or in the whole marketplace.

Step 2: What strategy is being employed. When possible, information from books, seminars and special reports and expound on the formula.

Step 3: The trade. What exactly did we do with the stock or option.

Step 4: The expected results or actual results (when appropriate) of the trade.

Three excerpts from WIN:

JUNE 21, 2000　8:22 AM PDT

Good morning everyone! This is Team Wall Street™ reporting from the Wall Street Workshop in Philadelphia, PA.

One of our Facilitators opened a Simutrade Bull Put Spread on JDS Uniphase (JDSU) while the stock was trading around $128^1/_2$. Our Facilitator placed an order to sell 10 contracts of the July $125 puts and to buy 10 contracts of the July $120 puts, for a net credit of $\$^5/_8$. The July $125 puts were trading around $1 x $\$1^1/_{16}$ and the July $120 puts were trading around $\$^5/_{16}$ x $\$^1/_2$. This trade was based on yesterday's news off the I.Q. Pager™ of the stock being added to the S&P 500 Index, and the Facilitator liked the premiums on the spread for today.

JUNE 27, 2000　10:27 AM PDT

The Trading Department did a trade off of today's Covered Call list on Boston Communications Group, Inc. (BCGI). We bought 500 shares at $14^5/_8$. We did this trade on the strength of the uptrending stock and the tradable fundamentals of this company. We then sold five contracts of the August $15 calls (QGBHC) for $1^7/_8$. The rate of return is 25.64% and if called out it would be 30.76%.

JULY 6, 2000   12:43 PM PDT

The Trading Department has been watching Adobe Systems (ADBE), with the stock trading upward trying to breakout of an upward pennant from $135. We opened a Bull Put Spread by selling 10 contracts of the July $125 puts (AXXSE) for $3^1/_8$ and buying 10 contracts of the July $120 puts (AXXSD) for $2^1/_{16}$ for a net credit of $1^1/_{16}$. We might look to open a long call position if the stock continues to show strength and breaks out above the $132 level.

We are Wade's staff. We get to hang around him every day and nobody is as focused on helping people as he is. He is dedicated to this educational process. The money is nice, but only if it helps our students actually increase the quality of their lives. Another way of looking at this is to fit your trading style to a great lifestyle, not the other way around.

Okay. We could give thousands more. You can even look at our archives. Now we want to make a big deal out of the challenge—"who else puts all their trades out like this?—indeed, who has the guts to do so?" We want to shout out that the Security Trader's Handbook said this about WIN, "the site with the most new investment ideas." We want you to see hundreds of WIN testimonials, but our concern is for you.

You'll learn very quickly that we always get off our side of the fence and onto our students' side of the fence. To be the #1 financial educators in America (might we say the world) we must do so. So, putting aside our bragging rights, what does this mean to you? Let's go there. Has your stock broker ever showed you how to take $500 and make $7,000 in three weeks? Read this:

I just wanted to let you know, that I was able to play one (rolling) stock over a three week period, seven times, and was able to realize a $7,000 profit from a $500 investment.

–THOM A., TX

When Thom came to our Wall Street Workshop we didn't promise him this kind of profit, but he did it anyway. Do you need promises or results? We help you get results, and you don't need much to get started.

> *I've made $100,000+ in 5 months starting with $5,000.*
>
> —RICKY I., VA

$5,000 turned into $100,000. Wow. What could you do with $100,000? If you would then switch to a safer 10-15% monthly cash flow formula, this will generate $10,000 to $15,000 (or $20,000 to $30,000 if you trade on margin) by using our "Writing Covered Call" formula. Is your IRA (or pension money) making 5% to 10% monthly cash flow returns? Could you quit your job in six months to a year—even starting with less than $10,000? These students did:

> *Retired within one month of first Wall Street Workshop September 1998. Made more in 1999 than ever working for a living.*
>
> —DAVID B., WA

> *At age 50, my wife and I have now been retired for six months. Trading is making it possible to take time for ourselves, our children, and our community. (Our trading strategy is) conservative, but it makes us about three times our money each year.*
>
> —JOHN S., WA

> *I have been able to retire and live wonderfully off of selling covered calls on large cap stocks.*
>
> —LEE H., TX

You need WIN today and forever. It's just $3,600 per year. That's peanuts for the quality and value you get. Just one medium trade gets you this back and more. To some, this $3,600 is a chunk. We hope within a few months you'll realize what the value of this is. Oh, we realize we're probably the most expensive Internet site in the world. But this cliché definitely holds true here: you get what you pay for. You don't need mediocrity. You don't need a half-done job. You need results. We get results!

*I can give away enough money to feed a man for a day
or I can teach him how to earn enough to feed himself for the
rest of his life.*

—UNKNOWN

Look at what we generated in all of our publicly traded corporate brokerage accounts. We didn't do this by following the old style formulas found by the national and local market gurus (i.e., your stock brokers). We're so different and so very happy to be so. If you want their kind of results–go with them, BUT if you want our kind of results then make a slight change in your trading team–put us on your teaching staff–align yourself with us and get going.

I am an RN...for a labor and delivery unit. I mentioned to a friend (he sells life insurance for New York Life) that I was learning so that I could start investing in the Stock Market. His comment was, "Leave the stock market to the big boys." This rather incensed me and became the catalyst to learn all I could so I could be successful and prove this friend wrong.

–SUZANNE E., CA

Seriously look at the box on Page 196 and see what $10,000 would do our way over one year (1999) as compared to using their way–even if you would have been fortunate enough to choose all the stocks in the NASDAQ group.

Can you afford these guys, or is it time to take your own financial "bull market" by the horns? Stop and think about your own lifestyle:

WHAT WOULD YOU DO WITH MORE MONEY?

Had to retire and then discovered I had prostate cancer and needed surgery. Insurance ran out and I was cancelled. Now 'high risk' insurance is $850/month. Trading pays for it and a lot more. I have peace of mind.

–DAVID E., CA

I am a single mom. Sold my business within one year of taking my first Wall Street Workshop. I'm now trading full time at home,

WADE COOK FINANCIAL CORPORATION
ALL BROKERAGE ACCOUNTS

YEAR ENDED 12/31/99 AUDITED
RATE OF RETURN RESULTS
WADE COOK FINANCIAL CORP.   127.59%
*includes all realized & unrealized gains/losses

AVERAGE IN BROKERAGE ACCOUNTS   (MONTHLY)
WADE COOK FINANCIAL CORP. $2,917,816

REALIZED/UNREALIZED GAINS
WADE COOK FINANCIAL CORP. $3,722,950
Realized Gains $3,255,760
Unrealized Gains $467,190

WADE COOK FINANCIAL CORPORATION
VS. THE MARKETS – Year End 12/31/99

Return on S&P 500   19.53 %
   Return on DOW   25.22 %
Return on NASDAQ   85.59 %
WADE COOK FINANCIAL CORPORATION   127.59 %

NOW LOOK AT POTENTIAL RESULTS

IF YOU STARTED WITH $10,000
ON JANUARY 1st, 1999
                                                    value on 12/31/99

S&P 500 $11,953
DOW $12,522
NASDAQ $18,559
WADE COOK FINANCIAL CORPORATION $22,759
                    Your results will vary

and spending more time with my 13 year old son, and doing things together that we love to do. I just bought an SUV Benz and a Rolex watch to go with it! Wade's seminars have changed my life.

–SUSAN R., HI

ARE THERE PEOPLE IN YOUR LIFE WHO NEED HELP?

I trade full time, (bought) 6 bedroom home with swimming pool and tennis court, helped others who needed work (they work on my house now and I pay them with what I make in the market). I know if I lost everything, I could start with enough to buy one contract and make it from there.

–GARLAND H., FL

CAN YOUR CHURCH OR FAVORITE CHARITY USE MORE MONEY?

My life has changed by spending less time running my computer business and more time with my family. This has also allowed my wife and I to sponsor many new programs through our church. My minister wanted to put 100 teenagers through a program about waiting until marriage for sex. We (anonymously to all other members) offered to match ALL donations received to this program for two weeks. The other members donated enough to send 75 teens through the program. With our matching funds, our minister was able to do 150 teens or 150% of his goal.

–DWAYNE G., OK

Donations: $25,000 to son's school building fund, $25,000 to church building fund, both this year on stock account gains.

–RAYMOND B., FL

ARE YOU LIVING A GREAT, NOBLE LIFE OF COMPASSION AND PASSION? HOW WOULD MORE TIME AND MORE MONEY HELP?

Helping others, gave over $30,000 in last four months to charity from earnings!

–LARRY K., MI

These success stories are real. We want to help you become your own success story. That's how we measure our effectiveness. But frankly, we cannot help you if you do not attend our Wall Street Workshop. We can hook you up with dynamic and far-reaching methods of wealth enhancement, but we can't do this if you don't come.

You see, you have a choice. (1) Learn these strategies on your own! (2) Don't learn them (in fact, if you do not attend a Wall Street Workshop™, you will not even know they exist); or (3) learn the strategies from people with experience, passion and achievement.

> **Some drink at the fountain of knowledge…others just gargle.**
>
> –ANONYMOUS

The best choice is to walk with people who are walking the walk. To quote from a special report I wrote called *Wise Choices*:

> *In the Bible is a series of wonderful lessons on gaining wisdom. A simple lesson stands out: 'walk with wise men.' [Proverbs 13:20] It stands true of listening to and following God's word in spiritual matters, as it does in other matters.*

May we interrupt Wade again? If you choose this "best choice," you will walk with achievers in the industry. Don't let the criticism of a few jealous stock market gurus and misguided journalists separate you from the potential you are about to achieve. After all, "Great spirits have always had violent opposition from mediocre minds."–Albert Einstein. Back to Wade.

> *Through the commendations and the condemnations, I will stay the course. I will help others honestly so as to win their recommendation of my services to their friends.*
> –WADE B. COOK

You should not settle for second best. Your family is too important, your retirement is too close; your life too worthy to surround yourself with mediocrity. To be sure, Wade Cook's Wall Street Workshop is one of the most expensive courses, but again, what are your alternatives?

> *Experience is the best teacher, but it's so darn expensive.*
> –ANONYMOUS

> *Experience is a hard teacher, because she gives the test first, the lesson after.*
> –VERNON LAW

Why, you ask, is this course so good? And why should I give you two days (three with the B.E.S.T. Seminar) of my life? What can I possibly learn in that time that would let me retire in a year or so? We'll answer these questions with a question–If you keep doing what you've been doing to build up your wealth, increase your net income and retire at 32, 42 or 52, will you make it? Do you have a good answer?

Well, we do. However, our answer will not be what you think. Please don't judge your future potential by your past. You'll miss a major point, and missing the point will be detrimental to your financial health.

So what is the point? The information is awesome, but that's not it. The methods are results oriented. No, though important, the methods aren't the difference. Maybe the insights and exit strategies are it. Nope, they're wonderful, but it's much more than this.

Simply put, it is our unique and fantastic method of delivery. It's not what we teach, but *how* we teach—indeed, it is how you learn that makes all the difference in the world.

> *To teach a man how he may learn to grow independently, and for himself, is perhaps the greatest service that one man can do another.*
>
> —BENJAMIN JOWETT

We use an efficacious "Tell, Show and Do" experiential learning process. You learn, see and then do (on paper or for real) the actual strategies. It's undisputed we are the best at teaching you our methods. No one can show and explain these processes like we do, BUT, if that were all, we'd be like dozens of others. The "Do"—getting you to do the deal, or into the trade, and as much as possible, we "watch over" you and help you truly "get it." If there was a better educational delivery method we'd adopt it. THIS IS THE BEST. You learn, you see the trades done, then the whole class goes on break, or is excused to go (on the phone or online) and make the trade. Most students do these on paper until they become proficient. You've heard that "practice makes perfect." That's a half-truth that breeds many failures. You can practice something for years and if you are practicing wrong or ineffectively, you've still got it wrong.

"Perfect practice makes perfect." This works. We put on our wonderful Wall Street Workshop on a regional basis to help people learn how to practice perfectly.

> *Practice yourself in the little things, and thence proceed to greater.*
>
> —EPICTETUS

Do not delay coming to this class. Even a one or two month delay could cost you tens of thousands of dollars ($$$). That's the kind of money most people only dream about. We'll help you make your dreams gone blue become dreams come true. We do it all the time.

Thank you Wade!! We made money enough to travel throughout Western Europe because of your strategies. We fulfilled a lifetime dream. Thank you, Thank you, THANK YOU!

–PATRICIA J., CA

For five years, my husband has worked 300 miles away Monday through Friday. We commute on weekends to be together. Our small town has no good paying jobs, but is an excellent place to raise our three children. Pete is quitting now and returning home! I have been trading options for just over one year, and have been quite successful. We plan to travel extensively during summer vacations. We've already been to the Bahamas twice for a month each time, but without Pete. Now he'll be joining us! I should add that Pete has been in a very stressful job that has been wearing on his health and our marriage. We both look forward to our future now. I have also been able to give heavily to my church – something I've always wanted to be able to do. Thanks Wade!

–SUZANNE G., CA

I began attending Wade's seminars my junior year in college. I graduated in 1999, and I did not get a job. I will never have a job in Corporate America. Just in the Fall of 1999 I have already nearly made the average starting salary of a college grad. Thanks to all of you. I am living every man's dream, I am 24 years old!

–DAN D., TX

Another knowledge point. We want you to not only learn the "how," but the "why."

The man who knows how will always have a job. The man who knows why will always be the boss.

–DIANE RAVITCH

To come to this kind of understanding where else could you go? We contend–"**There Is No Place Like Our Home**." Please come visit.

There is a critical aspect to this educational process that will bear you much fruit once you employ it. We'll get to it after you look at the topical agenda for Wade Cook's two day "experiential learning" Wall Street Workshop:

DAY ONE

GETTING STARTED

- What you expect and what you will get.
- Strategies of Engagement: Take notes, hang around positive people, working lunches, papertrading.
- Three-step training process: Tell, Show, and Do.
- Learn the basics and practice, practice, practice!
- Creativity: If there is a way, take it; if not, make it.
- To whom are you listening? Sources for information and advice.

BUILDING A GREAT PORTFOLIO

- Trading basics: Buying stock safely, how we make money, making effective decisions, yield calculation.
- Choosing a brokerage firm and a good personal broker.
- Market Makers: who they are and how they work.

ROLLING STOCKS

- Benefits, definitions and rules.
- Tools for finding (WIN, TC2000®, etc.).
- Assignments: research, real trades or Simutrades™.
- Review.

OPTIONS

- Benefits, definitions and rules.
- Risks of doing options and how to avoid losses.
- News: Other Motivating Factors (OMFs).
- LEAPS®.
- Examples and review.

STOCK SPLITS

- Benefits, definitions and rules.
- Why companies split nad how to find them (WIN, IQ Pager).
- Options on stock splits, five times to get involved.
- Examples, assignments, review.

WRITING COVERED CALLS

- Benefits, definitions and rules.
- Wade Cook formula for writing covered calls.
- Finding the good ones.
- Examples, assignments, a nd choices.
- Covered call power strategies: buy/write, clean house, in the money, buy back and roll out.
- Examples, questions and concerns, review.

DAY TWO

EARLY BIRD SESSION

- Research, call brokers, do the deals (real or simutrades).

SELLING PUTS

- Benefits, definitions and rules.
- Examples: a strategy where you can't lose money.
- Three things to do if the stock is put to you.
- Cost basis and margin requirements.
- Tandem plays: stacking the deck in your favor.
- Bull put spreads (if time permits).

PEAKS AND SLAMS

- Benefits, definitions and rules.
- Dead cat vs. dead dog bounce.
- Can the price be sustained? Has the news played out?

BARGAIN HUNTING

- IPOs: How to find them, when to buy and the 25 day rule.
- Turnarounds: Why are they down? Why should they go up?

- Spin-offs: Examples (Pepsi etc.), advantages.
- Penny Stocks: advantages and disadvantages.
- Range Riders: up, down or sideways; news, moving averages, money flow, events.

PULLING IT ALL TOGETHER

- Tracking sheets – start using the words "open and close."
- Combining balancing strategies.
- My four step plan:
  Is my trading personality safe or aggressive?
  Choosing a favorite strategy.
  Research for that strategy.
  Practice.
  Monitor, monitor, monitor.

DAY THREE: B.E.S.T.™: BUSINESS ENTITY SKILLS TRAINING

OVERVIEW

- The goal of wealth enhancement.
- Trader's update – advantages and disadvantages.
- Key areas for success – divide and conquer.
- Three solutions for protecting assets.
- The power of entities.
- Protections, growth and tax reduction.
- The basic structure of the legal entities.

CORPORATIONS

- The basics of corporations.
- Corporate benefits – estate tools.
- Corporate structure for family dynasties.
- Who runs the store? Shareholders, directors and officers.
- Tax brackets, benefits and movement.
- The pre-tax difference.
- Corporations and the IRS.
- Splitting income.

- Why Nevada?.
- B.O.S.S. (Business Office Suite Service)

THE LIMITED PARTNERSHIP

- Tax benefits.
- Income and tax distribution.
- Ownership vs. control: general and limited partners.
- Asset protection and estate tools.
- Unearned income: getting out of the social security system.

THE LIVING TRUST

- Trusts, wills and probate.
- The courts and your estate: the problems of probate.
- How to avoid probate: die as a pauper.
- What about control? Trustees and beneficiaries.
- Tax benefits and family ramifications.
- Will vs. Living Trust: examples.

TAX MINIMIZATIONS AND DEFERRAL TECHNIQUES

- Making tax free investments.
- Pensions: creating a tax-free entity.
- Charitable Remainder Trusts (CRT).

It is so much fun to show this. When you really think about these topics–seven of the major ones in the Three Step Process of "TELL, SHOW and DO"–you'll realize how comprehensive this immersion learning course is. I think it's comical, yet pathetic, when all these brokerage firms spend millions on their radio and TV ads to convince you that they enable or empower the individual investor. I beg to differ. I've gone to their websites; I've seen their brochures and the only thing they do is educate you on the next thing they want to sell. It's sad.

> *It's like the Wizard of Oz. You learn that the big Wall Street guys are hiding behind the curtain, peddling a contraption to generate enough noise and sound to be convincing enough to keep you afraid and away from the truth.*
>
> –TIM W., VA

My staff and I, on the other hand, have as "our heart and soul" the education (enabling), the processes (empowering) and the methods (achieving results) that the other pros probably don't even know exist. And why? Do you get the feeling that they don't want you to know? In all actuality, a more educated trader is a better trader, and will make them more money (commissions), but still, you'd think they're either hiding something or they truly don't know.

Along comes Wade Cook, and says, "Hey Americans, you're not stupid. You can learn and master these splendid methods of cash flow. I'll learn them from the Billion Dollar Traders and share them with the Average Guy." Is it any wonder why a typical retail stockbroker, who hasn't the foggiest idea of how the stock market really works, shoots down these ideas? If they're not up on it, they're down on it.

An interesting thing happened at the Wall Street Workshop™. I am a licensed general securities broker, licensed insurance agent, and a CFP (certified financial planner). And compared to (the instructor), I don't know jack! It just proves that institutionalized knowledge and street knowledge is about a $1,000,000+ per year difference in money making capability. Thanks for presenting difficult to understand material in an incredibly absorbable and fun way. Bravo Wade Cook strategies!

–CHRISTOPHER K., FL

As Wade's staff, we would like to ask, why would you ever surround yourself with people who do not know, and have not made hundreds of thousands of dollars? Yes, use them to effectively place trades. They should save you more than their commissions by getting you purchase and sale prices in the spread, or by getting a better price. Things you simply can't do repeatedly with online trading–electronic trading costs too much in lost deals, bad prices and bad fills. But don't expect your broker to be what he is not. We are *your* education machine. We will help you build up your income–indeed, create, as Wade so fondly puts it, "your own Wall Street Money Machine."

I took $4,000 to $80,000. My wife and I pulled it out and built apartments. I have $10,000 now to do it again.

–KEN M., CA

We made $230,079 today, January 12, 1999. We made it on CMGI, a tech stock. In fact, on January 11th, we made $47,855 and on January 7th, we made $46,644. We've made $372,725 in just the opening days of this month…

−JOEL AND JENNIFER D., CA

Our December (99) statement showed that we had taken a $17,000 account to $120,000. In January (00), we'd made (my husband's) annual salary plus a portion of mine!

−VIRGINIA M., NJ

A CASE MADE FOR ZERO TO ZILLIONS™: HOME STUDY MEGA-COURSE

It is such a rush for us to put these events on, almost all with real audiences, so our students are part of the action and feel the passion. We see people listen, review, retain, share with their family these time-honored, in-the-trenches ways to build up their income.

I took $4,000 with the tapes only and in $2^1/_2$ months, doubled my money.

−MARILYN M., TX

I was very unhappy with a holding of RXSD which was going nowhere. I was just going to sell it around $11 or so, when I listened to (the) Zero to Zillions tape(s). I sold a $12 call for $1^3/_8$. I was called out of seven contracts. Just listening to the tapes garnered me an additional $1,300–paid for much of the course so far.

−STANLEY G., FL

Approximately $9,000 by just listening to Zero to Zillions and doing: 1) $800 Rolling Stock. 2) $6,600 Writing Covered Calls in two months. 3) $2,400 Dividend Capturing. All done in two months of active trading…

−SIMISOLA O., MI

To add to the excitement, take a look at this extensive list of topics in a most remarkable home/car study course that explains, expounds on, elucidates, fills in the gaps and is all-in-all the most powerful and effective "college on wheels" ever assembled.

VOLUME 1

CD #1: Treat The Stock Market Like A Business: Introduction to Wade "Cash Flow" Cook, and what makes him tick. The need for more cash flow and how to turn the stock market into a profitable business. (Income machine.)

CD #2: Building A Great Portfolio, Part 1: Making wise decisions. Company P/Es and how to effectively measure stock valuations. Understand a "Fun-damental" approach to better portfolio building.

CD #3: Building A Great Portfolio, Part 2: More great information put forth in a "down-in-the-trenches" format. Understanding what moves stocks, why some prices contract while other prices explode.

CD #4: Building A Great Portfolio, Part 3: A technical approach to making better entrance points (open positions) and exit points (close positions). Then on to OMFs–Other Motivating Factors–the "why now" behind stock option movements.

VOLUME 2

CD #5: Stop And Go–More Cash Flow: The ultimate presentation on the quarterly "newsy-go-round." Don't do anything until this information enters your brain. Earnings Seasons are only a limited part of the story.

CD #6: Rolling Stocks–Repeated Waves: This is a lively presentation to bring more life to your trades. The Three Rules explained. Examples given. Charting, tips, hints, methods that work: understand three types of roll patterns.

CD #7: Stock Splits: Capitalizing On Big Moves: Stock Splits. You'll soon be able to harness the power of this workhorse. You'll thoroughly go through the five times to get involved and then uninvolved. You'll learn to watch out for Split Strategy #2. This powerful event has become a cornerstone of many other events.

VOLUME 3

CD #8: Options (Introduction): Safer Than Stocks? Part 1: Low-cost, limited-risk options are safer than stocks in some ways. Get the jargon down. Use leverage for magnified profits. Control without ownership and protective profit-making techniques.

CD #9: Option Optimism, Part 2: Understanding more on option/stock relationships. See price swings and gain an understanding of problems and pitfalls to avoid. See how basic options can be used in a variety of strategies.

CD #10: Option Pricing And Volatility, Part 3: Options: a unique demonstration of how option prices move. Stock movement is just part of the story. Learn the three components of Option Market Makers and computer pricing models.

CD #11: Making Options Work Hard, Part 4: Moving on up. Option knowledge and expertise most of the pros don't have. This intermediate level comes as a must for serious investors.

CD #12: Stockbrokers: Choosing (Training) A Good One: An effective team is essential. A good stockbroker, one who truly knows how to get in the spread prices, does cross-market trades, and knows the components of the cash flow formulas is invaluable.

VOLUME 4

CD #13: Writing Covered Calls, Part 1: This powerful cash-flow formula is a must in every trader's tool chest—even if most trades are made with more aggressive methods—this "calm-down, get the monthly check" will grow anyone's portfolio and cash flow.

CD #14: Selling Calls, Part 2: Way too much for one CD (#13) this seminar continues with more precise techniques for strengthened profits. Problems to avoid and overcome. How to better choose strike prices and expiration dates.

CD #15: Writing Calls: Cleaning House, Part 3: Only someone with hundreds (even thousands) of trades could share this information. These powerful insights for extra (get more cash now) income are creative, yet simple to implement. Buy backs, roll outs (up and down) are explained with pertinent examples.

VOLUME 5

CD #16: LOCC–Large Option Covered Calls, Part 1: Part of Wade's Lifestyle Investing Series. Certain stocks produce huge four to six month out option premiums–sell these, generate big time income–this seminar shows you how to get your stocks for FREE–yes, get the stock market to pay for your stocks.

CD #17: LOCC It Up, Part 2: Pick off (pre-capture) large option premiums now. Offset stock purchase prices. Switch to plan B for more cash flow. Retire within one year (if you have $25,000 to start) or two and a half years (if you have $5,000 to start). Also, explained is the stock repair kit for down stocks–this is awesome!

CD #18: Puts For Income And Protection: Puts have a definite place in every trade arsenal. Protect large upside moves in your stocks by buying puts. If stocks dip, puts go up in value–sell for cool profits. Also, learn about puts for bear market trading.

VOLUME 6

CD #19: Spreads For Safer Cash Flow: The amazing bull put spread is Wade's favorite cash generating strategy. Build on basic selling puts– buy insurance with this credit spread. (Credit means you get paid cash to put it in place–yes, you get paid.) This is a wonderful way to go for the safety conscious, and it's oh-so-simple.

CD #20: Bargain Hunting, Part 1: Don't delay listening to and studying this information. These deals, turnarounds, spin-offs, slams and peaks are available on a daily basis. Wade's creative insights are powerful, not to mention necessary for finding and playing these detailed formulas.

CD #21: Bargain Hunting, Part 2: Huge discounted, undervalued stocks are out there if you know what to look for. Wade moves on with street wisdom in regards to IPOs (Initial Public Offerings). The problems with trying to get in, but then the 25 day (quiet) rule is explained.

CD #22: Make More, Keep More, Part 1: Asset protection and wealth enhancement the entity structuring way. You learn about Nevada Corporations, Living Trusts, Pension Structures, the (Family) Limited Partnership, and the effective CRT (Charitable Remainder Trust). This is an extremely informative event.

CD #23: Make More, Keep More, Part 2: Grow your wealth and protect your assets as you pay less taxes, lower your exposure to lawsuits and other problems, and prepare for a great retirement. The best of all worlds: cash flow, tax write-offs, and growth. These entities are blended together for unequaled efficiency.

Plus, Two Bonus CDs

Hidden Wealth™: A passionate presentation on structuring your financial affairs–for beginners and everyone else. Also, an introduction to the Wealth U.

Building A Quality Life™: Wade's heartfelt seminar for enhancing the nobleness of our life is wonderful. Based on the Bible with use of powerful quotations, stories and experiences. This is great for teenagers and anyone else wanting help in achieving great results.

This course also has four videos. Again, you can sit and watch me at work, in a professionally set studio–most with live audiences–and professionally taped and executed. You get the best information quickly, using sight and sound, but given at a pace for you to emotionally awaken to the extent that your emotions, your history, your own skills and your desires step up and go to work for you.

Look at a brief description of the four videos:

On-Growing Stock Market Profits™

This video alone is worth thousands, seriously. I come at stock market trading in a whole different way: I explore how people learn and use some of these different mechanisms, coupled with real life examples to bring these systems alive–to hit home with you in a way that will affect you and cause you to gain the attributes of trading success. Seriously, these formulas can be used repetitiously for on-growing (not just continuing, but increasing) cash flow.

Position Trading™

Do not go near the stock market until you watch and absorb the knowledge (wisdom) in this video. I explain the "news/no news" cycle. As CEO of a publicly traded company, with SEC reporting requirements, I've discovered the anticipation of news inside the company versus outside news, and when it starts and ENDS. You'll learn how to get your money out of harm's way to stop losses, and also how to get your money in the way of progress.

It's what I call "position-trading," or "posi-trading." It makes so much sense. This video could help you make an extra $200,000 to $400,000 a year.

Enhancing Your Wealth™

As a former financial planner, I thought I knew a lot about securities and the market. As a current attorney, I thought I knew a lot about companies and securities. Now I know I knew nothing about companies, securities, and the market.

–Michael R., WA

Back in the studio I went, to put out the most concise strategies for asset protection, tax reduction, risk avoidance, and estate structuring. This video presentation will help you gain a working understanding of:

Nevada Corporations: secrecy, privacy, tax reduction and estate planning capabilities

Living Trusts: extensive probate avoidance, tax savings, good for the family, yet estate-sharing limitations.

The (Family) Limited Partnership: asset protection, distribution of assets, awesome tax ramification and bequeathment attributes.

The Pension Plan: tax deductibility, control, tax free growth of all types of income, acceptability.

CRT or Charitable Remainder Trust: deductions, cash flow and asset control, growth and income and possibly an awesome "tithe" on your build-up of wealth. This last one, the CRT, is my favorite. It's awesome (in every cliché of this word "awesome.")

I'm into entity structuring and design. Truly you'll hear a symphony when you see and know how to use these different "instruments" to produce notes, then chords, then beautiful music.

After a decade of being in practice as a surgeon, I found myself in the classic American mode: a holder of assets that demanded always

more cash, forcing me to work longer and harder so I could continue to add to the legacy of government taxation—now more than $1,000,000 since I had begun my practice...

Enter Wade Cook.

...I learned that my malpractice is only another sandwich spread on the buffet table for the ravening wolf known as a trial lawyer. After the malpractice insurance has been collected in a suit, a doctor's home, practice, stock accounts, or any other assets are fair game to take. The best way around that was to incorporate, and distribute one's assets in a number of legal entities so nothing was owned, but all the powers of decision were retained. Where was this stuff ten years ago?! Why didn't my friends and legal advisors tell me about these things?! I had to learn it from a taxi-cab driver! Not only would I be shielded from lawsuits, but from taxes. "No, you didn't have to pay the government that million dollars," I heard. (I had to ask that twice.) So immediately that day I paid the $6,000 to start the creation of my legal entities. It was a bargain, even if $60,000. Thanks Wade!!

—DR. STEVEN N., OR

PRECISION TRADING™
PRESENTATIONS OF OUR SUPPORT SPEAKERS

We want to be the company that will stick with you until you make it. We won't abandon you. Our Team Wall Street™ instructors, originally chosen and trained by Wade, branched out into their own designs and profitable methods. They built on his foundation, but now have fine-tuned various aspects of trading. They're wonderful, and so passionate. When you see the precise discoveries they've made, and their effective ways to enter and exit trades, you'll simply wonder what you've been missing—so will your stockbroker.

TOPICS

Stock Splits: More insights, trading methods and tips.

Sector Trades: Get in the way of movement as the money moves from one arena to the next.

Charting: Use trends, support lines, money flows, gaps and much, much more.

Spreads and Safety for Income: See and earn maximum profits with leg-ins and outs, emotionless trades.

News Trades: Develop expertise to use tools (IQ Pager and WIN) for daily profits.

Tax Saving, Asset Structuring: Even more effective ways to make more and keep more money.

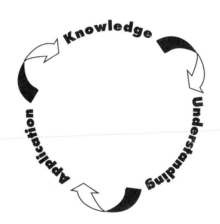

You would never think of hiring on a new employee without training. Could you imagine a farmer expecting a tractor to plow straight rows without someone behind the wheel guiding it? Trading is no different. You earn from a formula just in proportion to how much you learn from it. There is no substitute for knowledge, understanding and application on a never-ending cycle of quality improvement. We live in a society and economy with so much available information. But how do you learn to profit from it? How do you capitalize on you? Where our company rises and shines is in bridging the gap between knowledge and understanding. In this never-ending cycle, we facilitate the application process to increase your understanding and the cycle goes on and on and on.

Why Home Study Courses?

You get seminars personally tailored to fit your time and schedule. With videos, you can literally design your own workshop, picking and choosing what strategies to focus on. Review as much or as little as you choose, whenever you can!

You get the visual dimension. See the charts being explained, follow along with the examples, and get the facilitator's full instruction. Using sight and hearing at the same time increases attention and comprehension, and that leads to more successful trades! Most of our courses have blank manuals for your notes plus a filled-in version.

You get instant replay! If you miss something, run the tape back and watch the example again. Stop the tape, try it out, come back and review immediately to see the right result. You can go over a concept or strategy as many times as it takes to really be comfortable with it.

Share the education with your friends and loved ones, for no additional charge. You can take just one volume or the whole course anywhere you want to watch it. Only video provides every chart, strategy, tip and technique as you learned them (except for the live experience). If you can't get folks to the Workshops, take the Workshops to them!

Video copies of Wade Cook's seminars and workshops are like getting free college courses forever when you pay for just one semester! Every time you review a strategy you learn something new. Our most successful students attend courses every month. Having your own video copy essentially allows you to attend as often as you want at your own convenience.

You can review on demand. Did you ever have a trade go wrong and wonder what happened? Would you like to have a mentor on hand any time of the day or night to go over the strategy with you? That's what video makes available–the opportunity for immediate course correction any time you get off track, for years to come.

The handsome multi-volume reference libraries keep you in action toward your goals. Just by sitting on the shelf, our video sets remind you of what you could be doing with your time and money to achieve your dreams. And you'll be able to act on them, whether you want early retirement, freedom from debt or simply a better lifestyle for your family.

Zero To Zillions Is A Must

Here, in one extensive, detailed course, exists 23 full-blown audio CDs, plus two wonderful bonus CDs, and filled-in manuals with charts, diagrams, explanations, analysis and seminar notes–after all, these are seminars, workshops, demonstrations and presentations. You'll be there, to some degree, learning, reviewing, pondering these formulas, methods, systems, concerns, techniques–and then, yep, you figured it out– you'll use these new-found strategies when you place your orders; when you eliminate bad trades, and as you make more money.

A Comprehensive System

You are just a quart or two of knowledge away from having and keeping the cash flow necessary for a great lifetime of giving. Ask yourself: if I don't get this knowledge what will I do? I don't like any answer or scenario you'll experience without knowing and using these powerful tools.

Zero to Zillions is worth way more than the low cost of $1,695. You'll make that back in a trade or two. You'll make more, keep more, and have more growing for you to produce income now and more income later–when you really need your money to work for you.

> *It is the glorious prerogative of the empire of knowledge that what it gains it never loses. On the contrary, it increases by the multiple, of its own power all its ends become means; all its attainments lead to new conquests.*
> —Daniel Webster

Our promise is to give you "fox-hole soldier" information, not ivory-tower, useless mumbo-jumbo. You deserve the best, most effective knowledge and a delivery system to match.

At the time this special report was written, Zero to Zillions was given for FREE with paid attendance at the Wall Street Workshop. It's worth the whole $1,695 and much, much more, but we were trying to prove a point: "We always give more than we promise."

Call our number and see if this offer is still available. If not, ask if it's on sale. We've put it on special for $1,295. Again, peanuts for what you get. You need this knowledge.

We, as the seminar/product staff cannot let this opportunity pass. Wade has a tough time touting his own product. We can assure you that Zero to Zillions is not some namby-pamby, wishy-washy collection of barely usable trading strategies. It is heavy-duty, industrial strength techniques, commentary (the why-to's as well as the how-to's) and functional investing and trading methods.

If you want a motivational seminar, or personal development tid-bits you should look elsewhere. When Wade is called, "America's Premier Financial Strategist," it is well deserved. $1,695 is a small price to pay for such well-thought-out, dynamic systems. In fact, every three to five minutes you'll think, "Wow, this one idea itself is worth way over $1,695. You probably will have 300 to 500 such experiences.

When we say the price is $1,695, we're not talking the cost. The cost is possibly $100,000 to $2,000,000 in lost profits if you say no. You can watch a lot of offers come and go, BUT NOT THIS ONE!

When we heard that Wade offered to throw it in for free with the Wall Street Workshop we flipped! This will not last long. This is a great course to prepare you for the two/three day event.

The CDs, videos and manuals are packed with information–in some cases even more details than the Live Wall Street Workshop. Why, then, is the tuition for the Wall Street Workshop so much more? Because it's a live, do-the-deals, get you ready by practice trading, and get you going workshop. It's a workshop, not just a seminar. It's like learning pottery. We help you mold the clay, work it, put it in the kiln and make something beautiful–and much more than an ashtray. Get the BRAIN POWER to make consistent monthly income.

We made $230,079 today, January 12, 1999, on CMGI–a Tech stock. In fact, on January 11 we made $47,855, and on January 7 we made $46,644. We've made $372,725 in just the opening days of this month...we've never lost a dime when we followed the rules as taught at the Wall Street Workshop™. A year ago today we were living on 20 plus credit cards and had a second loan out on our home. Today we're down to two or three credit cards and that second loan has been paid off. And we don't owe much on the cards. A year ago we didn't know if we were going to

keep this damn house. Now it's paid for. All due to the lessons we learned at [Stock Market Institute of Learning, Inc.]!"
—JOEL & JENNIFER D., CA

YOUR EMOTIONS AND THE STOCK MARKET

"People don't ask for facts in making up their minds. They would rather have one good, soul-satisfying emotion than a dozen facts."
—ROBERT KEITH LEAVITT

Here are a couple of major dilemmas I have in trying to convince you to "take the bull by the horns," get trained and learn by experiencing my trading methods.

Dilemma number one – one of the easiest ways to sell an item, especially if that item is not well-known by the customer, is to compare it to something that the customer can relate to. It's sort of an "it tastes like chicken" scenario. The Wall Street Workshop has no equal–it literally stands alone. There is no other seminar in America that is done in this workshop format, wherein we use real-live stock market experiences, actual examples from what is going on that day, and even that minute, in the marketplace. We could use hypothetical situations, but it is so much more interesting and educational to use real live stocks. So if we're buying a call option or selling a call option on a stock, it is best to use a real stock, even though that stock price is just a snapshot in time.

But the students get to see a real deal being done. Then, as they're excused in the TELL, SHOW, DO format, whether they're doing paper trades or real trades, they can go out and get a stockbroker on the phone and get real live quotes, and start to get a feel for how the deals are really put together.

The teacher's task is not to implant facts but to place the subject to be learned in front of the learner and, through sympathy, emotion, imagination and patience, to awaken in the learner the restless drive for answers and insights which enlarge the personal life and give it meaning.
—NATHAN M. PUSEY, PRESIDENT, HARVARD

We have Direct TV at my home. It is hooked up to our TV, which is hooked up with a VHS, DVD, stereo (*et cetera*) system. My wife and son point, click, relax and enjoy the show. Not me. I can sit there for 30 minutes moving the buttons, pushing, clicking, and then step 5–go get my wife or my 13-year-old son to help me get my show on.

I ask them for help! They grab the remote gadget and in six to ten seconds the show is on. I say, "No, let me hold it." At first, they still reached over my shoulder and pushed the buttons. I was frustrated. I said, "No–stand over there and tell me how to do it. Let me push the buttons. *Let me learn how to do it myself.*"

It was hard for them, I know, to let me do it myself. I needed to see it done, then do it. TELL, SHOW and DO. That's how we teach. You study, practice, understand and do.

One comparison that might shed a little light on this would be reading a cookbook, as compared to attending a cooking class, where you actually make a soufflé, or a cake, or meatloaf. Again, I think everyone knows that you can just learn so much more by doing. It's wonderful to read, it's good sometimes to watch a video, but to use another comparison, if you're going to learn how to snow ski, there is just no substitute for buckling the skis on and hitting the slopes. All the books in the world, all the videos in the world, will not help somebody become a master at snow skiing. So while there is no other course like our course, there are a few comparisons that help people see what we do to try to bring the stock market to life in the lives of our students.

The second dilemma is this: every sale is an emotional sale. The purchase of a car or stereo was done to satisfy some emotional need.

I've tried to get you to think about getting rich. I've attempted to show and teach you in this brief format, strategies for cash flow. I've used testimonials of big bucks being made, others of steady income, others to show you don't need much money to start. I used others from stockbrokers and financial planners to give credibility and credence to my methods. Have they worked? Did they produce an emotion in you to grab the phone, take your financial destiny into your own hands and get to a class?

Things may come to those who wait, but only the things left by those who hustle.

—ABRAHAM LINCOLN

I've tried to get you to not judge your future by your past–to come with us as we train you in our simple, easy-to-follow formulas.

Did that work? I showed you results, dollars and percentages made. I am trying to get you to make a wise choice–because truly it's a wise person who can see through the eyes of another. You can leap-frog your way to wealth–of course in small leap-frog bounces (we can't forget the meter drop–making millions in small, bite-size pieces). Did I make you feel that you (*you*) can do it, and do it now, and do it where you are? Does the fact that we've helped tens of thousands matter to you?

Does our track record of actual trades, developing new and thrilling educational methods and dedication to your success move you?

Does it help when I show you how WIN works and that some months of WIN are available FREE with your tuition? You get this tutorial, do-the-deals site for your profit convenience. Can you see the wisdom and power of having Zero to Zillions so you can master these processes–and turn all that wasted time in your car into instructive, constructive time? Time that will now help you make more money. We get really emotional about this for our students. Are you focused on the hard work necessary to gain these skills, or on the thrill and fun of achieving results?

No steam or gas ever drives anything until it is confined. No Niagara is ever turned into light and power until it is tunneled. No life ever grows great until it is focused, dedicated, disciplined.

—HARRY EMERSON FOSDICK

I need help here. I can't do this alone. I need you to get emotional. You need to do your part. So sit back and ponder with me.

Imagine a big 'ol huge check–a few times a month–in your mailbox. You didn't have to go to work and punch a time clock. Your money produced this extra money. Does this feel good, or just okay?

Imagine quitting your job. Again, how does this feel? The fear–don't worry, you'll have extra, extra, extra cash flow for medical/dental insurance. Remember–your financial future is controlled by you, not your boss, not a union, not a fading industry.

Are you still with me? Now imagine sitting in church this Sunday and paying a tithe of $10,000 (and it's not even much of a sacrifice), because there's more on Monday. Imagine donating $25,000 to the American Heart Association.

Picture yourself in your car. A Mercedes passes on your left. Now sit in a new Mercedes dealership and write out a check–$86,000 and it's yours. No credit approval, no filling out credit apps. No debt. All cash. Turn the radio up, roll your window down–let the wind blow through your hair.

Now let's keep thinking. Look around your house. Now close your eyes and imagine a beautiful home with a huge yard for your kids. Mentally sit on your new beautiful furniture. Kick your feet up and relax.

Imagine paying cash for your kids to go to college; or helping your mom and dad retire more comfortably.

Can you feel it? Can you see yourself in better circumstances? We can–that's what we help people do.

Thanks Wade, I now work the market as a business daily from my home. I was a former stockbroker working for a bank brokerage. I now have financial independence and freedom to be with my family and travel.

–RICHARD P., AZ

A year ago today, we were living on 20 plus credit cards and had a second loan out on our home. Today, we're down to two or three cards and that second loan has been paid off. And we don't owe much on the cards. Up till August 1st, we did not have a computer. A personal message for Wade Cook with regard to each and every one of his critics: MAY ALL OF HIS CRITICS GET A TERRIBLE CRAMP IN THEIR TONGUE!!! That's a very old Yiddish curse. But his critics deserve no less. Much thanks for helping to turn our lives around!

—JOEL AND JENNIFER D., CA

My husband has worked two full time jobs since our son was born three years ago. He put his aspirations for a career and education [on hold] so I could be home with our son. Since I started trading with real money in 12/99, he has been able to quit a job and will be starting school to be a computer network engineer. Quite a big deal for a farmer from El Salvador who came here looking for asylum. Without stock trading, we would have to live on low income or dump our child in daycare.

—GAYLE G., CA

You pick out and *use the emotion you need.* Don't delay! Riches and cash flow await you. Our place in this is simple. We'll teach you. We'll inspire you. We'll cheerlead you. We're in your corner. We're behind you and we want the job of helping you make it big time.

If you don't choose us to help you, then who? If not now, when? If not this current stock market and our workable cash flow ways, then what? When will it be your turn? Yes, most people are not rich because they don't deserve it. What experiences have they had, what knowledge have they gained which qualifies them to be rich? It's time to give up the heavy baggage that doesn't work. It's time to ditch old stale formulas and it's definitely time to give up the excuses.

You can make money or you can make excuses, but you can't make both.

—DON BERMAN

So, lets move some earth. Please read this carefully. This should shake up your thinking a bit—maybe a lot.

Companies already dominant in a field rarely produce the breakthroughs that transform it.

—GEORGE GILDER

I have been criticized by some of the most influential financial "gurus" in the country. Their attacks are relentless, because they represent the status quo for the firms in the industry, and I must apologetically say about them, they do not want to help or serve the little guy. They have their job, I have mine.

When their negative attacks get to the point that potential customers are affected I simply offer the challenge in the following box. It's a wild challenge. You see, I have hundreds of thousands of students. You would think that these journalists and pundits would relish the opportunity to embarrass me. Read on.

Dear Sir,

Owing to the many reports about our great company, and in our humble effort to set the record straight, we hereby offer the following challenge:

$10,000

If you can find one person who has attended our Wall Street Workshop™, used our strategies exactly as they are taught, and then lost money, we will pay a charity of your choice $10,000.

We would like to use your findings to show the public and help people continue to learn the machinations and dangers of the market place.

Sincerely,
Wade Cook

In regards to our <u>one time</u> $10,000 challenge, here is information so you know what we teach our students, and therefore what you're up against:

1. *Surround yourself with a good team – a knowledgeable stockbroker is a must.*

2. *Choose, study and learn one of 13 formulas.*

3. *Do not use <u>real money</u> until you thoroughly understand and then have paper traded (simulation trade) this strategy fifteen times, and then, only*

after you have paper traded this particular method ten times successfully in a row–again, on paper–then and only then use real money.

4. *Use basic wisdom with help from fundamental analysis, technical analysis and trade on OMFs (Other Motivating Factors) to make better entrance points and exit points.*

5. *Diversify with the different formulas. For example, use very little money on low-cost, limited-risk options, as they are time sensitive and therefore carry an added element of risk. Specifically, if one has $100,000 to invest, only $4,000 to $5,000 should be used in options.*

Then this $4,000 should be used in four different $1,000 trades, i.e., even incremental trades.

Learn the "two in three chance of making money by selling" strategy.

Put spreads in place on sell positions to limit downside risk.

6. *Consistently learn:*
   a. *Check and evaluate results.*
   b. *Look at similar trades on WIN™ for tutorial insights.*
   c. *Continue to read and study.*

If you think you've found someone who has followed our strategies and lost money, we reserve the right to interview that person to ensure that our strategies were indeed followed.

We know you are seeking the truth and we hope this helps.

Hello again. Staff here. No one has taken us up on this challenge. It's remarkable, because Wade has more, way more, than his fair share of detractors. What he teaches works, when done the right way. Once in a blue moon we get a letter from someone who lost money on a particular trade. These comments come in so very seldom that we scarcely know how to deal with them. Almost always these students make comments like these:

When I stick to Wade's strategies, I do great. If I use my derivatives of Wade's strategies, I lose my behind...go figure?

—SHAWN L., TX

Biggest lesson learned–FOLLOW THE STRATEGIES!!
–DEBORAH K., MT

I have been very successful as long as I do my homework & follow the strategies. When I get too "cocky", I get my head handed to me in the market. So, I go back to the basics.
–KERT P., WA

June '99 to February '00 (I) turned $6,000 into $286,000 and thought I was an advanced trader. March-May has humbled me, and (I) realized I wasn't following certain strategy rules. Didn't lose a lot, but standing still. Thank you Wade Cook!
–PEGGY F., CA

More than anything, you have shown me just how much I don't know, how much more I need to learn, and where to go to learn it.
–ORION H., NJ

Last year I made approximately $400,000 trading using Wade's strategies. But if I had used trailing stop losses, I would have made another $200,000.
–DARREN D., CO

If this $10,000 challenge does not cause a reaction on your part, maybe you should get a good night's sleep and read it again with a fresh, clear mind. Who else is so brazen as to offer such a challenge? We don't consider it brazen at all. We're just confident. Back to Wade:

One of the most unique aspects of how our company works and the products and services we purvey is the fact that virtually everything we do is centered on our customer's needs. Many times people only know us for one thing, but as they really get to know us, they see the comprehensiveness of our products and services. We help our customers where they are, giving them the tools they need to fix their wealth.

I expect to pass through life but once. If, therefore, there be any kindness I can show, or any good thing I can do to any fellow-being, let me do it now, and not defer or neglect it, as I shall not pass this way again.

–WILLIAM PENN

Look at the six-fold mission of our company:

1. Help people make more money in Business, Real Estate, and the Stock Market.

2. Seriously reduce exposure to risk and liability.

3. Help businesses and people reduce their tax liability.

4. Help prepare people for a great retirement.

5. Make sure people's families or churches are bequeathed all possessions in a "TLC" way.

6. Conduct business using Biblical standards.

Now, what does this have to do with selling the product at hand? A lot. Let's use a problem/solution format with graphics (see page 226) to make the point. You'll see that we've got you covered.

TO SUMMARIZE: We're the bus, boat, plane and train that can truly help you get where you want to go. Oh, and it's flat out okay to get rich in this great country.

Keep away from people who try to belittle your ambitions. Small people always do that, but the really great make you feel that you, too, can become great.

–MARK TWAIN

We relish the opportunity to share all that we have and all that we are with you.

Let's review my attempt to educate; to help you find out more about yourself; to cause you to see that we can help you; and to take action (get registered for the first available Wall Street Workshop–even if you have to travel). Let's see how I've done.

YOU'RE THE ONE...

1. Do you have a need for more income in an effective useful way?

2. Do you want to find ways to understand effective wealth accumulation methods?

3. Do you have an ongoing need for methods to reduce taxes, lower risk, bequeath assets and protect those assets?

8. Do you need to associate with doers and achievers and people dedicated to helping you come out on top?

OUR "EXPERIENTIAL LEARNING" WALL STREET WORKSHOP

B.E.S.T. BUSINESS ENTITY SKILLS TRAINING

BOOKS, NEWSLETTERS, SPECIAL REPORTS, OTHER EDUCATIONAL MATERIALS

YOU

ZERO TO ZILLIONS (HOME/CAR STUDY COURSE) AND A HOST OF OTHER PRODUCTS

W.I.N. (OUR INTERNET TUTORIAL SITE) WEALTH INFORMATION NETWORK

4. Do you want effective ways to build wealth safely and exponentially?

7. Must you have up-to-date information from the "streets." Knowledge that works when you need it?

6. Do you need a way to turn your spare time into instructive time with CDs, videos, etc. to propel your education?

5. Do you need ongoing and precise tutorial help–to see the deals, grasp the process and make it work–in changing times?

And here's the best part:

1. You can start where you are–use what you know and build from there.

2. Proceed at your own pace. Review and retain at your personal speed.

3. Learn, practice and only proceed with caution, expertise and conviction.

4. Blend different learning methods to master all these skills of income generation, asset protection and wealth enhancement.

5. Involve your family in this wonderful process.

- I've used knowledge: what a strategy is, when to use it and who should use it.

  ⇒ *Did this get you going and make you feel that you can do it?*

- I've tried logic and reason—and hopefully have brought the American Dream back into reach for you.

  ⇒ *Have you picked up the phone and called?*

- I pointed out baggage that needs discarding and used quotations, testimonials and maxims to help you see new ways of thinking and acting.

  ⇒ *Has it worked? Or are you still wedded to the past?*

- I've used as many emotional appeals as I thought necessary.

  ⇒ *What did you think? Are you ready to "damn the torpedoes, and go full speed ahead?"*

- I've included FREE items, discounted the price for a short time and put together a comprehensive package of knowledge, ways to get understanding, and how to best apply this information for results.

  ⇒ *Have you bought it? Are you ready to move on?*

- I've painted a picture for the future quite different from the one ahead of you, if you'll learn, earn and grow.

  ⇒ *Are you now ready to do what it takes—pay the price—for this new lifestyle that is yours for the taking?*

> **Getting an idea should be like sitting on a pin. It should make you jump up and do something.**
> —Kemmons Wilson

It's time to jump up and get going.

One last thing. I have been very, very successful in my life, and I hope I can make a difference in your life. I want to be the very best, but I want to be here to serve people. I don't want to charge a price that is so inexpensive the class won't be valued.

Every time I attend a Wade Cook Seminar I realize how little I know. Thank you Wade for giving of yourself to help us students achieve this wonderful course in stock market strategies. I attended my first Wall Street Workshop in Boston in 1998. I made $8,000 on PFE. It paid for my course plus. Thank you!

–VICTORIA K., CT

So let me give you all the incentive you need to take action on your future and get yourself into this incredible event! The Wall Street Workshop retails for $6,295. Keep reading–you're about to be blown away…

I know travel involves extra expense, and I want to help in every way I can, so I'm offering a $1,000 (*one thousand dollars!*) *Travel Discount.* Since my staff can't possibly book everyone's travel, I decided to keep things simple and offer you this $1,000 discount. The Wall Street Workshop is such a dynamic event, if it isn't in your town, get on a plane and get there–your trip has just been covered!

If you think I've already done enough, think again–I want to do more! I know how hard you work. I know everyone expects to pay for their education. I know some people even pay more for their education than it's worth. Well *you* are going to get more education than you pay for! I am offering right now, for a very short period of time, one additional Scholarship Discount. Anybody who calls right now, I will knock another $1,000 off the price! That puts the Wall Street Workshop within the realm of virtually everyone! I don't want you to say no. These two discounts cannot be used in conjunction with other specials.

I feel like I've been in college for one year but I've only been in class (Wall Street Workshop) just two days!

–BARBARA D., TX

At $6,295, we knocked off $1,000 for a discount for travel, and now we've knocked off an additional $1,000 for this Scholarship Discount! Now, you don't have to take this discount. You can say, "I want to ignore Wade's Scholarship Discount, and I'll pay the extra $1,000." But, I'm offering it to you, and I would love for you to take advantage of this. I want you to say YES!

I don't have any secrets—I could make a lot more money trading in the stock market for myself, but I have such a love, a passion for sharing this information! I was going to say "teaching," which I used to believe in, but I don't believe in it anymore. There's an old proverb that says "When the student is ready, the teacher appears." I believe in learning. I believe in education, but all you will learn something when you need it, and you'll learn at your pace. I want to be a facilitator in your life, helping you along that path to wealth, those stepping stones to success.

The American Dream is alive and well! I want to be one person in your life that will lead the way and help you get it; help you get the understanding, the knowledge and the application skills that will help you re-enter the American Dream. You deserve it! What are you waiting for??

> *Knowing is not enough; we must apply. Willing is not enough; we must do.*
>
> —JOHANN VON GOETHE

Okay, if you still need a kick in the pants, there's one last thing I want to do for you. The spouse, or companion rate (and I *really* recommend that you come as a family) right now is $3,695. Usually the spouse rate is about half, but I'm going to do even better than that. I just knocked off $2,000 from your price for the Travel Discount and for the Scholarship, and I'm going to knock off *another* $2,000 from the spouse rate! So, it's only $1,695 for your spouse or your Mom or Dad, or your business partner. And, what's more, I'll honor that price for *two more people*! So if you want to bring a spouse *and* your Mom and Dad, their price will only be $1,695 each!

You will get the $1,695 Zero to Zillions, and when you get that, you will say that this one item is worth every penny of the entire package price. You're also going to receive three months of WIN, our incredible Internet tutorial service (a $900 value). What I'm trying to say here, is anything that my company can do to help move you through this educational process, we will do it. It's all part of our desire to stick with you until you make it. At the time of printing, we were offering more than three months of WIN. Call to see if "more" are still available.

That's right. All this for a price that one good trade will pay for. I know it's hard to believe, but I realize we as Americans want value and quality. Come learn with us, and you'll have value, quality and abundance fill your life to overflowing.

By wisdom a house is built, and through understanding it is established; through knowledge its rooms are filled with rare and beautiful treasures.

–PROVERBS 24:3-4

People say "Is this guy real? Is he just using the Bible because it's convenient?" I'm serious, I get that question every now and then. People come to my seminar and say "OK, you talk about the Bible; do you live it?" I say "Well, talk to my employees. Talk to my family. Talk to my students."

I am so grateful for people like Wade and his terrific (staff)…this is the stuff that will make it possible for anyone who wants it, to have a better life. Thanks so much to all of you. After my first Wall Street Workshop…my account went from $2,500 to $60,000 in about nine or ten months.

–TRISH K., AZ

So, if you like my style, and if you like me, I invite you to this experiential learning workshop. Put us to the test. We want to get you through this learning curve, and again, help you to make all the cash flow you need so you can truly live a great lifestyle. A lifestyle of nobility. A lifestyle of quality. A lifestyle of caring and sharing for those people in your life. And if there's anything that my staff or I can do to help you in this endeavor, then please join with us. If you're going to buy stocks and bonds, take stock in knowledge and bond with us!

Abundantly Yours,
Wade B. Cook

I am very encouraged by the Wade Cook Seminar System. Most people I talk to want to go out and make some things happen so they can afford the seminar and that is backwards because it will cost them money [not to go] and they may get discouraged and they won't get the education. I'm endorsing [the] Wade Cook seminars because every time I go to one, my income goes up. If my income is going up, why shouldn't I be excited? I'm writing covered calls, buying a few options and doing rolling stocks, just the basics. I am finding a 20-30% per month income. I am simply implementing the tools provided and the teachings by the staff [at the Stock Market Institute of Learning™]. Everyone thinks that there is an easy way out. I will tell you that I've never seen anything easier than following within the guidelines of the Wade Cook seminar system. Wade, in his wisdom and tenacity of going after knowledge and never letting down, has created something that will live a long time. We can provide for our family–generations and generations deep. This is SINCERE, REAL, DO-ABLE, can be done, and should be done. Why waste another minute in your lives without seeing the potential and the fruit on the tree?

–DAVID E., FL

GLOSSARY

A

ASK The current price for which a security may be bought (purchased).

AT THE CLOSE The last price a stock security trades for, when the market stops trading for the day.

AT THE MONEY An option where the strike (exercise) price is exactly equal to the trading price of the underlying security.

AT THE OPEN The price a stock security trades for, when the market starts trading for the day.

B

BEAR MARKET Term describing a long-run, downward-moving securities market.

BEAR SPREAD The purchase of a combination of calls and puts on the same security at different strike prices in order to profit as the security prices fall.

BETA Measures the volatility of a share of stock. A high beta stock, for example, will rise more in value than the stock market average on a day when shares in general are rising. And it will fall more sharply than the average on a day when shares are falling. The Standard & Poor's Composite Index of 500 Stocks, an index that represents large-company stocks, has a beta of one.

BID The current price at which a security can be sold.

BOOK VALUE A company's total assets minus intangible assets and liabilities such as debt. A company's book value might be more or less than the market value of the company.

BULL SPREAD The purchase of call or put contracts and the sale of a higher strike price call or put. As the name implies, this is a bullish strategy.

C

CALENDAR SPREAD When you buy a longer term option and sell a short term option against the long term option. It is similar to a covered call except you use an option to cover instead of buying the stock.

CALL An option contract giving the owner the right (not the obligation) to buy 100 shares of stock at a strike price on or before the expiration date.

CALL PRICE The price paid (usually a premium over the par value of the issue) for stocks or bonds redeemed prior to maturity of the issue.

CALL SPREAD The result of an investor buying a call on a particular security and writing a call with a different expiration date, different exercise price or both on the same security.

CASH ACCOUNT An account in which a client is required to pay in full for securities purchased by a specific date from the trade date.

COMMISSION The fee an investor pays or buying or selling securities.

COST BASIS Original price of an asset, used in determining capital gains. For example if you bought Novell (NOVL) at $9^1/_2$ and sold the May $10 call for $1, then your cost basis in the stock becomes $9^1/_2 - $1 = $8^1/_2$.

COVER Can be either options purchased to offset a short position or being "long actuals" when shorting futures.

COVERED CALLS A stock strategy in which you own a stock and write (sell) a call at the next strike price above the current stock value.

COVERED CALL WRITER An investor who writes a call and owns some other asset that guarantees the ability to perform if the out is exercised.

D – E

DAY ORDER The stock or option order that is good for today only.

DELTA The percent an option's value changes in relation to the underlying security. For example, if an option has a delta of 50% and the underlying stock increases by $1 you would expect the option to increase by 50¢. Put options have a negative delta because as the underlying security goes up, the option value will fall. Most full service brokers can access a delta screen and can give you the data. The software program "Trade Station" also has delta information.

DISCOUNT BROKER A broker that provides less investment help but will take orders for your account at a discount price in comparison to full service brokers.

D.U.C.K Dipping Undervalued Calls. Trend lines are essential to determine if it is a DUCk or not.

EARNINGS PER SHARE (EPS) A company's profit divided by its number of shares. If a company earned $2 million in one year had two million shares of stock outstanding, its EPS would be $1 per share.

EQUITY The market value of securities less any debt incurred. Also funds provided to a business by the sale of stock.

F – G – H

FULL SERVICE BROKER A broker that provides advice and recommendations and works for a major brokerage house.

FUNDAMENTAL ANALYSIS The analysis of the financial side of a company to decide on an investment strategy. Common Fundamental Analysis includes Earnings, Sales, Debt, Dividends, and Profit Margin.

GOOD-TIL-CANCELED ORDER (GTC) An order to set a specific buy or sell price and which will be good until you cancel it. The broker's computer will remember it. They expire 60 to 90 days after being placed depending on your broker.

HEDGE A securities transaction which reduces the risk on an existing investment position.

I

INDICATORS Charting techniques that use price volume and momentum to predict future movement in a stock. Indicators are used when performing technical analysis on an investment decision.

IN THE MONEY For a call option, it means that the current market value of the underlying interest is above the exercise price of the option. A put option is said to be in-the-money if the current market value of the underlying interest is below the exercise price of the option.

INITIAL MARGIN REQUIREMENT The amount of equity a brokerage customer must deposit when making a new purchase in a margin account.

INTERNET BROKER A brokerage house that has Internet investment service available online

INTRINSIC VALUE The amount, if any, by which an option is in the money.

L

LEAPS® (LONG-TERM EQUITY ANTICIPATION SECURITIES) Long-term equity options traded on U. S. exchanges and over the counter. Instead of expiring in two near-term and two farther out months as most equity options do, LEAPS® expire in two or three years, giving the buyer a longer time for his strategy to come to fruition.

LIMIT ORDER An order to buy or sell an equity at a specific price. The order go unfilled unless it can be filled at the specified price or better.

LOCC™ Large Option Covered Call. A covered call on a highly volatile stock with expiration out five to six months.

LONG Either owning the security on which an option is written or a person's position as the writer of an option.

LONGHORN SPREAD A covered call with a wide spread and expiration out three months.

M

MARGIN Allows investors to buy securities by borrowing money from a broker. The margin is the difference between the market value of a stock and the loan a broker makes.

MARGIN ACCOUNT An account in which a brokerage firm lends a client part of the purchase price of securities.

MARGIN CALL A demand for a client to deposit money or securities when a purchase is made in excess of the value of the margin account.

MARKET ORDER An order to buy or sell a security at the current trading price.

MOVING AVERAGE Takes the closing price of a stock for a set amount time to indicate the direction that the stock appears to be moving. Once a stock starts moving in a particular direction it tends to gain strength and doesn't reverse easily. This indicator helps reduce the daily fluctuations in a stock's price so that a smooth trend line can be seen. The Moving Average is an excellent technique to filter out the market noise and uncovering trends.

N

NET PROFIT The difference between the total price you paid for a security, with the brokerage commission you paid, and the current value. It will show either a profit or a loss.

NUMBER OF SHARES The number of stock shares that a company has outstanding.

O

OPEN INTEREST The total number of option contracts outstanding for that specific option at the close of market.

OPEN ORDER An order to buy or sell a security by an individual investor. That open order stays active until it is completed or the investor cancels it.

OPTION The right to buy or sell a specified amount of a security (stocks, bonds, futures contracts, *et cetera*) at a specified price on or before a specific date (American style options). We don't advise putting all your money in options, but rather only 5% to 10% of your risk capital should be in options at any given time.

There are two different types of options, cash settled options and physical delivery options. Cash settled options refer to puts and calls on the index options like the S&P 500 (SPX) or the S&P 100 (OEX). Physical delivery options are written on specific stocks and may be exercised or bought and sold for cash. Cash settled options are more expensive.

OPTION CYCLES The sequence of months assigned to a company's options.

OUT OF THE MONEY When the exercise price of a call is above the current market value of the underlying interest, or if the exercise price of a put is below the current market value of the underlying interest.

P

PAPER TRADING Doing make-believe trades on paper as if you had really done them. This can be a great way to refine your trading skills.

P/E A stock's price-to-earnings ratio: the share price divided by earnings per share for the company's most recent four quarters. A projected P/E divides the share price by estimated earnings per share for the coming four quarters. P/E ratios are helpful when comparing stocks in their same industry or group. For example, if Intel has a P/E ratio of 25 and AMD has a P/E ratio of 203, then Intel is a better value.

PORTFOLIO Where the equities you own are held.

PREMIUM The value of an option on an exchange. This represents the cost if you are a buyer or cash in if you are a seller.

PRICE SPREAD A spread involving the purchase and sale of two options on the same stock with the same expiration date, but with different exercise prices.

PUT An option contract that gives the owner the right to sell a specified number of shares of stock at a specified price on or before a specific date. Usually you buy a put if you think the stock is going down, with the intention of selling it when it increases in value. Usually you sell a put on a stock if you think it is going up, with the intention of letting the option expire worthless and you getting to keep the entire premium. Puts also are powerful hedges in such strategies as covered calls, giving you protection if the underlying stock plummets. The Chicago Board of Options Exchange has an excellent article on using puts for hedges.

PUT SPREAD An investment in which an investor purchases one put on a particular stock and sells another put on the same stock but with different expiration date, exercise price or both.

R

RATE OF RETURN The sum resulting from dividing the cash in (your cash taken in, or profits) by the cash out (your investment).

RESISTANCE LEVELS Levels that the stock seems to rebound off of. They can best be seen using trend lines. For example an advance to a price, say 45, which is repeatedly followed by a pullback to lower prices is said to be a resistance level of 45. The notion is that there are buyers who purchased at 45 and have watched a deterioration into a loss position. They are now waiting to get out even. Or there are sellers who consider 45 overvalued and want to take their profits. One strategy is to attempt to purchase near support and take profits near resistance. Another is to wait for an "upside breakout" where the stock penetrates a previous resistance level. Purchase on anticipation of a further upmove.

RETURN ON EQUITY Measures the return, expressed as a percentage, earned on a company's common stock investment for a specific period. It is calculated by common stock equity, or a company's net worth, into net income. The calculation is performed after preferred stock dividends and before common stock dividends. The figure shows investors how effectively their money is being used by managers.

ROLLING STOCK™ A stock that fluctuates between its high and low price points for long periods of time and whose history makes it seem to be predictable. We typically like rolling stocks that roll at least 50¢ or more.

S

SECURITIES & EXCHANGE COMMISSION (SEC) A federal agency that regulates the U.S. financial markets. (Web address is http://www.sec.gov.)

SECURITY A piece of paper proving ownership of stocks, bonds, and other investments.

SETTLEMENT DATE When an investor must pay for the purchase of shares by the third business day after he or she buys securities in U.S.

financial markets. And an investor must deliver an investment that he or she has sold by the third business day after the transaction.

SHORT A condition resulting from selling an option and not owning the related securities.

SHORT INTEREST The total number of shares of a security that investors have sold short–borrowed, then sold in the hope that the security will fall in value. An investor then buys back the shares and pockets the difference as profit.

SHORT STRADDLE The position established by writing a call and a put on the same stock with the same strike price and expiration date.

SPREAD The gap between bid and ask prices of a stock or other security. There is also a number of strategies used that make use of different spreads between calls, puts and the underlying stock.

STOCK TICKER A lettered symbol assigned to securities and mutual funds that trade on U.S. financial exchanges.

STOP LOSS ORDER A brokerage order that executes a trade if your equity falls to a predetermined value. This is to limit a loss on a specific equity investment.

STRIKE PRICE The price at which the underlying security will be sold if the option buyer exercises his/her right in the contract.

Market makers will inflate or decrease option prices sometimes based on such things as volume of contracts or their perception of strike price direction. It sometimes has no relation to stock price, especially out of the money options. Once the option is in the money, they tend to follow the stock much closer. Sometimes it helps to get quotes on options further out in time and compare prices. For example: option X for May is $1, and the option price for July is $1^3/_4$. The May option is probably inflated, and for only $$^3/_4$ more you can buy two months more of time. Time value on most options averages about $$^3/_4$ per month. (This is a rough estimate and definitely not set in stone)

SUPPORT LEVELS Levels that the stock seems rebound off of. They can best be seen using trend lines. Suppose a stock drops to a price, say

$25, and rebounds, and that this happens a few more times. Then $25 is considered a support level. The concept is that there are buyers waiting to buy at that price. Imagine someone who had planned to purchase and his broker talked him out of it. After seeing the price rise, he swears he's not going to let the stock get away from him again. One strategy is to attempt to purchase near support and take profits near resistance. Another is to wait for an "upside breakout" where the stock penetrates a previous resistance's level. Purchase on anticipation of a further upmove. The support level (and subsequent support levels after rises) can provide information for use in setting stops.

T

TECHNICAL ANALYSIS The use of price and volume charts and indicators to make trading decisions. Technical analysis attempts to use past stock price and volume information to predict future price movements. It also attempts to time the markets. You should consider delaying purchase of stocks whose chart patterns look bad, no matter how good the fundamentals. Equities Analytics has a good tutorial on a wide variety of technical indicators.

TICK A change in the price of a security, either up or down—as in uptick or downtick. ("–" denotes down, "+" denotes up)

TICK FOR TICK The consistent correlation between the price of a stock and the price of its options.

TICKER SYMBOL A trading symbol used by a company to identify itself on a stock exchange.

TIME VALUE The premium of the option in addition to its intrinsic value.

TRADING HALT Sometimes the SEC or one of the markets stops the trading of a security. Trading of a stock, bond, option or future contract can be halted by an exchange while news is being broadcast about the security, or if the market drops a great number of points suddenly.

TREND LINES Lines used to display the direction that a stock is moving. We focus on changes in trend to make trading decisions.

V

VALUE The current price of the security multiplied by the number of shares you own. If you own 1,000 shares of Intel, and the shares are selling for $95, the value is $95,000.

VALUE STOCK A stock perceived by the marketplace to be undervalued based on criteria such as its price-to-earnings ratio, price-to-book ratio, dividend yield, et cetera.

VOLATILE When the market or security tends to vary often and wildly in prices.

VOLATILITY Can be figured as an indicator by using the annualized standard deviation of the logarithm of returns.

VOLUME The daily number of shares of a security that changes hands between a buyer and a seller in a specific period. It can be used as an indicator to confirm the direction of the trend.

When the price plot has the same pattern as the volume goes–high price with high volume, low price with low volume–then the market will have the same trend as before.

When the price plot has the opposite pattern as the volume goes–low price with high volume, high price with low volume–then the market will have the opposite trend as before.

W

WALL STREET The common name for the financial district at the lower end of Manhattan in New York City, where the New York and American Stock Exchanges and numerous brokerage firms are headquartered.